A Guide to
Hunting
Pennsylvania
Whitetails

2nd Edition

Tom Fegely

Published by

**krause
publications**

700 E. State Street • Iola, WI 54990-0001
Telephone: 715/445-2214
Web: www.krause.com

ISBN 0-9643278-0-5
Library of Congress Catalog Number: 00-107843

DEDICATION

**To Betty Lou, my friend and
companion at home and in the
deer woods.**

TABLE OF CONTENTS

ACKNOWLEDGMENTS

A project such as this, requiring painstaking research and many years of gathering information, photographs and keeping up with happenings indoors and out as they affect deer and deer hunting, is not done on a whim.

The initial interest in doing a book on Pennsylvania deer hunting was sparked more than 20 years ago. But other matters — not the least of which were daily deadlines for newspaper, magazine, TV and radio projects — kept that spark from igniting into full flame. Then, in January 1994, when snows piled deep outside the office window and deer nibbled corn from the pile I'd scattered there, I wrote the first word. That was followed by many hours at the computer and a few hundred letters, phone calls, faxes, e-mails and visits to the library and state offices.

My wife, Betty Lou, an integral part of the project, kept the embers burning. Spring brought travel and an increased load of deadlines, and another lull in the operation. In mid-summer, we began devoting every spare minute to gathering information on public hunting lands, scrutinizing photo files, making dozens and dozens of phone calls and picking up all the loose ends which eventually filled this guide.

Many others also played supporting roles. Among them are Keith Kaeppel who was responsible for illustrations and layout of the entire County Profiles section. Bruce Whitman and Joe Kosack of the Pennsylvania Game Commission's information and education division, and others, were also invaluable in providing me with information.

A "job well done" also to my editor, Kevin Michalowski of Krause Publications, for his efforts in hastening this project to completion.

Thanks also to the editors of *Pennsylvania Sportsman, Pennsylvania Game News, Buckmasters, Whitetail Hunting Strategies, Outdoor Life, Rural Sportsman* and other publications for providing their blessings in using information previously published under my byline.

Invaluable also, are the many memorable days spent at Green Tree Lodge in Carbon County, Mountain View Camp in Bradford County and other deer camps across the state over the years. They were sources of information, inspiration, unique experiences and photos galore.

Now the book is in its second printing with considerable updates and many new photos.

I hope you enjoy it and benefit from "A Guide to Hunting Pennsylvania Whitetails."

T.D.F.

FOREWORD

Deer and deer hunters are part and parcel of my heritage, passed down from my mother's ancestors who hunted whitetails long before white man ever set foot in North America.

Is it any wonder that deer and hunting deer is such a large part of my life?

They hunted to live ... to survive. I hunt because I enjoy the time spent afield. Taking an animal has become secondary for me.

I began hunting with relatives at age 8, but didn't graduate to carrying a gun for another 4 years. I can vividly recall going with my father to two places owned by my aunts, and also to my grandfather's farm in Perry County. When deer season was on the horizon, I just couldn't wait.

Today, some hunters claim Pennsylvania lacks enough deer. As president of the Pennsylvania Deer Association, I've had people tell me they hunted the entire opening week of buck season and didn't see a buck or doe.

Fact is, there are more deer in the Keystone State than ever. Their areas of abundance may have changed but deer remain in healthy existence nearly everywhere. In fact, the problem now is far too many deer. The largest harvests and biggest deer densities come from different portions of the state — namely the Southwest and to a lesser extent the Southeast — than previously. When I was growing up, the Northcentral wilderness held the largest numbers of deer.

Those aren't the only changes that have taken place in Pennsylvania deer and deer hunting over the years.

In "A Guide to Hunting Pennsylvania Whitetails," Tom Fegely provides helpful and often intriguing information that both novice and experienced hunters should know. Even the one-day-a-year hunter will benefit from the wide-ranging material Tom provides in more than 300 pages of text and eye-catching photography.

If you want to be a smarter hunter (and that's what you need to be if you want to harvest a Pennsylvania whitetail), this book is a must. Originally published in 1994, Tom has revised and updated his best-selling guide with the goals of helping readers (1) learn more about deer and (2) become more proficient hunters. It matters little if you're a bowhunter, gun hunter or blackpowder hunter. It's all here ... and more.

In the 1994 edition of this Pennsylvania hunting guide, Lou Hoffman, former publisher of *Pennsylvania Sportsman* and an honored and respected hunter-conservationist-naturalist, penned this foreword. Lou was taken from us a couple years later, far too soon, for he had so much to give and so much to share.

I think about what he wrote and I cannot say it better: *"Trophies are more than monster bucks. The best trophies are hidden inside our minds. They are the personal images etched from experiences that needn't be compared or debated."*

With that, I leave you to enjoy your time hunting Pennsylvania's white-tailed deer.

And Tom Fegely leaves you with a one-of-a-kind book detailing the past, the future and the present of Pennsylvania deer, deer camps and deer hunting, traditions we must all strive to pass on to our children ... and theirs.

Hunt safely and make yourself a pledge to — sometime soon — introduce a kid to the great outdoors.

James B. Seitz, President

Pennsylvania Deer Association &

1998 Pennsylvania Outdoor Writers Association Youth Mentor Award

PREFACE

Why another deer book?

Surely enough titles are on the market and dozens of magazines, some devoted specifically to whitetails, stand sentry at newsstands.

Since 1976, when I began my tenure as outdoors editor of *The Morning Call* in Allentown, I've fielded countless letters and calls from readers on every conceivable aspect of the outdoors. Many focused on deer and deer hunting.

Nearly a million Pennsylvanians hunt deer, unmatched in any other state. They're an insatiable bunch. If not actually deer hunting, they talk or read or argue about deer hunting. Even in summer they find excuses for weekend "work party" visits to deer camp.

In September, they patrol back roads spotlighting deer, previewing what will be available in the local deer woods at the start of the bow and gun seasons. They live for opening day, often leaving home after eating Thanksgiving dinner to "get ready" for that cherished buck opener. They devour news of changing deer laws, season revisions, spread word of local buck "legends" that someone's seen or shot, read countless magazine articles, attend post-season "buck clubs," argue about what they think is best for the herd. They're also found on the range all year long firing muzzleloaders, scoped shotguns and sweet-shooting rifles, or aiming bows and arrows at 3-D targets.

In all my travels for whitetails, nowhere have I seen the overall passion and devotion to deer as here in Pennsylvania. For some it's a family affair. For many it's a lifestyle. For others it's an annual reunion.

Then, too, we need to recruit new hunters, young and old, to the ranks. Many of them are in need of guidance and, unable to find mentors to lead them gently into the sport, may seek other avocations.

That, alone, is reason enough for a book devoted entirely to hunting in the Keystone State. I've not taken up precious pages with details not pertaining to the Pennsylvania scene nor does this guide enter into analysis of topics to which entire books have been devoted.

Rather, it's as the title implies — a guide. It's a reference on where to go, how to get started, how to make the most of the seasons afforded Pennsylvanians and out-of-state guests and where to get specific information, with addresses and phone numbers galore.

It's my hope, also, that readers will page through this book when they need a dose of "buck fever." I've tapped the minds of some well-known hunters who patrol the state's deer woods and looked back at game laws and deer hunters of the past — and crystal-balled the future.

The book is illustrated with photos of some of the state's biggest bucks — both wall-hangers and others running wild and free.

Indeed, one regret is that this book is not another 100 or 200 pages longer. That's about how much more material I've written and photos I've shot. But it is not economically wise.

Much has happened since this book was first published in 1994. In six short years the philosophies and needs in managing deer — and managing deer hunters — have done an about face. With the new millennium comes a revolutionary educational and ecological thrust, so necessary if deer hunting is to be a part of our grandchildren's and great grandchildren's lives.

I trust that you will enjoy reading as well as benefit from the information, advice and memories — of deer, deer hunters and deer camps — provided on these pages.

Tom Fegely
Walnutport, PA
May 30, 2000

SECTION I
WHITETAILS
AND WHITETAIL HUNTERS

A game protector checks a hunter during the 1953 doe season in Allegheny National Forest, Warren County.

Chapter 1

DEER CAMP
A Pennsylvania Tradition

Deer camp.

The words ring magic in hunters' ears.

On the eve of opening day, windows in deer camps all across the state will glow as woodsmoke from seldom-used chimneys curls into the night-sky.

Deer camp is a place occupied for a only a few days each fall while holding a place in the minds and hearts of Pennsylvania hunters all year long. On the hottest days of August and the most frigid nights of February, hunters sip iced tea or steaming coffee and talk of deer camps past and present.

I vividly recall my first deer camp experience in Sullivan County in 1959. It was here I got my first taste of the spirit and camaraderie of the hunt. Consider it a move toward manhood if you will — a male bonding as old as the hunt itself. A tentative acceptance into the clan.

And more.

For one, to be a good deer camper you've got to be able to take a joke. Like someone hiding your hunting license. Sure panic.

Or taking a portrait of you perched in the outhouse. Sheer embarrassment.

Or some clown sneaking into the cook's bedroom and turning his clock ahead three hours.

That happened at one Cameron County camp I know. The cook climbed from bed, dressed, switched on the coffee pot and began frying eggs and pouring pancake batter. Problem was, it was only 2 a.m.

It took him and the rest of the crew a few sleepy-eyed minutes to realize what had happened as they staggered about wondering where the night had gone. The unhappy campers grumbled and returned to their bunks, vowing to find out who did the foul deed.

But they never found out and no one ever "fessed up," although there were a few prime suspects.

Funny how time can mellow such happenings. What was cursed in December becomes hilarious in July.

Of course, the essence of deer camp is seeing old friends and loved ones. Sons, brothers, parents, college friends and others taken afar by jobs and marriages are brought under one roof in buck season.

The firm handshakes. The smiles. The jokes. And reliving past hunts, of course.

While deer camp memories are strong, details somehow meld and blur over time. That's why, many years back when I hunted with a bunch of Lehigh Valley friends at Greentree Lodge in Carbon County, we began a tradition that makes history of deer camp happenings. It's in the form of several scrapbooks.

Who was there and who shot what?

Who bagged the biggest buck in 1971?

Who got lost in Lime Hollow?

Whose treestand was gnawed off by a porcupine?

Included are jokes and barbs. The camp menu. The lucky campers who filled their tags each year. And pictures. Lots of pictures.

When Lou starts bragging about the monster 8-pointer he shot in 1967, someone pulls out the official log book. It shows Louie proudly posing with a small Y-buck.

"Oh yeah," he admits sheepishly. "Guess it grew a bit since then."

It matters little whether deer camp is a rustic cabin in the backwoods, a motorhome, a leaky tent lit by Coleman lanterns or a plush lodge tucked away in a mountain retreat. The surroundings may vary, but the smells and spirit are the same.

Hoppe's No. 9 strokes the nostrils as it did 40 years ago. Morning coffee wafts through the bedroom, making alarm clocks unnecessary. A restless night dreaming about big-racked bucks is nipped by the roar of sizzling bacon in the camp kitchen.

Nervous jokes break the tension. More teasing. Checking for extra shells. Now where did I put that drag rope? Five extra shells oughta do it.

Someone sets bare feet on the porch to check the sky, then offers a forecast. Nervous chatter grows as the magic hour draws near, until the cabin finally falls silent as hunters head to their chosen stands.

You nestle against a familiar tree and await the deer hunter's dawn — none so special as on opening day.

Oh yes, every once in a while someone shoots a buck. But that's the bonus.

Deer camp is, more than anything, an escape. A celebration. A joy. An initiation. A reminder of what life and good times and buck hunting and friends are all about.

The nostalgic times take on new meaning as one moves along the trail from rookie to graybeard ... the gray accompanying a wisdom of the whitetail woods.

For hundreds of thousands of Pennsylvanians, it just doesn't get any better than this.

And what better way to start — and end — a book of tribute to Pennsylvania's deer and deer hunters than to honor its richest tradition?

Deer camp.

In a more modern scene, a Jayco motorhome is transformed into a "portable" deer camp in Bradford County.

The stuff of which buck hunter's dreams are made.

Members of Shoemaker's Camp in the Iron Run area of Clinton County pose at the meat pole, circa 1910.

Chapter 2

LOOKING BACK
The Evolution of Deer Hunting
in Pennsylvania

Charting a careful course for the future is largely dependent upon understanding the past. And nowhere is there a richer and more colorful history of whitetail hunting and management than right here in Pennsylvania — from the first game law more than 300 years ago through the ever-changing realm of more complex seasons and licenses of the past decade or more.

Today, deer numbers in the state match or surpass the populations of the early 1930s, more than 1.4 million, biologists estimated. But it wasn't always that way. Venison was the "beef" of pioneers and Indians, the source of buckskin coats and antler tools. Market hunters and others later shot them by lantern-light (called "jack-lighting), with snares, gun traps, dogs and by any other workable means.

Though exploitive, don't compare that to the poachers of today. Back then it was simply a way to make a living. Venison was a big city treat, selling in Pittsburgh markets for a mere two cents a pound.

Add to that an insatiable lust for wood and wood products during which much of the state was cleared. Stripped mountains, erosion and fires continued to wreak havoc with whitetails and other wildlife for many years.

By the turn of the 20th century deer had become rarities. From 1906 through 1924 nearly 1,200 deer were stocked from Michigan, Maine, New Hampshire, New Jersey, Ohio, Kentucky and a few from Pennsylvania breeders, hauled on railcars to their new homes. For 16 years doe hunting was banned.

The stocking efforts and work to protect deer by law were successful, although not without cost. Natural succession brought regrowth of seedlings and saplings, all within reach of whitetails. By 1930 the state hosted an estimated million deer.

Then came the crash. As forests matured to pole stage, producing minimal food, deer competed for what was available. Two severe, back-to-back winters in the mid-1930s caused mass starvation. That was followed by another period of growth, creating the need for a doe season, a wise yet misunderstood and controversial, management tool.

Since that time a mountain of changes, in both deer management and hunting laws, have been set. Some are controversial. Others are widely accepted. And they keep changing as we cautiously step into 21st century.

Following is a brief chronological history of whitetail hunting, deer laws and management from yesterday's "good old days" — to now.

1681 — Charter granted by King Charles II of England to William Penn to found a colony in the new world, later to become known as Penn's Woods or Pennsylvania.

1683 — Hunting is permitted on all lands under William Penn's charter; first bounty is established, 10 and 15 shillings for wolf scalps.

1721 — Pennsylvania's first game law enacted to protect deer from January 1 to July 1; fine of 20 shillings established to penalize violators.

1730 — Pennsylvania Rifle (later to be falsely dubbed the "Kentucky" Rifle) developed in Lancaster, York and Lebanon counties.

1749 — Illegal to hunt deer on Sundays except in "cases of necessity."

1760 — Deer may be hunted from August 1 to January 1.

1828 — The United Bowmen of Philadelphia, the country's first archery organization, is established.

1840 — Hunting deer in Monroe, Pike and Wayne counties legal only for Pennsylvania residents.

1850-1885 — Venison and other game becomes standard fare on free-lunch counters in better saloons in Philadelphia and Pittsburgh.

1867 — Last native elk killed in north-central Pennsylvania.

1873 — Use of dogs for deer hunting outlawed; all Sunday hunting banned.

1878 — Deer hunting in Pike County banned for three years.

1887 — President Teddy Roosevelt founds the Boone & Crockett Club.

1895 — Pennsylvania Game Commission established and authorized to hire 10 game protectors.

1897 — Salt licks and hounds are forbidden for deer hunting.

1900 — Congress passes Lacey Act forbidding the interstate transportation of wildlife taken in violation of state law.

1903 — Nonresident hunting license first established ($10).

1905 — Pennsylvania becomes the first state to protect black bears; buckshot banned for deer hunting; dogs chasing deer declared a "public nuisance" with permission for anyone to shoot them.

1906 — Fourteen game protectors are shot at with three killed, three seriously wounded, one slightly injured and one citizen killed while aiding a game protector; first deer stocked (50 from Michigan).

1907 — Pennsylvania becomes the first state to ban the use of automatic guns in hunting game; only bucks legal, 300 killed; does given absolute protection.

1909 — Bucks declared legal "with horns visible above the hair."

1911 — Game Commission authorized to appoint 30 game protectors.

1913 — Resident hunting law enacted, calling for a $1 per year license fee; bucks declared legal with "antlers two inches above the hair."

1915 — Game Commission authorized to appoint up to 60 game protectors.

1917 — Law passed making it unlawful to hunt from an automobile; camp limit for deer established; night hunting of all game animals, except raccoons, forbidden.

1919 — Legislature passes law to permit the Game Commission to purchase property to be known as "State Game Lands;" Game Commission authorized to hire up to 80 game protectors.

1920 — First State Game Land tract purchased in Elk County — 6,228 acres, for which the commission paid $2.75 per acre.

1921 — Bucks declared legal "with antlers four inches above the top of the skull."

1923 — Landowners are given the right to kill deer for damage to crops; first special doe license established and commission given the right to establish antlerless deer seasons; Legislature makes it illegal to "kill bucks unless with two or more points on one antler or with an antler at least six inches long from the top of skull;" Game Commission given authority to establish an antlerless deer season; first open season on elk brought from Yellowstone National Park and private game

Pike County hunters pose proudly with their bucks strapped to the fenders in a 1940 photo.

Woolrich-clad hunters check their kill at a 1941 Potter County deer camp.

A 16-year-old hunter poses with his first buck in 1943, location unknown.

propagators; resident hunting license fee raised to $1.25; non-resident license raised from $10 to $15.

1925 — Deer law amended to declare a buck illegal "unless it has two or more points on one antler;" farmers permitted to keep deer for food when killed while causing crop damage; cost of antlerless deer permit reduced from $5 to $2.

1927 — 185 antlerless deer killed by "special agents" in Cumberland and Lycoming counties to reduce crop damage.

1928 — First statewide season on antlerless deer, except in 16 counties which were closed; only deer that exceeded 50 pounds (field-dressed weight) legal.

1929 — Bow and arrow legalized for hunting game; field officers get their first uniforms.

1930 — First issue of official Game Commission publication, "Pennsylvania Game News," published in mimeographed form.

1931 — Elk given complete protection; maximum per acre purchase price for gamelands set at $10; first open season on both bucks and does with only spike bucks protected; kill recorded at 24,796 bucks and 70,255 antlerless deer.

1932 — Gypsy moth caterpillars appear in Pennsylvania, infesting a 400 square mile area of Lackawanna and Luzerne counties.

1935 — Unlawful to cast artificial light upon big game while possessing means of killing it ($100 fine).

1936 — Sales of timber from state gamelands authorized; first student class "in the world" enrolled at game protector training school, with 27 graduates.

1937 — Maximum purchase price per acre for gamelands increased from $10 to $30; archery preserves first established, one each in Forest and Sullivan counties; bounty removed on wildcats (bobcats); minimum age to purchase a hunting license reduced from 14 to 12.; loaded guns in vehicles forbidden.

1939 — Guns discharging .22 or .25 caliber rimfire cartridges prohibited for big game hunting; cost of antlerless deer permits reduced from $2 to $1.

1940 — Record deer harvest set at 186,575 — 18,056 from Elk County alone.

1942 — Hunters urged to donate deer skins to make vests for members of armed forces; licenses made of vulcanized fiber instead of aluminum.

1949 — Resident hunting license fee raised from $2 to $3.15.

1951 — Special season authorized for deer hunting with bows and arrows (Oct. 15-27) with $2 archery tag needed; county quota system authorized for issuance of doe licenses, 60 percent of tags issued by county treasurers and 40 percent by the Department of Revenue in Harrisburg.

1953 — Bucks declared legal "only with two or more points to one antler or spike three inches or longer."

In 1953, bucks were declared legal "with two or more points to one antler or a spike three inches or longer."

Hunters check the wares at the gun rack while others tend to dinner in these vintage photos.

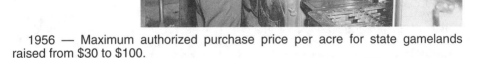

1956 — Maximum authorized purchase price per acre for state gamelands raised from $30 to $100.

1957 — Hunting of deer of both sexes authorized for bowhunting season; special antlerless license requirement dropped.

1958 — Commission inaugurates firearms and hunter safety education program with N.R.A.-qualified instructors; Safety Zone program created with cooperation of private landowners.

1959 — White-tailed deer named official state animal.

1961 — New law limits group hunting deer together shall not consist of more than 25 persons.

1963 — Hunting license fees increased from $3.15 to $5.20; junior license fee set at $3.20, $25.35 fee for non-residents.

1964 — Six-day antlerless deer season initiated in Southeastern Pennsylvania; winter archery season established in certain sections of the state (expanded in 1967).

1965 — Millionth acre of state gamelands purchased; establishment of deer record program in cooperation with Pennsylvania Outdoor Writers Association.

1967 — Record buck harvest set at 78,268; first statewide winter archery season set.

1968 — Spotlighting prohibited between midnight and sunrise.

Ed Kauffman of York County wears the Woolrich garb that's been a Pennsylvania standard since 1830.

1969 — Hunter safety training made mandatory before youth under 16 can purchase a license.

1971 — First Game Commission meeting open to general public.

1972 — Game Commission studies conclude that winter feeding is "of little value;" agency mandates that 50 percent of a county's doe license allocation shall be reserved for that county's residents for the first month of sales (rescinded later the same year).

1973 — Cost of antlerless deer license increased to $2.35; compound bow legalized; hunters required to mail in a deer harvest report within five days of kill.

1974 — First flintlock-only season established on certain state gamelands; 65 does and four bucks harvested in three-day hunt on 37 state gamelands.

1975 — Muzzleloader hunters take 174 deer on five hunting days.

1976 — 20 day muzzleloader season on 39 state gamelands yields 340 deer; damage to trees from treestands on public and private lands (except with written permission) subject to fine.

1977 — Record 146,078 buck/doe harvest set; winter deer feeding adopted stressing population control (winter feeding permitted only under extreme conditions); doe season held on Friday and Saturday following buck season; flintlock season open on 60 gamelands with 866 deer killed.

1979 — Flintlock season extended statewide, 2,459 deer taken; deer management system improved by incorporating carrying capacities of varied forest types.

1980 — Deer hunters required to wear at least 100 square inches of fluorescent orange on head or chest and back (later increased to 250 square inches on head, back and chest combined).

1981 — Record reported flintlock harvest of 8,246 whitetails; motorists permitted to pick up road-killed deer but must report it to Game Commission within 24 hours.

1982 — All first-time hunters, regardless of age, must take hunter education course; mechanical release for bowhunters legalized.

1984: Hunters forced to choose either a muzzleloader stamp or doe license, but not both.

1985 — Record 161,428 buck/doe harvest set; record bow harvest of 7,467; hunting license fee increased from $8.50 to $12.50.

1986 — Hunter education course expanded from 6 to 10 hours.

1987 — Illegal to spotlight from 11 p.m. to sunrise; battery-operated scopes legalized; Game Commission permitted to pay up to $400 (from $300) per acre for gamelands.

1988 — Record buck kill of 163,106 and record all-time buck/doe harvest of 381,399; "bonus" deer tag (leftover doe permits) program begun; big game hunters required to wear a minimum of 250 square inches of safety orange.

1989 — Record buck kill of 169,795; record all-time buck/doe harvest of 388,601; record allocation of 806,100 doe licenses; archers break all-time record for fifth consecutive year with harvest of 11,008 whitetails.

1990 — "Second bonus" doe permit program starts, permitting hunters to take three deer, two of which must be antlerless

1992 — Pilot program for killing antlerless deer during buck season on approved lands in four counties.

Jeff Heller of Lehigh County was among a number of properly-licensed hunters who were permitted to take three deer — two antlerless — beginning in 1990.

1993 — Fall archery season expanded to six weeks; elk herd expands to 205, highest ever; Pilot Deer Damage Program (during buck season) expanded to 16 counties; all hunters, no matter which hunting instrument is used, required to purchase doe tag to harvest antlerless deer; safest hunting year on record since 1915 when record-keeping began.

1994 — Game Commission approves deer control permit system allowing year-around culling by certified persons in suburban municipalities; harvest of antlerless deer (with proper license) on Deer Damage Areas during buck season expanded to all counties; state gamelands acreage approaches 1.4 million acres; Pennsylvania again leads nation in hunting license sales with 1,173,428.

1995 — Game Commission celebrates 100th anniversary; deer depredation program instituted; highest buck harvest of century recorded (182,235).

1996 — State's first Becoming An Outdoors Woman program held in Somerset County; archery safety zones reduced from 150 to 50 yards in Special Regulations Area counties.

1997 — Toll-free poacher hotline instituted (1-888-PGC-8001).

1998 — Gov. Tom Ridge signs legislation increasing license fee from $12 to $19 and non-residents, $50 to $100; hunters take second highest buck harvest ever (181,449); only Southwest counties eligible for surplus doe permits; 328,193 bow permits sold.

1999 — New license fees go into effect July 1; Nov.18-20 flintlock season for antlerless deer in Special Regulations Area; bowhunters take record 37,709 bucks and 34,362 antlerless deer.

2000 — Dawn of a new era in deer management.

Appreciating the evolution of deer laws and conservation attitudes of our grandfathers and great-grandfathers provides us all with a perspective of where we've been — and where we're going.

For more background on Pennsylvania's hunting history check out the fascinating and enlightening account of the agency's history in the hardcover book titled **The Pennsylvania Game Commission: 100 Years of Wildlife Conservation** by Joe Kosack. For credit card orders, call 1-888-888-3459. Cost is $13 with state tax and shipping included.

The fluorescent orange requirement was still **10** years off when Ray Greenbaum (left), the author (center) and Bob Greenbaum carried a doe from the Carbon County backwoods on a birch pole.

In some parts of northern Pennsylvania deer have devoured the understory.

Chapter 3

LOOKING AHEAD
Calling a Truce to the Deer Wars

When I was a kid, not yet old enough to hunt, I'd listen closely as my father, uncle and their friends argued over whether or not does should be legal game.

Those opposed (and most hunters were opposed in the 1950s, as I recall) claimed that for every doe killed the following year's population is reduced by three. One doe + two fawns = three deer, they reasoned.

Others (the minority) countered that deer in the "big woods" country to which they traveled each year for buck season could not live with too much competition for food, especially in severe winters when the snowmelt brought rotting carcasses in every spring seep in the northern tier.

My hometown then, near where I continued to make my home in southeastern Pennsylvania up until 1997, had only scatterings of deer. They weren't rare by any means, but surely not as common as today. The sighting of a big buck, any buck, brought plenty of chatter at the country store or the local taproom and before long everyone knew that "Homer saw a big 8-pointer cross Limeport Pike last night" or "Felix saw a 10-pointer and four does in his corn Wednesday morning."

Then, harvesting antlerless deer in the farmland and woodlot region might well have been counterproductive. Today, of course, all that has changed with not enough hunters having access to far too many deer.

The arguments still rage today, although some bold moves accompanying the arrival of deer management into the new millennium are resulting in revolutionary changes in the state's whitetail management program.

It's been nearly 10 years since David deCalesta, a research biologist for the U.S. Forest Service in Warren County, told game commissioners that "once deer get above 20 per square mile they begin to destroy their food base and begin to starve to death."

"If antlerless season is dropped, just for one year as many hunters have asked, the deer herd will soar from 1.1 million deer pre-season to about 1.6 million," said deCalesta.

Pennsylvania Farm Bureau spokesman Mel Eckhaus at the same time voiced similar opposition to any doe license reduction, stating that such a move "would devastate farmers."

At the same meeting, representatives from the Pittsburgh and Philadelphia areas urged the commission to work with them to reduce deer numbers in the suburbs. One request suggested a year-around season to placate the homeowners whose losses of ornamental shrubs and garden plants, as well as the increased chances for vehicle collisions with deer, are intolerable.

If farm and forest interests have a problem, consider the more recent testimony by David Robertson of the Pennypack Ecological Restoration Trust in Montgomery County:

"Our trust lands have about 150 deer per square mile and zero forest regeneration," he told the commissioners. "We need both new programs for urban deer and immediate increases in the number of antlerless licenses."

The point of all this is that deer hunters are no longer the only ones with a vested interest in the whitetail. Wildlife management through the ages has become a highly complex, scientific and sociological issue. Yet, the conflict caused by too many deer, specifically does, remains an embarrassing and costly Pennsylvania "tradition."

All that is taking an abrupt change of pace as we enter the new millennium as outside interests make demands on the Pennsylvania Game Commission and its million-plus "stockholders" to take some drastic measures to keep deer numbers — and costly deer damage — under control.

Biodiversity, economics and whitetails

Only months prior to the dawn of the new millennium, a diverse contingent of people — from hunters to anti-hunters and biologists to farmers and foresters — met in Camp Hill, Cumberland County, for the first-ever "Conference on the Impact of Deer on the Biodiversity and Economy of the State of Pennsylvania."

The conference, attended by more than 200 concerned conservationists, would set the stage for some truly revolutionary proposals into the year 2000 and beyond.

Here's what was revealed on that warm, October day as speakers, one after another, spelled out the problems as they saw it in past and present deer management policies and the cost inflicted on private sectors by the refusal of game commissioners to substantially reduce deer numbers statewide.

More deer, less habitat

Lesson one is that setting the table for Pennsylvania deer costs the forest industry more than $75 million a year and farmers absorb another $70 million in losses.

"Forest regeneration in Pennsylvania has been turned upside down by the white-tailed deer," concluded Dr. Susan Stout, a U.S. Forest Service silviculturist based in Warren County. "Renewal of forests in some places is impossible."

Deer nip seedlings in the bud, preventing them from establishing viable woodlands. High fencing, which is being utilized by the forest industry, costs $150-$200 per acre to erect and requires monthly maintenance, said Stout. It is not financially feasible for large tracts.

Lebanon County farmer George Wolf said too-numerous deer "cause as much as $7,000 to $9,000 losses for the average farm family." He said the farmer's greatest concern is out-of-balance deer numbers, followed by hunters who abuse the privilege of access to private lands. However it's the hunters, he acknowledged, who are the best and only tools for bringing deer numbers under control.

"We (hunters and farmers) must work together," Wolf challenged. "This us-and-them mentality must stop."

Cal DuBrock, chief of the Game Commission's Wildlife Management Bureau, said yet another $80 million in annual losses is caused by deer colliding with vehicles, adding to the $150 million in losses by foresters and farmers.

"We have many stakeholders — agricultural, forestry, deer hunters, businesses and services, legislators, motorists, homeowners, landowners and others — who are some way involved with deer," said DuBrock. "There are changes in the wind but those changes are not crystal clear."

At century's end, deer numbers across the state were estimated at 1.4 million with annual harvests by hunters and other mortalities totaling around 400,000.

Another speaker, Byron Shissler, an independent wildlife biologist from southwestern Pennsylvania, challenged groups and agencies to "consider science, values and opinion (and) incorporate them into the deer management program."

"Deer management isn't and never has been driven by science," said Shissler. "It's driven by feelings, ideas and the political process."

At the core of the problem Shissler noted, is a failure to consider the variety of entities and interests in the traditional system of managing deer for abundance.

"Hunter's expectations have resulted from an agricultural paradigm," Shissler, a hunter himself, noted. "The trees are a pasture and the deer a crop — managed to have as many as possible for hunters."

A question of biodiversity

At the core of any new deer management philosophy and program, Shissler and others emphasized, is a need to manage the ecosystems to include ALL of its components, not just deer. The diversity of members of any plant-and-animal community — called biological diversity — directly influences the longtime health of such systems.

What's the hunter's role in such an approach to land management? Will managing for biodiversity alter the hunter's traditional role as a "predator?" How do deer compete with other wildlife, like birds, for example?

"Such a system can use hunters to restore the natural process of predation which is an essential ecological service for a healthy herd," suggested Shissler.

A notable example of one member of an ecosystem (deer) negatively affecting another (birds) was posed by Bill McShea, an ornithologist with the Smithsonian Institute.

"Deer don't eat birds but they do alter the understory vegetation where some birds nest and feed," said McShea. "There is a definite competition."

Studies in some locales have shown zero survival of ground-nesting or low-nesting species because the insatiable whitetails have opened up the understory, thereby aiding predators in finding nests.

The problem, through Dr. Ann Rhoads' eyes, is simply "too many deer eating too many plants."

"We are losing biological diversity as deer seek out and consume highly-preferable plant species," said the University of Pennsylvania professor. "Deer are dictating the structure of natural communities and it's gone on so long and it's so profound that reversing it will be quite a challenge."

She cited studies showing that deer first eat preferable foods, then shift to less desirable items which may include rare ladyslipper orchids, white trilliums or Canada lilies. That's followed by deer devouring nearly anything palatable, in so

Deer will eat wildflowers, such as the painted trillium, when more preferable foods disappear, reducing a habitat's biological diversity.

doing having a negative effect on organisms that most people would not think are influenced by deer.

Dr. Rhoads believes that the ravages have gone on so long that just reducing deer numbers may now not be enough.

"We will need to seed because the plants are no longer there to produce their own seeds. In many places you can't begin to grow a new forest until you've fenced the deer out."

Through the hunters' eyes

Steve Trupe, representing the Pennsylvania Deer Association, said some of Pennsylvania's near-million deer hunters "perceive managing for biodiversity" as a threat because it will reduce deer numbers."

He cited four categories into which today's hunters fit, each with a somewhat different perspective on deer hunting.

One group wants a deer behind every tree, Trupe believes.

"These are typically older hunters who saw the revival of the herds and then their decline in the last two decades. They are the most vocal. They pay the bills and they want to see lots of deer."

A second viewpoint is held by rural-dwelling hunters who support scientific wildlife management "but not where I live."

Group three concedes that scientific management and biological diversity are the right things to do "as long as it doesn't affect their hunting." Trupe suggests. They typically back the Game Commission and are more environmentally aware than groups one and two, but they're also the least vocal.

The fourth group, says Trupe, is composed of the "enlightened deer hunters." They're more knowledgeable, understand the biology and behavior of deer, recognize the importance of healthy habitat and will support the concept of biodiversity.

"Problem is," Trupe comments, "these hunters are the least numerous of the four factions."

Deer in the suburbs

Of course, deer are no longer just rural concerns. Six Special Regulations Area counties — Allegheny, Bucks, Chester, Delaware, Montgomery and Philadelphia — and the urban sprawl of other Pennsylvania towns and cities has accounted for bucks and does in backyards nearly everywhere.

Deer in the suburbs continue to cause big problems.

"Suburban people are becoming more and more frustrated," said Bob Wallace of the Friends of the Wissahickon in Philadelphia's Fairmount Park. "Today there's more people and deer conflict than ever."

He cited vehicle collisions resulting in injuries or deaths, a high incidence of deer hosting ticks which carry Lyme disease, damage to gardens and domestic plants and other problems caused by super-abundant bucks and does. Biological and social considerations clash when lethal controls (hunters or hired sharpshooters) are proposed. Non-lethal methods, specifically immunocontraception, is not yet considered effective "and still has a long way to go as a viable option," said Wallace, even though anti-hunting factions cling to it as a cure for whitetail overpopulation and a way to eliminate hunting.

While some anti-hunting suburbanites insist on protecting deer, "others are welcoming hunters in treestands," said Wallace, citing a slow but legitimate change of attitude from just a few years ago.

Scott Williamson of the Wildlife Management Institute and head of the Pennsylvania Deer Management Working Group, said the first order of business in resolving deer conflicts "is to improve dialogue between stakeholders."

"Although they are diverse groups, there are a lot of similarities in the issues and concerns," said Williamson, underscoring the belief that "hunting is essential to the long-term sustainability of Pennsylvania's ecosystems."

"We can assure hunters they are valued and necessary and that they will play an important role in restoring an ecological balance," seconded Donald Gibbon of the Sierra Club. "But it's going to mean taking a look at the whole ecosystem, not just deer."

Cindy Dunn, executive director of the Pennsylvania Audubon Society, summarized the landmarks workshop.

"In one room today we gathered a preponderance of evidence and credible perspectives on the impact of white-tailed deer on Pennsylvania's ecosystem," Dunn concluded.

"Maybe we, as conservationists and sportsmen, can now move forward and start talking about solutions."

New leadership, new ideas

It wasn't long thereafter that Dr. Gary Alt realized he wouldn't be getting much sleep during the first few months of the new millennium.

Dr. Gary Alt takes time to answer questions about his deer management plans following a presentation in Allentown in March 2000.

Within three months following the workshop, Alt was on the road, presenting slide programs to more than 15,000 sportsmen and others across the commonwealth. More than 50 presentations in 80 days filled his January to April calendar.

But this wasn't just a traveling show.

At stake was the future of deer hunting in Pennsylvania.

It was all part of a massive educational campaign by the Pennsylvania Game Commission, for which Alt created a black bear management program which became the envy of the continent's game and wildlife agencies. Now, at the request of PGC Executive Director Vern Ross, the charismatic biologist is undertaking what he calls "the challenge of my life" as leader of the Deer Management Section.

His mission? To convince a million deer hunters that some big changes must be made for their sport to survive.

Not wasting any time in grabbing the problem by the horns, Alt was surprisingly candid, showing an honesty that came to be respected even by the commission's most vocal critics.

"The Pennsylvania Game Commission has not properly managed deer since the 1920s," Alt told his audiences. "In fact, Pennsylvania has long been held in low esteem by other biologists from throughout the country ... we've been a laughing stock."

Pennsylvania continues to be known for its numerous but small deer, bucks in particular, even though its reputation for larger bucks is often understated. Seventy-five percent of the antlered deer shot in the bow, gun and blackpowder seasons are but 18 months old. In some counties, these 1-1/2 year old bucks may compose as much as 90 percent of the kill. Alt considers that unacceptable.

Add to that the longstanding furor over high doe license allocations in the commonwealth's traditional hunting grounds, largely in the northcentral region, where whitetail numbers have plummeted due to ravaged habitats.

"We must think more and more about habitat and less and less about deer," said Alt, echoing the stances taken by various farm, forest, sporting and conservation organizations ."The very future of the Pennsylvania Game Commission and hunting depends on fixing whitetail populations and habitat."

One of Alt's most convincing visuals is of a deer exclosure in Elk County several years after it was clearcut. On one side the high fence is a treeless bed of ferns with little else growing taller than knee-high. On the other side, inaccessible to deer, is lush vegetation, including many trees beyond the seedling and sapling stages, which deer otherwise nip in the bud.

Knowing the dramatic effect demonstrated by deer exclosures, the commission is in the process of establishing them on state gamelands across the state where

This deer exclosure was constructed on State Game Land 44 in Elk County in May 1996, nearly a year following a clearcut. Photographed in spring 1999, the devastation wrought by deer (right) is dramatically demonstrated.

The browse line in the background is an indicator that the deer population is too high.

hunters and others can see for themselves what happens when whitetails run amok, destroying their habitat.

What Alt continually refers to as "fixing" the deer problem by focusing on habitat has historically been under fire by a relatively small but vocal faction of hunters. They have cursed the liberal allocations of antlerless deer permits, insisting that deer numbers in the traditional mountain counties must be restored to their former numbers.

Problem is, many areas are so lacking in food and cover that deer numbers cannot possibly build. Alt understands the quandary. That means taking populations even lower, hopefully providing a recovery period to jump start the forest's growth once more. But Alt knows he'll be criticized in some circles, as will his fellow deer biologists Bret Wallingford and George Kelly, on whom Alt relies for advice.

"A lot of these hunters remember the days when they'd go to places like Potter County and push 40 deer by on a drive" says Alt. "But if you counted the number of bucks there was only one or two ... and that alone tells you something was seriously wrong, even back then."

The problem wasn't created in two or three years nor will it be solved in two or three years. However, in early 2000 several changes to "tradition" were approved by the board of game commissioners.

The process of change

New for Keystone State's million deer hunters were the following changes for the 2000-2001 seasons.

• One of Alt's most interesting proposals was to offer muzzleloader hunters the opportunity to take antlerless deer nearly two months prior to the traditional mid-December doe season. The conservative management hunt served to reduce doe numbers prior to the November rut and before being bred, not after. In turn, the buck-to-doe ratio is brought closer, as occurs naturally in health herds.

• Add to that the benefits of having fawns born at the same time the following spring, not scattered across 3-4 months as occurs when a substantial number of does do not get bred until they go through two, three or more estrus periods. One of several new studies involves the radio-collaring of fawns to determine how many survive into fall.

In the wind as this is being written is the prospect of expanding the fall doe hunt to rifles and shotguns beginning in October 2001. Before any such proposal, the Game Commission will be taking a close look at the biological benefits derived from the initial blackpowder hunt. Another consideration to be taken into account before an October doe season is proposed will be the potential "danger factor" of hunting when the woods and fields are still in heavy foliage.

• To provide more opportunity for hunters to fill their doe permits, the December 2000 antlerless deer season was approved for opening on the second Saturday of the buck season. Traditionally, the doe season ran for three days beginning the Monday following the buck season.

• During certain seasons, properly licensed hunters will be permitted to take more than one deer per day. However, the initial kill must be removed from the field before a second deer may be hunted. The measure will apply on the last day of buck season 2000 and at other times deemed legal by the commission. Informal talk of making the entire buck season into an "any deer" hunt has also been heard, but no formal legislation had been proposed as of the summer of 2000.

• The battle over the sale and utilization of unsold county doe tags — at one time referred to as "bonus" licenses — was partially resolved with the provision that the leftover permits will be sold only for use on private land. The change is expected to alleviate the hunting pressure for antlerless deer on state gamelands and state forest lands, except when certain public lands are managed under a special Game Commission program.

Approximately two or every three deer killed in Pennsylvania come from private lands.

• Holders of Junior (age 16 and under) and Senior (age 65 and older) hunting licenses in possession of appropriate county doe tags were permitted to hunt for both bucks and does during the 2000 buck season. More recreational opportunity and greater efficiency in the filling of doe tags, which are allocated on a county-by-county basis, is seen as a hunter benefit for both youngsters and oldsters.

• Another change which will surely draw much debate in 2001 or 2002 is a minimum antler point provision, such as has been instituted in Arkansas and Mississippi.

"That's a possibility we're going to be exploring," said Alt. "It's one thing that can put bucks into older age classes and that's needed here."

Alt said Pennsylvania hunters kill a greater proportion of their bucks than any other state. Three of every four bucks harvested each year are but 18 months old.

"As a biologist, that scares me to death," says Alt. "Most of our bucks don't live long enough to grow good racks. Bucks grow their largest antlers between four and eight years, but here only one of every 100 bucks gets to 4-1/2 years old."

Problem is and has been traditionally, most hunters will not permit any legal buck (holding at least one 3-inch spike or a branched antler) to pass their stands.

Letting immature bucks "walk" includes an attempt to identify and not shoot button bucks in the antlerless deer season.

Pennsylvania bucks with proper nutrition, and allowed to grow 3-1/2 years or older, will usually be of trophy proportions.

"A more conservative antler provision such as that will constitute a huge culture change and it may be hard to do," Alt believes. "But letting bucks get older is what may be needed to put more of them into older age classes."

Alt said he's examined more than 15,000 bucks in the field, at locker plants and hunting cabins over the years and the oldest buck he's ever checked was 6-1/2. Only one of 100 Pennsylvania bucks ever gets to 4-1/2.

"We have the genetics," Alt assures. "It's the age structure that we don't have. And we'll only solve that problem by letting smaller bucks walk."

• In 1999 the commission began a "link" program to put hunters in touch with landowners needing assistance in keeping deer numbers in check. It's one part of the new system to micro-manage, where possible, and shift hunting pressure to areas needing it the most.

• Also under consideration is the creation a demonstration area or two across the state "to show just what a Pennsylvania buck can do when it gets older than two or three years," says Alt. A suitable gameland, perhaps, would become a model for Quality Deer Management practices in which only older bucks — with antler minimums — would be harvested.

"This promises to be the most massive habitat renewal program in the history of the state," Alt forecasted.

"We must build better relationships — among ourselves and non-hunters. If there's one thing I've learned it's that people who are presented with the facts will support the program. We simply cannot go on fighting deer wars as we did in the past."

"We are going to fix those forests," Dr. Alt pledged. "And as hunters, we will provide a free ecological service in keeping deer numbers under control."

Deer Management Units

For the past few years a map of Pennsylvania's new Deer Management Units has appeared in the regulations digest accompanying every license sale.

The map designates a new concept — although it's been discussed for many years — to get rid of county management units and, instead of political boundaries, begin to manage deer based on habitat similarity.

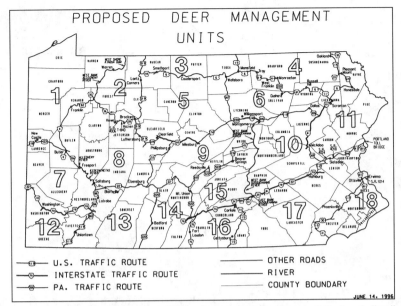

The 18 proposed units are based on forest distribution, public land distribution, human population densities and the age structure of the deer dwelling in each of the units.

As of the year 2000, the county system was still in effect. However, the inclusion of the DMU map in the regulations digest hints strongly that it may soon be instituted.

For now, the commission is asking that hunters report, on the card issued with the license and on the ear tag, the DMU in which a buck or doe was taken.

Expect even more revolutionary changes in the years to come as Pennsylvania's concerned hunters, naturalists, conservationists and others become more responsible managers of farmland, forests and other public and private lands, and as stewards of whitetails and all wild plants and wildlife.

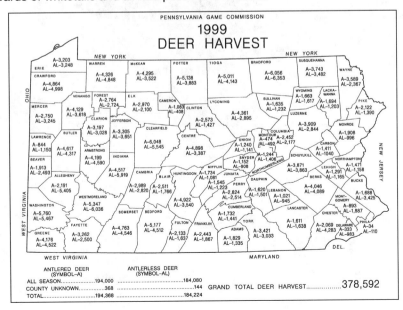

Deer hunters are required to wear a minimum of 250 square inches of safety orange during the buck and doe seasons.

Chapter 4

IT'S THE LAW

Deer Hunting's Rules and Regulations

Having hunted waterfowl, upland birds, deer and other big game in 30 states over the past couple decades, I've learned one important facet of pre-hunt preparation: Homework.

Part of that is knowing the game laws in the states or provinces in which you hunt.

Game laws vary dramatically from state to state as do license costs, season dates and the many rules and regulations within game laws. In recent years the Pennsylvania Game Law has become increasingly complex.

In my job as outdoors editor of a major eastern Pennsylvania newspaper since 1977, I receive several hundred calls annually about everything from applying for doe licenses to whether coyotes may be hunted during the deer season or if it's legal to spotlight deer during the archery season.

Many of these questions are answered in this chapter.

It's the hunter's responsibility to learn game laws before setting foot in the field. Ignorance of the law isn't a valid excuse for infractions, although it is frustrating when a hunter believes he or she has operated legally only to find that a law has been broken.

Following is a thumbnail guide to varied aspects of Pennsylvania deer hunting laws, regs and seasons of which sportsmen should be aware.

Deer hunting seasons

Although dates change from year to year, deer seasons in Pennsylvania are typically scheduled as follows. The listings are based on the 2000-2001 seasons.•
Archery season begins the last Saturday of September or the first Saturday in October.

• Buck season begins the first Monday after Thanksgiving and runs an additional 11 days, Sundays excluded, ending on a Saturday.

• Antlerless deer season, starting in 2000, begins on the final Saturday of the buck season and continues Monday and Tuesday.

As laws and regulations are subject to annual change, do not rely on the following information as the gospel, although many items stay the same year after year. Refer to the timely booklet accompanying the sale of each hunting license for official information.

• The late archery-flintlock season begins the first legal hunting day after Christmas and runs through mid-January.

License costs

Licenses (with exceptions as noted) are available from local issuing agents, county treasurers, the six regional Pennsylvania Game Commission offices and the main office in Harrisburg. Or they can be purchased by mail (on proper forms) through the Pennsylvania Game Commission, License Div., 2001 Elmerton Ave., Harrisburg, PA 17110-9797. The following list includes the $1 agent/handling fee for each license.

Gov. Tom Ridge has also allocated funds for instituting on-line hunting and fishing license sales. Access the PGC's HomePage — for license information and other Game Commission news — at www.pgc.pa.us.

Resident Junior	Ages 12-16	$ 6
Resident Adult	Ages 17-64	$20
Resident Senior	Ages 65 and older	$13
Senior Lifetime Resident	Ages 65 and older	$51
Nonresident Adult	Ages 17 and older	$101
Nonresident Junior	Ages 12-16	$41
Resident Archery	All ages	$16
Resident Muzzleloader	All ages	$11
Nonresident Archery	All ages	$26
Nonresident Muzzleloader	All ages	$21

• Muzzleloader firearms of any type and/or bows and arrows may be used during the regular firearms season without muzzleloader and/or archery licenses. Muzzleloader licenses for the special flint lock seasons must be purchased by Aug. 31.

• Senior Resident Lifetime licenses are available to hunters who reach their 65th birthday during the "year of application," defined as July 1 through June 30. They're available only through commission offices.

• Licenses are valid from July 1 to the following June 30, inclusive.

• A resident applicant must show satisfactory proof of residency, such as a valid driver's license, when applying for a hunting license. A Hunter Education Card or license from a previous year must also be shown.

Antlerless deer licenses

All hunters wishing to hunt antlerless deer must possess county permits. The initial application period for such licenses begins, by mail only, the first Monday in August. Leftover doe licenses are sold later, traditionally two weeks after the initial application date for "leftover" licenses, when available. Non-residents may apply for doe licenses beginning two weeks after the initial application date.

Each doe permit consists of a license to be displayed on the back and an ear tag and harvest report card.

A hunter purchasing a muzzleloader stamp need not give up his or her antlerless deer permit application, as in the past. Muzzleloader stamps must be bought prior to the day doe permits go on sale.

A doe license may be used in any season during which it is legal to harvest an antlerless deer.

Permit applications for Special Regulations Area counties or any other counties that may have been approved for "bonus" permits in a particular year can be found in the digest accompanying the sale of regular licenses. A county surplus tag permits a properly licensed person to take an additional antlerless deer during any season in which does are legal game.

Antlerless deer licenses ($6.00) are available only through county treasurers' offices.

Applications must be sent in the official pink envelopes issued by license issuing agents. All others will be rejected.

Anyone purchasing a license for the first time must complete a 10-hour Hunter-Trapper Education Course.

Landowner licenses

An eligible landowner who owns 80 or more contiguous acres open to public hunting in a cooperative access program with the Pennsylvania Game Commission, or an immediate family member living in the same household, is entitled to a Landowner Hunting License.

Eligible owners of 50 contiguous acres or more are also entitled to one antlerless deer license at the regular fee.

Junior licenses

Persons under 17 must present a written request to the license issuing agent, signed by a parent or legal guardian. Eleven-year-olds who have successfully completed a Hunter Education Course may apply for licenses if they will turn 12 by December 31 of the license year. The legal hunting age is 12, however.

Youths 12 or 13 must be accompanied afield by an adult (age 18 or over) member of the family or by a person serving in place of the parent. Youngsters 14-15 must be accompanied by any adult age 18 or older. Adults "must be close enough that verbal guidance can be easily understood" while afield, according to Game Law.

Hunters 16 or older may hunt alone.

Replacement licenses

If a license is lost, a replacement may be purchased by application to any issuing agent (preferably by the agent from whom the original license was purchased) or at any Game Commission office. Cost is $6.

Lost doe licenses can only be replaced (at original purchase cost) by county treasurers who issued the original tag.

Hunter Education Courses

A person who has not held a hunting license lawfully issued in this Commonwealth or another state or nation or does not possess a certificate of training shall be required to attain accreditation in a Hunter/Trapper Education Course before a hunting license is issued.

Regardless of age, persons who have not previously owned hunting licenses must take and successfully pass the 10-hour course. Such courses are offered throughout the state, usually by local sportsmen's clubs, by trained instructors. Most sessions are scheduled from spring through fall. Check local newspapers for course offerings or call the toll-free numbers of any of the six regional offices for information.

Handguns

A Sportsman's Firearm Permit or a license to carry a firearm is required to possess a handgun, concealed or in a motor vehicle, while hunting in Pennsylvania. The latter licenses are issued by county sheriffs or chiefs of police.

Applicants are required to appear in person. The Sportsman's Firearms Permit is issued only by county treasurers. The permit does not legalize the carrying of a loaded handgun in a vehicle nor at any other time than while hunting or traveling to or from a target range.

Carrying a loaded handgun while spotlighting or after having taken the lawful deer limit is prohibited.

Safety orange

Anyone hunting deer during the regular firearms seasons for deer must wear at least 250 square inches of fluorescent orange material on the head, chest and back combined. Bowhunters must wear an equal amount of the safety material during any overlap with fall turkey seasons, while moving. The orange may be removed when the archer is in a tree or ground stand. At that time a 100-square inch or greater band must be displayed within 15 feet of the hunter's location.

During the traditional post-Christmas flintlock season, muzzleloader hunters are not required to wear blaze orange. However, 250 square inches of the material must be worn during the new October flintlock doe season.

Safety zones

It is unlawful to hunt, chase or disturb deer within 150 yards of any occupied residence, camp, industrial or commercial building, farm house or farm building, school or playground without the permission of the occupants. This provision applies across property lines. While many lands open to hunting are posted with Safety Zone signs, their absence does not suggest the distance law does not apply.

The exception is in Special Regulations Area counties in which the minimum for bowhunters only is 50 yards.

Possession of road-killed deer

Pennsylvania residents may possess deer killed by motor vehicles at any time of the year. A permit must be secured from the Game Commission within 24 hours after taking possession of the deer. Antlers must be turned over to a Game Commission officer.

Firearms and vehicles

It is illegal to hunt from a vehicle, shoot at deer on a public road or right-of-way open to public travel, shoot across a road (unless the line of fire is high enough to preclude any danger) or alight from a vehicle to shoot, unless the shooter is at least 25 yards from the road.

Live ammunition in the chamber or attached magazine is illegal in any vehicle, parked or moving. Nor can a loaded gun be propped against or rested on a vehicle.

For the purpose of transportation, muzzleloaders are considered unloaded when all powder is removed from the flash pan or the percussion cap has been removed from the nipple.

Unlawful sporting arms/sighting devices

Automatic and semi-automatic rifles and handguns, air or gas-operated rifles and handguns, and crossbows (excluding hunters with crossbow permits) are not legal during the deer seasons.

A sight, scope or any other device on a firearm or bow that projects a beam of any kind from the sight onto the target is illegal. This does not apply to scopes with "dots" or "light-sites" which do not cast rays. Nor does it apply to external fiber-optic sights which retain but do not throw light.

Spotlighting/Legal hunting hours

Spotlighting deer is a popular recreational activity throughout much of the state. It is permitted until 11 p.m. each day throughout the year except during the regular buck and doe seasons. It is unlawful to spot deer while in possession of a bow-and-arrow or firearm. Also, casting the rays of a beam onto any building or farm animal is illegal.

Legal hunting hours for deer are from one-half hour before sunrise until sunset. Specific shooting hours for all parts of the state are published in the annual rules and regulations digest issued with hunting licenses.

Bait hunting

While legal in some states, baiting is outlawed in Pennsylvania. Such an infraction carries a fine and court costs plus loss of hunting privileges for one year if game is not killed and two years if a kill is made. Artificial or natural baits include hay, grain, fruit, nuts, salt, chemicals, minerals or other items deemed edible attractants.

In addition, hunting is not permitted on areas in which "baits" or supplemental foods had been placed 30 days previous, regardless of type or quantity.

Scents and lures

Up until the early 1990s the Game Law, strictly interpreted, made it illegal for hunters to use natural or artificial scents or lures (food, estrus, urine or other scents) while hunting, although the law was never fully explained or rigidly enforced.

The fine line between scent-use and baiting had hunters in a quandary for a time. However, the commission has since clarified the law, making it legal to use scents while hunting. The only exception is scents poured on the ground which leave a mineral or salt deposit to attract deer.

Mistaken kill

Any person who mistakenly kills a deer (shooting a doe during buck season, for example) shall immediately remove the entrails and deliver the carcass to a Game Commission officer in the county where it was killed. Deer must be tagged before removal from the area where taken. For turning in the mistaken kill, the hunter will be permitted to pay only a portion ($25) of the established fine for the infraction and will be issued another deer tag.

Special Regulations Areas

All of Allegheny County in southwestern Pennsylvania and Bucks, Chester, Delaware, Montgomery and Philadelphia counties in the Southeast are designated as Special Regulations Areas.

Rifles are not permitted here although muzzleloaders (including percussion sidelocks and in-lines), manual or semi-automatic shotguns 20 gauge or larger loaded with buckshot or slugs and bows-and-arrows may be used. Bowhunting-only is permitted in Philadelphia County and buckshot may not be used in Allegheny County.

In recent years, gun seasons in these counties have been very liberal. For example, in 2000 the deer seasons ran from November 27-December 12 and December 26 to January 13 with required antlerless licenses. Antlerless deer (with valid county doe permits) may be taken throughout all deer seasons.

Hunters may purchase unlimited numbers of licenses for these counties. Only one application may be sent in the initial (early August) application period. Surplus applications are accepted via mail or over the counter three weeks after the initial application period.

Deer Damage Areas

Designated properties under the Deer Damage Area program throughout the state which are registered with the Game Commission are open for antlerless deer during the regular buck season. Hunters are required to have valid county doe permits to hunt these lands, which are posted with special green signs.

Lists of cooperating landowners are available by sending a self-addressed, stamped envelope to the regional office in which the county is located. Request only locations of participating farms in the specific county or counties which will be hunted.

Legal bucks/does

Bucks are legal game as long as they hold two or more points on one antler or have a spike at least three inches long.

"Antlerless" deer are defined as having no antlers, or one or two antlers less than three inches.

Camp rosters

It is unlawful to hunt deer in groups of 25 or more persons. If five or more hunters from a permanent camp cooperate to drive deer, they must maintain a roster in duplicate. The drive leader must carry one copy and another must be posted at headquarters and remain displayed for 30 days following the close of the season.

The roster must include the license year, name of camp or hunting party, location, township, county, name of each party member and hunting license number, firearms caliber and for all game harvested, the date, weight, number of points (if applicable). Dates arrival and departure must also be listed.

Persons participating in drives or in any way aiding another licensed hunter, junior or senior, must have a valid Pennsylvania hunting license. A person driving deer for another person during the antlerless deer season must also have an antlerless deer permit for that county.

Any person who has harvested a deer may continue to take part in the hunt as long as he or she does not carry a loaded firearm or bow with a nocked arrow.

Damage from treestands

Hunters using portable or permanent treestands are breaking the law if, on public or private property, trees are damaged while constructing or using a stand or climbing device. The law goes so far as using or "occupying" a treestand (which someone else may have placed) which has damaged a tree.

This law does not apply to landowners building or otherwise using treestands on their own properties or others who have received written permission to use or construct treestands.

Tagging, transporting and reporting

Deer must be tagged immediately after harvest and before the carcass is moved. Tags attached to buck (regular license) and doe licenses must be filled out according to instructions on the tags and attached to the ear of the animal. It must remain attached until processed and when taken to a taxidermist. The tag must be attached while transporting the carcass, although unmarked parts of deer carcasses need not be tagged.

Issued with each license is a big game harvest report card which must be completed and sent to the Game Commission within 10 days after the harvest. A photocopy may be used.

Pennsylvania hunters have long been notorious for their non-reporting of harvests, hampering deer management efforts by agency biologists who must calculate estimated buck and doe kills each year. Reporting rates average only about 50 percent but are largely unenforceable because cards are sent via mail, with no guarantees on their delivery.

Interestingly, the commission has analyzed county by county reporting rates, ranking Montgomery (61 percent), Lebanon and Snyder (each 60), Lehigh (59) and Berks (58) among the most cooperative for returning their buck reports.

At the bottom of the list are Clearfield and Indiana (each 39 percent), McKean (40) and Allegheny (41).

To "calculate" harvests in each county, those percentages are used to determine more closely how many deer were taken when factored against license data gathered by conservation officers. Game Commission officials annually check ear tags and hunter license numbers and names at deer processing plants, hunting camps, in the field and at other locations. The information is fed into a computerized system to aid in determining how many successful hunters filed report cards.

Deer unfit for consumption

A hunter who legally kills a deer and discovers the flesh is unfit for consumption shall, within 12 hours, deliver the carcass, less entrails but with the head and hide, to any conservation officer. A written authorization will be given to the hunter to continue hunting for the remainder of the season.

Coyotes and foxes

Coyotes may be hunted during the regular antlered and antlerless deer seasons as long as the hunter holds a valid license with an unused deer tag. It is not legal to hunt coyotes during these seasons once deer tags have been filled.

A furtaker's license is not needed to hunt coyotes although it is needed to hunt foxes. However, it is not legal to hunt foxes during the hours in which deer may be legally hunted.

The author fills out the tag on his 1999 license after arrowing a Northampton County 7-pointer with his Golden Eagle Split-Fire and Satellite Broadheads. All deer must be ear-tagged before being moved.

Most people overestimate the size of a buck, which stands only about three feet from ground to shoulder.

Chapter 5

BIOLOGY AND BEHAVIOR
What Every Hunter Should
Know About Whitetails

Books could be written about the life of the white-tailed deer.

And hundreds have.

It's no secret that the most successful hunters are also students of the whitetail. They read more than merely "how to" articles and spend the off-season patrolling the deer woods, usually with camera or binoculars in hand, unraveling the mysteries of this complex animal.

Scientific Classification

The Pennsylvania whitetail is scientifically named *Odocoileus virginianus borealis*, from Greek roots. The genus name, *Odocoileus*, means, "hollow tooth," in reference to the depressions in the crowns of the deer's molars.

The species name, *virginianus*, is derived from fossils found in caves of Virginia. Hence, the name (once more commonly used than it is today) "Virginia whitetail."

All whitetails in North and Central America share the same genus and species name, but scientists have further classified them into subspecies, 30 of which range from southern Canada through most of the U.S. and into Mexico and Central America. Here, and in much of the Northeast, the *borealis* subspecies was originally found. It's considered the largest of the subspecies.

Although it's only occasionally heard today, the *borealis* subspecies is generally known as the "Michigan deer." However, reintroductions of whitetails into Pennsylvania from other states in the early 1900s, including Michigan, Maine, New Jersey, Ohio, New Hampshire and Kentucky, accounted for the import of both the *virginianus* and *borealis* subspecies, which are now heavily interbred.

Physical characteristics

In any talk of deer sizes, only averages apply. Some Pennsylvania bucks exceed 200 pounds and others barely reach 125 pounds. Of course, genetics is one reason for the differences but food and age are more important. Farm country whitetails with access to crops most of the year — "corn-fed bucks," hunters call them — will grow to larger sizes than mountain county deer which are more highly competitive, subject to severe winters and destined to lesser quality diets.

In Pennsylvania, the average adult buck weighs 140 pounds and stands 32-34 inches at the shoulder. Most hunters, quizzed as to a deer's height, will guess it is much higher.

Run a tape from nose tip to tail base and a buck will average 70 inches. The tail vertebrae add another 10-12 inches but the long, brown and white tail hairs make it seem a lot bigger — especially when one runs off following an errant shot.

Of course, deer weights vary with the seasons. A buck weighing 135 pounds at winter's end might easily weigh 175-185 pounds by rutting time.

Pelage

In summer, deer grow a thin, reddish coat which is shed, hair by hair, and replaced with a darker and heavier coat of hollow, insulating hairs and finer underfur for winter. Surprisingly, it's the summer coat that is made up of the most individual hairs.

In his book, *The Deer of North America*, my longtime friend Leonard Lee Rue III of neighboring New Jersey reveals that a single square inch of skin from the top of the neck of an adult buck shot in late November held 2,664 winter hairs. An equal-size piece of skin taken from a road-killed summer (August) buck had 5,176 hairs.

Rue went a step further with his calculations, concluding that a winter buck is covered with about 3.2 million hairs and a summer buck with about 6.2 million hairs. The summer pelage, of course, is much finer than the underfur and long, hollow winter hairs which trap body heat.

By the beginning of bow season in late September, most deer have shed their summer coats but it's surely not unusual to see some bucks and does that are "redder" than others well into October.

Although deer in their winter dress are less likely to be active on hot, fall days, it is not believed deer possess sweat glands as we do. They lose heat in various ways but sweating is not one of them, according to deer biologists. Yet, I've seen and photographed bucks — once on an icy, November morning in Lycoming County — that appeared to be soaked. No appreciable open water was nearby and, upon considerable thought, it occurred to me that the deer lost body heat in chasing does and when it contacted cold air, it caused condensation on its body.

Sight

Every hunter with more than a couple seasons under his or her belt has learned that deer have excellent eyesight. Flick a hand or move your head and the jig's up.

A whitetail's summer hair is notably reddish and thin.

This Lycoming County buck mysteriously appeared to be perspiring as it chased does on a chilly November morning. Deer, however, do not possess sweat glands.

However, as wary as they are, deer often do not recognize objects that do not move. I've had yearling does as close as 10 feet as I pressed my back against a tree, while I was dressed in abundant blaze orange. The deer were a bit curious but not frightened. Had I moved or had they picked up my scent, I'm sure they'd have fled immediately.

Unlike us, and many other predators, deers' eyes are located on the sides of the head, angled slightly toward the nose. The placement provides them the ability to see nearly full circle. It's believed a deer can see 310 degrees without moving its head. When focusing on an object, however, both eyes are used, permitting three-dimensional perception.

Despite their excellent eyesight, I've been able to stalk surprisingly close to lone deer feeding in fields and woods. When their noses are on the ground they're focused on feeding. Before lifting the head, they'll usually jerk their tails, the signal for you to freeze.

If a deer sees you and you don't move, it will often go back to feeding. But if it's even slightly suspicious, it will feign feeding, then quickly jerk its head upward to see if the object of its attention has moved. That, and stomping the ground with their forefeet at such times, are games deer love to play and hunters love to be part of. For the deer, however, it's a serious "game" of survival.

Do deer see colors as we do?

It's standard knowledge that deer see the world in shades of gray. However, recent studies at the University of Georgia and the University of California indicate blue and yellow may stand out vividly while reds and oranges blend with greens. That's good news to Pennsylvania hunters required to wear at least 250 square inches of the fluorescent color, which may appear as white or light gray depending on the habitat. On dull and cloudy days, however, the flourescent orange may contrast even more with a deer's environment than on a sunny day, readily revealing a hunter's position.

Hearing

No big news to anyone who hunts is that deer have an extraordinarily acute sense of hearing. Like radar antennae, they swivel their cupped ears to catch even the slightest sounds such as the snap of a twig or the scrape of a jacket against tree bark.

The deer's cupped ears which trap sounds account for its excellent hearing.

Whenever a deer's hearing sensitivity is reduced, such as when high winds cut across the woods and fields, they'll become nervous and cautious. Often they'll lay up in thickets under such conditions and become extremely difficult to hunt. The wise hunter, however, may be able to take advantage of the winds and the noise and movements it creates to slip in close to them.

Deer become accustomed to certain sounds but anything unusual will command their attention.

Scent detection

Not only is a whitetail's sense of sound adversely affected by brisk wind but they also have a more difficult time locating the source of wind-borne scents.

The world of smells in a deer's environment is every bit as important as what it sees and hears, perhaps more important. More deer have probably been alerted to hunters' presence via their noses than their eyes and ears.

Of course, deer smell not only humans but use their phenomenal scenting abilities to communicate with one another throughout the four seasons. Their ultra-sensitive noses pick up every odor — from other deer, predators and humans — carried in the breeze.

Sometimes such sensitivities are enhanced. A buck may be seen *flehmening* (often improperly called "flaming") during the rut. It stiffens its neck, raises its nose and curls its upper lip, testing the wind. The act traps the molecules of a doe's scent on the epithelial lining of the nostrils and the Jacobsen's organ, located atop the palate in the mouth. The act is used primarily to detect urine smells and determine whether or not a doe — even a few hundred yards upwind — is in estrus.

How far can a deer smell a human? It's probably safe to say that no one knows for sure but humidity, breezes and temperature all play a role. I've had deer I'm convinced didn't see me in a treeline stand raise their noses several times, then bound off in the opposite direction even though I was at least 200 yards away. On other occasions deer have been downwind 20-25 yards and seemed not to catch my scent.

An entire industry has been built on trying to fool deers' noses, some of which work to the hunter's advantage and others which defy their purposes.

SCENT GLANDS

Deer do more than detect humans and predators with their noses. They also communicate with one another via glands on the legs and head. Fresh droppings and urine also serve as tools of olfactory communication.

The next time you have the opportunity to check out a deer close up, spend a few minutes locating the following scent glands, each with a different function.

Interdigital glands

The interdigital glands are located between the hooves of all four feet. Spread the toes on your next kill and look for the small, sparse-haired sac which, to my nose, emits a "sour citrus" smell although others have described it as a "foul, rancid odor." The "cheesy" excretions from the sac aid deer in trailing one another and noting the presence of others in their territories.

The scent evaporates and loses its strength over time, which is why bucks trailing does, or even predators following a deer's trail, are provided clues as to how long in the past a scent trail was made.

It's believed that running deer emit more scent than they do when walking, as the hooves are splayed. It's also been ventured that deer pounding their front feet when disturbed, as when in a face-off with a hunter and not certain what they're looking at, will create a detectable interdigital scent to alert others that something's amiss.

Metatarsal glands

The metatarsal glands are set on the outside of a deer's hind legs, between the feet and knees. They're readily visible as white, oval patches of hair tufts surrounding the small, hairless pores.

The function of these glands is the subject of disagreement among biologists. Some believe the metatarsals' purpose is to leave scent on the ground when bedded. Others say its function has nothing to do with scent. Rather, it's been offered, their purpose is to enable deer to detect vibrations in the earth from nearby movement when the deer is bedded and the glands are in contact with the earth.

Tarsal glands

The tarsals are the best-known glands among hunters. This is the most important "communication" gland and hunters (bowhunters in particular because they hunt the early rut) should be aware of their location and function.

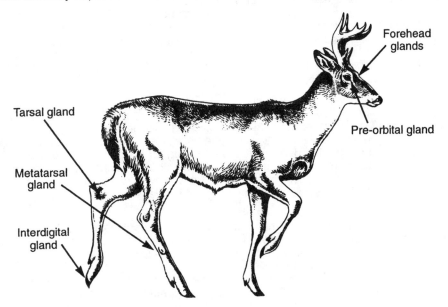

Forehead glands

Tarsal gland

Pre-orbital gland

Metatarsal gland

Interdigital gland

Tarsals are found on the insides of a deer's hind legs, on both bucks and does. The tufts of elongated hairs are readily visible, especially on rutting bucks when the excretions make the gland dark, oily and odoriferous.

Glands beneath the skin are connected to hair follicles which transfer the fatty secretions, called *lactose*, to the hairs. It's believed this is the "fingerprint" of whitetails, individualizing animals as to sex, age and physical condition.

During the rut, bucks urinate over these glands as they tend to scrapes. This process individualizes a buck's trademarked odor. The same holds for does, which allow urine to run down their legs at estrus time. Bucks sometimes rub their tarsals together while urinating, performing a bow-legged mating dance, of sorts.

The odor from a tarsal gland is enhanced when a deer becomes excited. Specialized muscles make the hairs stand erect, further releasing scent into the air. It also serves as a visible signal to other deer with which it may be traveling.

The odor of a buck's tarsals is most evident during the rut and I, as surely have other hunters, have experienced a "reverse," of sorts, in being able to smell their presence. On one occasion I located a bow-killed buck in a thicket as the breezes carried the blackened tarsal's scent to my nose.

Proper use of synthetic and natural tarsal scents has accounted for both bow and gun hunter's success in Pennsylvania hunting seasons.

Pre-orbital glands

The pre-orbital gland's secretion is one many hunters may have noted but, perhaps, didn't identify as anything more than a deposit at the lower corners of the eyes.

Also called the lacrymal glands, these are actually tear ducts. Check out a whitetail mount from a skilled taxidermist and the narrow slit below the eyes, where the glands are set, can be readily seen. The yellowish or whitish, waxy secretion is often visible on live deer.

It is believed the pre-orbitals emit scent which bucks will rub on overhanging twigs and ground vegetation.

Forehead glands

Forehead glands are a relatively new find among both biologists and hunters, although their function isn't fully understood. Many hunters have witnessed bucks making rubs, almost always brushing their foreheads against the scarred bark. Limbs, saplings and leaves are rubbed similarly.

The skin in the crown region contains scent glands which often discolor the forehead, staining it dark or, if cedars are present a rusty tint may be seen.. Deer visiting a rub will first smell the area, lick it and deposit their own forehead scent. The deer I've watched are seldom in a state of excitement, unlike the aggressive scraping of antlers on a bush or tree, but seem to be carefully and purposely depositing their individual forehead scent.

Saliva

Compared to studies done on glands and scents, very little is has been done to discover whether or not a deer's saliva is sufficiently distinctive for it to play a role in communication. Most hunters are aware of a buck's behavior of licking twigs above a scrape. It's possible the deer nibbles on the twig for the sake of depositing salivary scent. I've also watched captive bucks smell the "licking stick" above the scrape of another buck, hinting that saliva may play a role. That, however, will remain conjecture until some university biologist studies the phenomenon.

Population dynamics

As evidenced by the phenomenal growth of deer populations in suburbia over the past couple decades, it's known that they are capable of rapidly expanding their ranges and maintaining high reproduction rates in suitable habitats.

Predation from wolves and mountain lions is a thing of the past and even Pennsylvania's "new wolf," the coyote, seems to have only minor impact on population control. Hunting, of course, is the most important control method although the combined effects of deaths from vehicles, winter mortalities, disease, fawn losses, deer killed for crop damage and accidents are also taken into consideration by biologists.

Currently, the Pennsylvania Game Commission is attempting to control deer numbers by establishing density goals in each county (County lines are Pennsylvania's version of management units although that may change as the 21st Century progresses.). The desired density goals per square forested mile (see "In Brief" items in county profiles) is largely controlled by doe license allocations and hunter success rates.

Overpopulation accounts for delayed breeding ages, low fawning rates, fawn mortality, winter losses, low weights and small antler sizes.

Whitetail society

The whitetail is obviously a social animal, most comfortable when in the company of others of its kind. However, like many people, small groups are preferred over large gatherings. Yet, in some wintering grounds, deer numbers may exceed 100 at one place, largely due to available food.

More common is the "matriarchal" group of a "boss" doe, her fawns of the year and her yearling female offspring. Young bucks go their own ways, sometimes as far as 25 miles from their birthplaces, while their sisters remain dedicated to a closer home range. Forget the Disney version of a big-racked buck, submissive doe and a couple Bambis napping in the summer woods. It doesn't happen.

On occasion, several generations will stay together in a family group, although they don't necessarily travel with one another at all times. In May, pregnant does become solitary and later bear, then nurture, their fawns.

Bachelor bucks, which travel together summer through early fall, determine hierarchy as the rut period approaches. Simple antler-testing often decides which buck rules and which are submissive. Bucks of near-equal sizes, however, may get into full-fledged donnybrooks, often resulting in injury and, rarely, death. Sparring is largely a determination of strength, as are the outright battles among older bucks which frequently result in injury but only rarely in death.

The ranges of individual whitetails vary from season to season and within the diverse habitats which make up the state. While most Pennsylvania whitetails do not "migrate," studies show some long distance movements. As much as 50 miles may be covered during winter in the vast, contiguous tracts of forest composing much of the northern tier.

Smaller shifts in home range, which average 500 to 3,000 acres, are the norm. Rutting bucks and yearling fawns breaking off from their mothers exhibit the greatest range shifts.

Food choices

Pick up any hunting magazine devoted to deer and surely you'll find an article or two on scouting and locating feeding areas. Problem is, deer are catholic in their dietary choices, consuming a variety of plants. From season to season the menu changes. The serious hunter will pattern these changing food sources and adapt his or her stand or still-hunting locations to what's "ripe" at a particular time of the season.

Deer, like cattle, are grazers. That is, they're adapted to feeding on grasses and herbs and will choose non-woody plants when and where available. But they're also browsing animals, nipping leaves, buds and twigs as the wander, particularly in winter.

Clearcuts are prime examples of good whitetail country where the most varied menu is available. Seedlings and newfound, sun-loving plants on the forest floor entice deer from the deep forest and offer excellent places to hunt.

Grasses make up much of the spring diet followed by herbaceous plants (forbs) in summer and mast and fruits in fall. Winter brings a natural reduction in food intake as grasses, forbs, honeysuckle and other browse which hold leaves late into the year is eaten. Woody browse is sought when snows prevent grazing. In some places, volunteers working with Game Commission biologists will cut winter browse

White oak acorns are sweeter than those of the red oak family.

A good beechnut mast will keep deer in an area as long as they're dropping.

for deer, delivering the tender twigs from the crowns of saplings and other trees to the forest floor. In agricultural regions, corn, alfalfa, winter wheat and other crops are tapped, as they are throughout the growing season.

Like humans, deer become selective when a variety of foods are available. They make choices from whatever menu's at hand, although not all deer have a wide choice of entrees. Succulent plants are preferred over hardened vegetation. However, a Penn State study revealed that woody stems make up about one-fifth of the whitetail's diet throughout the year.

Of course, every hunter knows the beginning of bow season brings whitetails to oak ridges like squirrels to a birdfeeder. All acorns are consumed but deer show a decided preference for the sweeter white oak. Other commonly consumed carbohydrate and protein-rich mast and fruits include apples, beechnuts, blackberries, blueberries, cherries, dogwood, persimmon, hickory nuts, grapes and pears, among others.

At best, deer are opportunists with a taste for a wide variety of foods. Some, such as red maple, offer better nutrition and are more widely utilized than rhododendron or other foods eaten when high-quality nutrition is scarce and competition is high.

A cooperative Penn State-Pennsylvania Game Commission study revealed the following plants found in stomach content samples of wild whitetails. Some, of course, showed up more abundantly than others and a few, such as mountain laurel, may be classed as "starvation foods." But they're all part of the Pennsylvania whitetail's vast and varied diet.

Woody Plants

Apple	Grape	Pitch pine
Arborvitae	Gray dogwood	Privet
Ash	Greenbrier	Red oak
Aspen	Hawthorn	Red cedar
Beech	Hazelnut	Red maple
Birch	Hemlock	Rhododendron
Blackberry	Hickory	Multiflora rose
Black cherry	Honeysuckle	Sassafras
Black locust	Jackpine	Spruce

Blue beech	Juneberry	Sugar maple
Blueberry	Larch	Sumac
Cherry	Mountain laurel	Sweetfern
Chestnut oak	Mulberry	Teaberry
Coralberry	Oak	Tulip poplar
Crabapple	Orange	Virginia creeper
Deerberry	Partridge berry	White pine
Dogwood	Pear	Willow
Elderberry	Persimmon	Witch hazel
Elm	Pine	

Non-woody Plants

Aster	Ground cherry	Sheep sorrel
Bellwort	Indian pipe	Speedwell
Canada Mayflower	Liverwort	Spikenard
Cinquefoil	Mayapple	Spring beauty
Club moss	Milkweed	Trefoil
Cohosh	Panic grass	Violet
Crown vetch	Plantain	Wild geranium
Dandelion	Pokeweed	Wild mustard
Goldenrod	Ragwort	

Commercial Crops

Alfalfa	Clover	Soybean
Apple	Corn	Strawberry
Bean	Lettuce	Timothy
Cabbage	Oats	Tomato
Cantaloupe	Potato	Wheat
Carrot	Rye	

Reproduction

Yearling bucks will depart their mother's home range in September, acting like their fathers and other older bucks during the rut. Pennsylvania bucks become sexually mature their first fall and sexually active at 18 months, but many fail to breed during their first year due to competition from older bucks. Some doe fawns will go into their first estrus period at seven or eight months and, if bred during the post-rut, produce fawns in mid-to-late summer the following year.

The age and health of a doe determines her reproductive capacity. Simply, does living in prime habitat produce more fawns than those in poor range. As a doe

Corn is a favorite with deer, beginning with its milk stage in August.

Fawns are born following a 200-205 day gestation.

matures she stands a better chance of bearing twins or even triplets. According to Game Commission studies, young does will produce a larger percentage of male fawns than do older does.

Bucks are ready to mate in October but it's the doe who determines the timing of copulation. Bucks regularly tend small groups of does from late October through November, chasing after them relentlessly. Hunters sometimes interpret this as watching a doe "in heat" when she's actually fleeing the buck because she's not yet in heat (estrus). As the estrus period, which lasts only 24-28 hours, approaches, bucks will stick tightly to near-ready does.

Following breeding, the buck will often stay with the doe for several hours and more. Then he moves on to seek other receptive females, rogue that he is.

The gestation period is typically 200 to 205 days. Considering the mid-November peak of the rut, most births occur at the end of May and beginning of June. But some are born earlier and others later.

Does unbred during their short receptive period will again come into estrus 28 days later. Fawns resulting from such matings are born later in summer than the norm. On rare occasion, as I experienced in Bradford County on the gun season opener in 1989, spotted fawns will be seen well into fall. I also photographed a spotted fawn in Delaware County on the second day of the winter muzzleloader season (Dec. 27) in 1996. Its mother was nowhere in sight. Chances are the late-born fawn, which was probably conceived the previous May, did not survive.

Although few people ever witness it, fawn mortalities can be quite high. Besides accidents, such as getting stuck in fences or being hit by cars, there's also predation from bobcats, coyotes and free-running dogs.

Does stressed by the rigors of winter enter spring in poor condition and will give birth to fawns weighing less than the typical five to seven pounds. Small, weak fawns may not be able to stand and nurse or nutritionally-stressed does may not produce a sufficient amount of butterfat-rich milk. If a deer is weak and malnourished in winter, the embryos may be resorbed, a natural "abortion," of sorts.

An advantage at such times is the birth of a single fawn, which doesn't have to share its mother's milk with a sibling.

Antlers

The sizes and general shapes of antlers depend upon three factors — heredity, age and diet.

Even a buck with the genetic potential to produce a heavy, 10-point rack won't have much more than a scraggly adornment if it can't find nutritious protein-rich foods — especially those with sufficient minerals such phosphorous, potassium and calcium. Often, soil is the determining factor in an area's reputation for big-racked bucks. In my Lehigh Valley homeland, for instance, there's prime lime-stone soil for producing big antler growth.

It's usually not until a buck's second summer that spikes appear. In its first year, as a fawn, it will be a "button buck." Bumps on the head of a small, antlerless deer sneaking by your stand reveals its sex. Often such deer will be in the company of others, probably siblings and its mother. With sufficient nutrition, a buck's first rack may be thin but can have 4-8 points. In some counties, such as in the endless mountains of central and northcentral Pennsylvania, as many as 20-40 percent of the buck harvest has been composed of spikes in recent years, a sign of too many deer for the available food supply.

Not surprisingly, people who don't hunt or aren't otherwise exposed to wildlife harbor fallacies about antlers. Time and again I hear references to the number of points on a deer's rack being an indicator of its age — like rings on a tree. Of course, that's untrue.

Blood-rich velvet supplies nutrition and minerals to antlers well into August.

Some hunters continue to harbor the old belief that antler loss is caused by freezing weather. If that were true, few Pennsylvania bucks would still be holding their headgear by the end of the buck season.

The pituitary gland is the control mechanism that starts antler growth in spring and puts a stop to it in late summer, causing the velvet-covered bones to solidify and lose the fuzzy, blood-rich outer covering. The internal gland's activity is stimulated by the amount of daylight hours.

By mid to late August most antler growth is complete. By the first week of September most bucks will have rubbed the drying velvet from their racks, a process that may take less than 24 hours.

Once the fall breeding season is over, the decreased activity of the pituitary gland, triggered by the diminishing number of daylight hours, causes a drop in the buck's testosterone level. At this time a layer of cells at the pedicle (where antlers join the skull) begins to dissolve into granular form.

This process is phenomenally rapid. In *The Deer of North America*, Leonard Lee Rue III writes: "One day the buck's antlers are so solid they could not be broken off if you hit them with a pipe. The next day, after granulation sets in, one or both antlers may drop off by themselves."

On occasion, a deer will be seen or shot that has an unusual antler formation. Tines droop over the eyes, moose-like palms appear or a maze of tangles creates a truly unique rack. This sometimes happens when an antler is damaged while still in the velvet stage, as growth is occurring. Such racks are referred to as "non-typical."

Not all non-typical bucks have been subject to antler damage, however. In fact, most non-typicals receive their genes from parents with the code for such racks in their ancestry. Females, remember, also hold in their DNA the code for rack size and shape. Even though does (with rare exception) do not grow antlers, they do have a genetic effect on the sizes and shapes of their son's racks.

Sometimes non-typical deer have a great many points. The world record Boone & Crockett non-typical whitetail, a Texas specimen, had 49 points. Another find, a buck shot in Ohio in the early 1940's, had tines that looked more like deformed tree limbs than deer antlers. It held 44 points and had a 37-inch outside spread. The rack weighed 11-1/2 pounds.

Like Samson, a buck's personality changes abruptly when it loses its head adornment. Starting in December for some and stretching as late as March and even early April for others, the granulation process will occur and in a moment the stag that ruled the woodlot will be just another "bald" whitetail. Its aggressiveness will diminish along with the weight on its brow.

It will not produce testosterone until new antler growth begins in early spring, continuing through the peak of testicular activity in the fall rut.

Anomalies

In any wildlife species anomalies — deviations from the norm — occur. Whitetails are no exception.

Every once in a while a hunter will kill an antlered deer, then discover he or she has shot a doe. At one time a Game Commission biologist estimated that one of every 18,000 antlered whitetails were females. Additional studies indicate the frequency of "rack does" may be as common as one in 2,500-4,000.

Deer color has also been an object of interest among hunters for centuries, particularly white deer. Albino animals lack natural pigments, showing pink eyes as no coloration masks the blood in the eyes. Studies show albinos are ill-equipped for long-term survival with poor eyesight a side effect.

Some white deer are not truly albinos but, rather, are considered mutations. They're normal in all ways, including black noses, dark hooves and brown eyes. The gene for hair color, however, differs from the norm.

More common than fully white animals in Pennsylvania are piebald deer, also called "calico deer." Splotches of varying degrees of white throughout the otherwise brown or gray body are taken by hunters each year.

The sighting of an albino deer, such as this Lehigh County buck, is a rarity.

On occasion the opposite of albinism occurs. Melanism causes the pelage to be totally black. Although rare, the production of melanin, a natural pigment causing dark color in black squirrels, for example, is over-produced in such deer, rendering them notably darker than the norm.

Tom's Tips

-Bucks maintain strong ties throughout most of the year, except during the rut. Often they rub against and preen one another in a non-sexual way, in a sort of male bonding behavior.

-One perpetuated myth that, in my years of whitetail hunting, hasn't seemed to hold true is that bright moonlit nights mean heavy feeding and less chance of encountering roaming deer the next day. While arguable, it would seem reasonable that a deer's night vision is sufficiently honed to enable it to feed whenever it likes. Indeed, an old buck would probably feel safer feeding in an opening in pitch-black darkness than when the moon creates shadows and longer distance viewing.

-It's often possible to tell the sex of a deer that bedded in snow. Often, upon standing, a deer will urinate. If the yellow splashes are scattered chances are it was a buck, particularly at or near rut time. A doe's urine path is usually more confined to a single spot.

- How far do deer travel from their birthplaces? Surprisingly, documented cases of bucks and does being killed 90-170 miles from where they were born have been recorded.

-Most hunters know that a deer chews its cud but not many can describe what the "cud" really is. It's a wad of vegetation eaten earlier, about the size of a small orange, that's regurgitated into the gullet when a deer is at rest. It's a back-up system for helping masticate and digests foods that may have had to be eaten "on the run."

- "Forkhorn," "Y-buck" and "crotch buck" are all slang terms used by deer hunters to describe a (2x2) 4-pointer.

SECTION II
GETTING STARTED
BULLET, BALL & BOW

Dick Weaknecht of Weaknecht Archery in Berks County helps a youngster choose his first bow.

Chapter 6

THE RIGHT STUFF
Getting Started Bowhunting

Since 1970, Pennsylvania's bowhunting ranks have jumped by a phenomenal 125,000 hunters, bringing the number of people who "go with a bow" to about one of every three deer hunters, making the Keystone State tops among bowhunting's national ranks.

The record-setting year of 1998 saw 328,451 hunters purchase bow stamps. In 1999, when, at the urging of state bowhunting organizations, the archery license fee increased to $16, numbers declined, but only slightly.

Although success in all types of deer hunting depends in large part upon having the proper, personalized equipment, it's especially important to beginning bowhunters.

The Right Stuff

It's no secret that archers have brought a newfound bounty to bow businesses — from mom-and-pop bow shops to big retailers handling bows, arrows and other gear in their sporting goods departments. The best known manufacturers of bows and related gear are well aware of the influence and economic benefits of catering to Pennsylvania archers — all 325,000-plus of them.

Thirty years ago picking a bowhunting outfit presented few questions. Choices were meager. Affordable quality was questionable. But that's all changed.

So where do you start if you've decided you want to go with a bow? You ask the people who deal with bows and arrows every day.

I quizzed Sherwood Schoch of Reading, a lifelong bowhunter and archery distributor, and Dick Weaknecht of Weaknecht's Archery in Kutztown, one of the state's oldest bow businesses, for their suggestions in helping newcomer's take aim.

They both advised buying through a pro shop where service and advice go with the sale.

"A pro shop includes information and education with its product," said Schoch. "You don't get that with every store just because they sell bows and arrows. It may cost a little more at a pro shop but the service and advice you get with it is invaluable."

Studying and handling a selection of rifles before making a choice is a relatively basic operation, but not so with bows.

"Some bow shops have indoor or outdoor ranges of one kind or another to give the buyer a chance to first shoot the bow," said Schoch. "There are so many errors the new shooter can make — from getting a bow with the wrong draw length to getting disgusted because he can't make an arrow fly straight simply because he's using the wrong grip."

If you can shoot a bow before buying it, under the tutelage of a knowledgeable salesman, you're half way home, Schoch believes.

Consider that one compound bow may have three variations of draw lengths, a half-dozen different wheel sizes and several grip shapes or arrow rest designs. Learning which combination is for you comes with experience — the experience of a bow shop staff person.

"If there's one bit of advice I can give it's that anyone investing in equipment for the first time should decide how much he or she has to spend," Weaknecht suggests. "If I know someone can only bankroll a Ford Escort I'm not going to try to sell him a Lincoln Continental."

There's nothing wrong with inexpensive bows, Weaknecht assures, agreeing with Schoch that today's choices and their quality far surpass the selections of just a few years ago.

Visiting bow clubs, many of which today have paper target or 3-D ranges, is another good way to familiarize yourself with the variety of gear on the market. Most shooters are friendly and willing to answer any questions you may have.

So where does a new convert to archery begin to search for the right stuff?

Take 10
Following are 10 tips for choosing "the right stuff" as recommended by Schoch and Weaknecht.

(1) Have a reliable person measure your draw length. That's the distance from the bottom of the arrow nock to the front of the bow when the arrow is drawn. About three-fourths of an inch is added to permit broadhead clearance at full draw.

(2) Buy the best you can afford. Today's "low end" bow line is far better than the "high end" was 20 years ago. Set a limit as to what you can spend for a bow and add some extra for other necessities. Don't be embarrassed to admit your billfold holds $200 and not $500. Most retailers will work with you.

(3) Test several bows to determine that subjective feature of "feel and comfort." Your most comfortable draw weight will be established at this time. All compounds can be adjusted over a range of 10-15 pounds. Start with a comfortable draw weight and work up to heavier pulls as your muscles develop. If you don't want to

Some pro shops also have shooting ranges — John Glenn (left) of Archery at the Glenn in Allentown discusses a shot pattern with Shawn Duffy.

A variety of release aids offer a wide "comfort" choice.

tackle the job of readjusting the bow, should it be necessary, take it back to the pro shop from which it was purchased. It only takes a few minutes to do the job.

(4) Stick with prominent brand names. Companies stay in business because of past successes and consistent production of time-tested products. Be wary of product names you haven't seen in ads, articles or being used by fellow archers.

(5) About the only mandatory accessories are a sight system, quiver, shooting glove, tab or mechanical release and, possibly, an arm guard. Try different release types — and there are many of them — before making a decision. The arm guard keeps the bowstring from slapping against your forearm or catching on your sleeve and causing erratic flight in the arrows. A bow sight is also a good investment, depending on the shooting style you wish to develop. A simple 3-pin sight is a basic addition to a bow. Some archers also use peep sights to further refine their shooting. Many opt for the newer fiber-optic sights which are especially helpful under low-light conditions. Again, it's an individual choice.

(6) Be forewarned against "over-accessorizing." That is, the modern archery market is saturated with a great variety of sights, releases, quivers, silencers, stabilizers, rests, field points, broadheads, range-finders, carrying cases and plenty of gadgets and gimmicks. Reliable bow pro shop owners won't try to sell you something that's too intricate or advanced nor will they tout items you don't need for getting started. Many accessories refine shooting skills and may mean the difference between being an adequate archer or a skilled bowman. But don't get hung up on high-tech items just because you see other more experienced archers using them on the local range.

(7) As you wouldn't go afield with a 270 rifle and 30-06 ammunition, so too, arrows must be matched to bows. At one time wooden arrows were all that was available but now aluminum is the most widely used material with graphite, fiberglass, carbon and various composites also on the market. A bow shop pro will know the proper weight and length of the arrows you'll need along with matching broadheads and field points. Like sighting systems and release aids, broadhead styles also offer dozens of choices. Arrows built to shoot from a 40-pound bow won't perform well with a 60-pound bow. Arrow-making is another valuable service of a pro shop.

(8) Also buy a backstop for backyard target practice. A wide array of target butts made of rope-grass, ethafoam, burlap-covered impact material, mattress foam and old-fashioned (but effective) haybale backstops are available. Some targets, such as ethafoam, can take the slicing of broadheads but most are meant for use with field points.

Pick up a few of the multi-colored paper targets to pin to the butts and backstops. Or make your own with paper plates and felt-tip markers. Paper animal targets are also widely available.

Later, if there's room in your yard, you'll want to invest in a near-life-size deer target, such as those manufactured by McKenzie, Delta, Blue Ridge, Game Tracker and others. Or, nose out a local club or shooting range where field courses with as many as 24-36 targets are set up and made available for a nominal shooting fee.

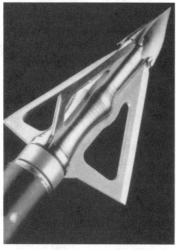

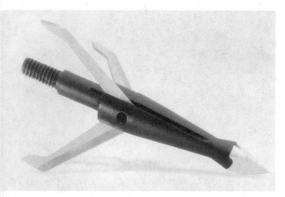

Each year more archers are trying mechanical broadheads, such as the Satellite Ventilator, which opens upon impact.

Broadheads, such as the Rocky Mountain Titanium, come in 80, 100 and 125 grain weights.

(9) Another big advantage of dealing with a pro shop rather than buying gear at a discount house, where the clerk probably doesn't know a broadhead from a bullhead, is the prospect of going back if you have additional questions or your equipment isn't performing properly.

(10) Before my initial trip to a bow shop I'd garnered enough information from friends to feel competent and confident in choosing the proper gear. I wasn't afraid to ask questions, regardless of how "stupid" they may have seemed.

"That's what we're here for," said Weaknecht. "It's a pro shop's business to make sure a customer goes out of here with equipment that will perform."

Numerous bow specialty outlets are scattered across Pennsylvania — from shopping center stores in the suburbs to home businesses in dusty country basements.

They're a newcomer's best bet for assuring that first shot at a whitetail is made with "the right stuff."

Tom's Tips

The hairs on velvet-covered antlers are believed to act as sensors in protecting the growing bone. The erect hairs "feel" obstructions as the deer attends to its daily rounds which may include everything from feeding in a thorny thicket to crawling under a barbed-wire fence.

-Few living tissues grow as fast as antlers. A buck's velvet-covered rack will grow about one-quarter inch a day. Elk antlers grow twice as fast, about a half-inch per day.

-A deer's antlers grow from the outside in, like a tree. The velvet lays down the bone on the outside, accounting for its gradual growth throughout the summer. Horns, such as on pronghorns, sheep, goats and cattle, grow from the inside out.

Tom's Tips

-Are your arrows flaring off the target upon release? Maybe you're squeezing the bow too tightly. Some archers who do well under the relaxed conditions of range shooting become tense when deer are in their sights. A heavy grip torques the bow at the moment of release, sending the arrow off to the left. Lefties will send their arrows off to the right.

-Using whiskers (silencers) on the string and assuring maximum quietness by tightening your bow's lockdown screws will minimize the sound at the arrow's release.

-During my introduction to bowhunting, my instructor frequently used the terms "porpoising" and "fishtailing" in reference to arrow flight. Not giving the terms much thought, I assumed they meant the same thing. It took a couple sessions before I finally realized that porpoising describes up-and-down arrow wobble while fishtailing indicates a side-to-side wobble. Porpoising, incidentally, is usually alleviated by changing the nock-point position. Fishtailing is often caused by a poor release, improper spine weight or the fletching striking the rest upon release.

-Confused by those identification numbers on aluminum arrow shafts? In a 2216 arrow, for example, the first two numbers (22) indicate the outside diameter in 64ths of an inch. The last two numbers (16) show the wall thickness in thousands of an inch.

-The white-tailed deer is the carrier of brainworm, a minuscule parasite acquired by eating vegetation on which small slugs and snails are present. The parasite is then passed on through a deer's feces. While the brainworm is fatal to elk, moose and mule deer, it's seldom fatal to whitetails.

-According to the National Shooting Sports Foundation, hunting contributes $14 billion a year (that averages out to $40 million a day) to the nation's economy. More than 380,000 jobs are directly or indirectly supported by hunting. Hunting employs as many people as Northwest Airlines with enough workers left over to staff Delta and USAir, according to NSSF researchers.

-Several years ago the Pennsylvania Game Commission received a thank you letter from an out-of-state hunter. He wasn't sure where to hunt opening day but decided that wherever deer crossing signs were posted along a highway was as good a place as any. He parked near one and within a couple hours was back at his car — dragging a fat buck. The hunter thanked the commission for "posting" the hotspots.

Betty Lou Fegely's bow shooting days came to an end when arthritis problems prevented drawing a compound bow. In her first year shooting a crossbow in Pennsylvania she grunted in and arrowed a 230-pound, 8-pointer on her Northampton County property.

Chapter 7

TAKING A STAND FOR THE CROSSBOW
Does it Have a Niche in Pennsylvania Hunting?

A law first passed in 1992 permitting the limited use of crossbows during the Pennsylvania archery seasons was liberalized on June 28, 1993 when acting Gov. Mark Singel signed House Bill 718.

The bill provides for any hunter who cannot draw a compound or longbow, based on a physician's determination, to hunt with a crossbow during the fall and late winter archery seasons.

Previously the decision to issue a crossbow permit was solely at the discretion of the Pennsylvania Game Commission. Eligible sportsmen and women then had to show proof of "amputation or limb paralysis." That left many deserving hunters who couldn't draw a regular bow without the benefit for which the legislation was created.

Rep. Robert Godshall of Montgomery County spearheaded the change which was backed by many Keystone State sportsmen's organizations.

"The law's importance lies in the fact that it opens doors to archery hunting to every physically-disabled individual," said Godshall, who led a resounding 197-0 House of Representatives approval of the measure. "The previous law did not address many individuals who suffer from conditions that make them physically unable to draw a bow."

Opponents of crossbow use, namely organized bowhunting organizations, are still not pleased with the law, charging that unqualified people can get a permit by "faking it" at the doctor's office. Indeed, their arguments may have some merit.

Like any change, the crossbow law created a flap and continues to do so, particularly among diehard bowhunters. While this is not to imply that diverse opinions deserve no credibility, I have hunted with the crossbow in other states while on assignment for magazines. My familiarity with the devices underscored my belief that most of its opponents know little about this controversial bow and are strongly influenced in their beliefs by peer pressure.

Currently, crossbows may be used in some form, often with restrictions, in more than three dozen states and five provinces or Canadian territories. They're fully outlawed in 14 states and six provinces.

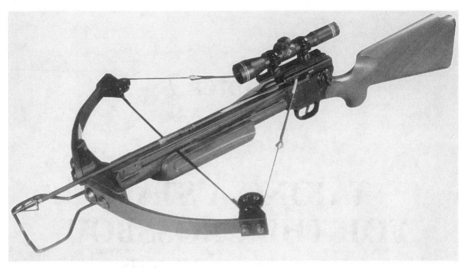

The crossbow is cocked and released with a trigger, but that's where any similarity to a gun ends.

According to U.S. crossbow manufacturers such as PSE, Horton, Bear, Barnett and others, much of the controversy reflects a gross misunderstanding of this device best described as a hybrid between a gun and a bow.

An Unbiased Look

"Maybe it would be better if we called it a cross-gun," said Mark Bower, director of operations for Horton Manufacturing Company, an Ohio business specializing in crossbows.

"The appearance of the crossbow has a whole lot to do with people's misimpressions and misunderstandings," Bower explained. "So people expect it to shoot like a gun."

It does in one or two facets. Far from it in all others.

One of the biggest misconceptions is that some opponents claim it shoots the same distance as a gun. Another stems from a crossbow's high poundage — 150-pounds or more. However, that doesn't mean it's three or four times more powerful than a compound bow. The short power-stroke on a crossbow must be balanced with a high poundage on the limbs to generate the equivalent energy of a 65-70 pound modern compound.

Another notable difference between shooting a compound bow and crossbow is the length of the arrow — called a "bolt" in crossbow terminology. A bolt measures 17-20 inches and weighs 445-490 grains, including a 126-grain broadhead. Arrow speeds have been chronographed at 225-260 feet per second when triggered from a 150-pound bow.

Like compounds, crossbows utilize a variety of sighting systems — telescopic or open sights, non-telescopic crosshairs, military V-sights and illuminator pins. The challenge and necessity of getting close to game is no different than that employed by compound-users.

Yet another notable difference — an important and valid one in the arguments posed by critical bowhunters — is that a compound or recurve-equipped hunter must draw and hold the string, sometimes for long periods, without being detected. This, they say, is the essence of practice and perfection in the making of a bowhunter — but it's not critical in successfully shooting a crossbow.

A crossbow requires considerable upper body strength to cock. A cocking rope reduces the pull needed to "load" the bow by about 50 percent. Horton, an Ohio

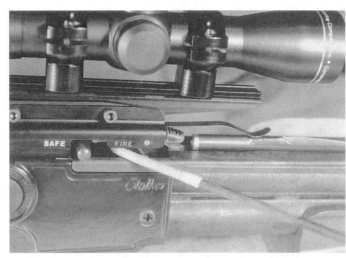

The Horton crossbow has a "no fire" safety which prevents the release of the string if a bolt isn't nocked.

company (a state in which crossbows may be used during all archery seasons), also offers a mechanical device which, depending on one's degree of incapacity, can be used to cock or slowly release the string.

For the most part, a handicapped hunter must adopt the "buddy system," having a friend accompany him or her afield. Often the "buddy" also aids in helping the hunter get into a treestand or ground blind and track deer or perform other duties. The same is typically done for physically disabled hunters carrying guns.

The crossbow's role next door in Ohio

What effect does crossbow use in other states have on deer harvests?

Since 1976, bowhunters and crossbow hunters in neighboring Ohio have been sharing part or all of the season, with just over half of the participants now using crossbows and many making use of both "stringed instruments." Fearing that crossbow legalization will adversely affect deer numbers has no basis in fact, as shown in Ohio.

Its role as a "poacher's weapon" also has little validity, according to Buckeye State law enforcement agents. However, it continues as one of the prime arguments against its legalization. It is countered, legitimately, that deer poachers show little concern for wildlife laws of any sort and, if crossbows were efficient poaching tools, they'd use them anyway. Their use (by poachers) is way overblown," said Jim Bunn, an Ohio Fish and Game Department wildlife officer. "A poacher wants to get in and get out fast, he's not going to want to track a deer."

"The crossbow has presented no problem here," Bunn adds.

A conservative trial crossbow season was begun in 1976, according to Ohio Forest and Wildlife Project Leader Bobby Stoll. In 1982 it was merged with the regular bow season. In 1998, Ohio's crossbow hunters accounted for 55 percent of the state's archery deer harvest. Longbow hunters claimed the remaining 45 percent of the kill. The figures have been consistent for the past 10 years.

Like baiting, the use of deer decoys, "modern" muzzleloaders that shoot sabot slugs instead of roundballs and other conflicts in which sportsmen become embroiled, the crossbow controversy is no exception.

Pessimists see no middle ground to its resolution. Optimists, however, look to a workable compromise — specifically the legalization of the crossbow during the regular firearms and muzzleloader seasons for those who wish to take it up. That, of course, could lead to its use by anyone so desiring during the fall bow season.

Special Regulations Areas — suburban landscapes in the Southeast and Southwest where the use of guns is limited — offer another alternative for crossbow use.

In addition to their legalization for disabled people, some hunters, this writer included, foresee a time in the near future when all holders of senior licenses will be given the option of shouldering a crossbow in the fall and winter archery seasons. For them, no license except an archery tag should be required.

It's this writer's belief that conflicts such as those perpetuated by anti-crossbow forces have no place in today's hunting atmosphere. In-fighting does nothing but waste valuable time and resources within our ranks. In the meantime, animal rightists continue to peck away at hunter's rights — no matter what their choice of gear.

Not everyone who may qualify for a crossbow permit in Pennsylvania may consider themselves "handicapped." An example is my wife who suffers from increasingly severe arthritis in her fingers and arms. She's able to draw a light pull on her compound bow but cannot hold it for any length of time, thereby making it ineffective for her as a reliable hunting tool.

In turn, she applied for and qualified for a crossbow permit in 1999. During the second to last week of the 6-week season, she was able to make a clean heart shot on a 230-pound, 8-point buck.Without the somewhat liberal "qualification" for a crossbow, she would not have been able to hunt the fall season at all.

What will be the role played by crossbows in the new millennium? It remains to be seen, but surely there's a slot that will satisfy not only crossbow users but those who currently oppose it, as well.

More than 20,000 Crossbow permits have been issued. As this is being written, the House Game & Fisheries Committee is hearing testimony for and against crossbows, with the possibility of a special season being discussed.

With deer numbers in dire need of control in many places, the once-controversial crossbow can surely fill a niche as both an effective recreational tool and an aid in managing whitetails in Pennsylvania's suburbs as well as its backcountry.

Applications, along with doctors' forms, are available by writing: Crossbow Permit, Pennsylvania Game Commission, 2001 Elmerton Ave., Harrisburg, PA 17110.

The application must be completed by the physician and returned to the game agency.

The applications are also available on the commission's Home Page.

Paul Haydt of Northampton County continues to hunt the fall bow season with his crossbow.

Tom's Tips

-Olympic Archery Gold Medalist Jay Barrs, who is also an avid deer hunter, recommends "daydreaming" as a way to help cure buck fever. Barrs frequently pictures a big buck in his sights as he mentally reviews the process of drawing, picking the kill spot and smoothly releasing the arrow. "Think about it enough and when the time comes it will seem like you've done it before," says Barr. "I used similar mental preparation to win the Olympics."

-When analyzing a blood trail, remember that pinkish fluid with small "bubbles" suggests a lung hit, bright red blood is most likely from the heart, a major artery or large muscle and dark blood probably means a liver shot. Green matter mixed with watery blood comes from the stomach or intestines.

-Camouflage face masks are standard items for many bowhunters but rarely found on the faces of gun hunters. Yet, the human face is second only to movement in attracting the attention of deer. When hunting in thick understory where a deer might be encountered at close range, a mask may mean the difference between being detected and getting a shot.

-Not all wounded deer drop their tails when running off after a shot. Depending upon where a deer has been struck, it may bound away as if nothing's happened — except for having been frightened by the sound of a shot or loosed arrow. Check for blood and/or hair after every shot, no matter what position the buck or doe held its tail.

-Rather than allowing your extra shells to jangle about in your pocket, roll them in the toilet paper you surely carry with you. Use a large rubber band to keep the shells from falling out.

- If the zipper on your hunting coat sticks, rub it lightly with paraffin or candle wax before going afield. It will lubricate the studs without adding scent or grease to your clothing.

-Lost in the woods with no compass? If the sun's shining, your watch can serve as an emergency compass. Point the hour hand toward the sun. South will fall in the center of the angle of the hour hand and 12. North is opposite, of course.

-Most hunters wear two pairs of socks — a thin pair next to the feet and heavier socks over the top, depending on the weather. Avoid the temptation of wearing cotton dress socks against the skin. Cotton retains moisture and can cause blisters. Opt instead for Orlon or Orlon-wool socks like hikers wear.

Pennsylvania's "Mr. Blackpowder," Dave Ehrig, a Berks County resident, hunts with muzzleloaders no matter what the season.

Chapter 8

MASTERING THE FINICKY FLINTLOCK
Lock, Stock and Barrel

Like the longbow of the archery purist, the flintlock is the choice rifle for many muzzleloader shooters. For some, its use is dictated more by necessity than intrigue as Pennsylvania law mandates flintlocks-only during the October and December-January blackpowder season.

In a Pennsylvania Game Commission hunter survey in the late 1980s, opinions were evenly divided on the legalization of percussion or "caplock" rifles, as are permitted in other states.

Guns triggered by both flint and percussion cap firing mechanisms may be used in the regular gun seasons but the flintlock continues as the sole arm for the "primitive" seasons. The modern in-line rifle is also legal during all but the muzzleloader seasons.

Muzzleloader hunter numbers have ranged from the low hundreds to about 125,000 since the initial flintlock season in 1974, when 69 deer (only four of them antlered) were taken. Hunter numbers leveled off at about 75,000 as the century approached its end.

While the more popular percussion or "caplock" rifle is far from foolproof, the flintlock can be doubly "persnickety," as the Pennsylvania German gunmakers who fashioned rifles in the 18th and 19th centuries probably referred to them.

I'm first to admit I've made my share of errors with the flintlock. But experience is the best teacher. If the experience comes at the expense of an escaped trophy buck, even more attention is made to perfection on the next hunt. On one memorable occasion my flintlock failed to fire due to a loose-fitting flint. It kept me from bagging a beautiful 10-pointer (at 25 yards) on a special hunt at the Middle Creek Wildlife Management Area in Lancaster and Lebanon counties in 1990.

It's an outing I'd rather forget. But never will.

Following are some flintlock basics for the "pilgrim" seeking to enter the blackpowder ranks.

Flintlock basics
It's necessary here to explain the method by which a flintlock operates.

The gun's cocking mechanism consists of a screw-tightened jaw holding a sharpened piece of flint. A patch of leather is inserted in the jaw for a firmer grip on the flint. When the trigger is nudged, the hammer falls swiftly with the flint striking a steel surface (the "frizzen") resting atop a shallow powder pan.

Upon impact, the frizzen snaps open, exposing the priming powder. Sparks from the flint striking the frizzen light the priming powder, in turn sending fire through the flash hole adjoining the pan.

At least that's how it's supposed to work. When it does, the gun fires.

If it's nipped in the bud, that frustrating click is the only sound you'll hear. Equally frustrating is the click followed by pffffft — the sound of igniting pan powder — and a puff of smoke.

All this happens only inches in front of a shooter's eyes, the anticipation of which can be quite disconcerting. The prospect of that flash of light and heat is the Achilles' heel for most newcomers to flintlock shooting, whether the gun fires or not. Add to that the minuscule lag time between ignition of the priming powder and the main charge.

While most shooters claim it's this micro-second delay that causes them to flinch, one experienced flintlock shooter claims otherwise.

"It's not possible to flinch in the time between the flash of powder and the gun going off," says Dave Ehrig, a well-known Pennsylvania writer and speaker and the author a book on building the Pennsylvania longrifle. Most "flinchers," Ehrig explains, "tense up as they're squeezing the trigger."

Ehrig notes that only five one-hundredths to seven one-hundredths of a second passes between the external powder's ignition and the firing of the gun, insufficient time to flinch — barring a misfire. But even misfires, preferably on the shooting range, teach lessons. Many flintlock shooters flinch even when the gun doesn't go off.

"It's the sign of a mindset when a person flinches," said Ehrig. "Mastering the flintlock means spending enough time shooting to feel comfortable with the gun. And that means more than just three or four shots before the hunting season."

Narrowing the odds

Through experience, blackpowder shooters learn to narrow the odds in Murphy's flintlock law, thereby lowering the prospects of misfires.

Ken French of Thompson/Center Arms refined the first standard flintlock with a removable breech plug. The gun also takes Pyrodex Pellets, which are not legal in Pennsylvania during the post-winter season. The gun, called the Fire Storm, is legal, however.

This hunter's priming charge ignited but not so the inner charge, resulting in the classic "flash in the pan."

For one, black powder is highly corrosive and can quickly foul a flash hole (also called the "touch hole"), preventing the spark from ever reaching the internal charge.

Some shooters use the newer and cleaner burning Pyrodex but it's not recommended for most flintlocks. The exception is the Thompson/Center Fire Storm, a gun introduced in 1999, that uses Pyrodex pellets and has a welcome removable breech plug for cleaning. It's legal in the Pennsylvania muzzleloader season but only blackpowder is permitted.

It's recommended that both range-shooters and hunters carry a pick with which to probe the touch hole each time pan-powder is changed. The pick may be anything from a piece of firm wire embedded in an antler tip to a simple paper clip. I keep a twist of piano wire attached to the zipper pull on my hunting coat or vest so as to avoid the need to prowl around the possibles bag each time I want to use it.

Flintlock aficionados like Ehrig recommend using only enough priming powder to half-fill the pan. Clearing a space between the touch hole and the powder is also advised. Accomplish that by tapping on the breech opposite the lock.

Ehrig uses 3F (FFFg) ignition powder instead of the next finer grain (4F) in wet weather. "The 3F works nicely and allows you to carry only one charge," explains Ehrig, although the larger 3F grains may ignite a touch slower than the finer 4F powder.

"It also doesn't seem to absorb moisture as quickly. The glazing is a bit thicker than on the fine grain powder."

Keep your powder dry

"Keep your powder dry" was often the parting phrase of mountain men heading in opposite directions after a rendezvous or a perchance crossing of paths.

It's also good advice today.

Foul weather is the flintlocker's number one enemy. Percussion firearms will also be influenced by humidity and rain or snow but extra care must be given to a flintlock as the powder is exposed to the elements.

Keeping the external powder dry, as Deron Erney of Lehigh County attempts to do, is a challenge in rainy and snowy weather.

To make matters worse, blackpowder is inherently hygroscopic. That is, it's water-loving and will quickly cake when moistened.

Hunters have come up with an intriguing variety of ways to keep their powder dry. They use makeshift covers of aluminum foil, plastic wrap, garbage bags and slices of innertube rubber over the locks. But simplicity and common sense are most effective.

"I always carry the gun under my armpit with the muzzle pointed down," Ehrig explains. "That's a natural way to carry any rifle and when it's raining or snowing the water will run down the barrel away from the pan. The lock area is also protected and kept from direct rain."

Ehrig changes powder several times a day in dry weather, every half-hour if humidity or precipitation is of concern.

He advises: "When you consider you're only losing 5 to 7 grains each time you clear the priming pan, it's not worth losing the chance at a deer just because you wanted to save a few cents worth of black powder."

Some purists go so far as to apply a sealant of beeswax at the jointure of the pan and frizzen to prevent water from penetrating.

Several companies make oiled leather lock covers to shield the ignition area but most are ineffective in heavy downpours. Water trickling down the barrel and gathering in the pan will instantly spoil a hunt.

Pick a quality flint

Another item demanding special concern is the flint. Specialty muzzleloader shops and mail-order houses such as Dixie Gun Works in Union City, Tennessee and Mountain State Muzzleloading Supplies of Williamstown, West Virginia offer several types, among the best of which is the black English flint.

"The black English flint is the best I've found," explains Toby Bridges, a longtime friend, blackpowder authority and author of "Advanced Muzzleloader's Guide" and other books. "This is the true flint. It can be knapped and a new edge can be created easily."

The French amber flint is another quality sparker, said Bridges, although it's not as abundantly available as American flints, which are supplied with most new muzzleloaders. The latter are prone to chipping and, while they provide a good shower of sparks, they require regular replacement. Extras should always be carried afield.

Mounting a flint in the lock's jaws may require some experimentation, Bridges advises. He prefers placing the flint so that the bevel is on the bottom, causing it to strike the frizzen sufficiently high to maximize contact in its swift downward motion without "kicking" the frizzen away too soon.

The flint must be aligned parallel to the frizzen so that the full edge-contact is made between the two components for maximum spark.

The possibles bag

Most accessories — "possibles" — carried by flintlock toters are the same as those found in any muzzleloader's possibles bag. But there are some items specifically for flintlockers.

One is a pan primer, used to add powder to the pan without spillage. The device, about the size of a 30-06 shell, holds sufficient 3F or 4F powder for many primings. Each time it's tapered spout is depressed against the pan a small amount of powder is released. An internal spring closes the primer when pressure is released. Some shooters fashion similar dispensers from eyedrop bottles, plastic 35mm film containers and spent rifle shells plugged with cork.

I also carry an old toothbrush which is used to clean the pan when a new charge is added, especially on wet or high humidity days. A stubby, wide-edge screwdriver is also necessary for adjusting or changing a flint while afield.

Developing the load

Developing an efficient and consistent load is of utmost importance. Each rifle holds its own set of peculiarities.

The first decision is which projectile to use. The relatively slow twists of most flintlock barrels best serve patched roundballs, which are required by Pennsylvania law along with conical bullets. Conicals were legal in the 1970s, then outlawed in the early 1980s. But in 1999 the Game Commission again approved conicals beginning with the 2000 flintlock seasons (October and December).

Official wording form the Game Commission is that "lead conical projectiles without a sleeve (sabot)" will be legal. This, says a PGC announcement, includes "what are commonly referred to as a mini-ball, which is a lead conical projectile with a concave base (or) a maxi-ball, a lead, conical projectile with a solid base."

For a 50-caliber rifle, a good round ball "starter" load consists of 60-70 grains of 2F blackpowder under a .490" round ball. But remember that this is only for getting started. My preferred Thompson/Center Hawken load with a patched ball is 90 grains of 2F. This powder is considerably more granular than the 4F powder used for priming.

As for the basic roundball, a .50 caliber projectile weighing 180 grains must be seated over the load with a tight-fitting patch of cotton (commercially available), linen or pillow-ticking. A commercial muzzleloader lubricant, of which there are many, will ease the patched ball down the barrel. Some shooters opt for pre-oiled patches.

The patched ball and conical bullets are legal in Pennsylvania but the sabot pistol bullet (far right) may not be used in flintlock season.

Most flintlock
hunters limit
their shots to
50-75 yards.

Many newcomers to muzzleloader shooting consider the patching process an incidental matter although, in truth, its tightness is often the most overlooked factor in developing an accurate load. A thin patch will allow for easy loading but permits gases to escape, thereby affecting ballistics and accuracy. If the patch is loose, the ball will not attain maximum spin in its flight down the barrel and beyond.

The ball must also be tightly seated against the charge. Black powder is most efficient when compressed. A loose-fitting charge can reduce velocity by 150 feet per second or more.

Another factor affecting accuracy is fouling. When working up a load, always swab the barrel between shots.

Conical bullets, which may weigh double that of roundballs, will require different powder weights. Conicals are not patched for tightness but the heavy bullets may need to be lubricated for loading, which presents a potentially dangerous problem. In a day's hunting, a conical bullet may drift away from the load and create a gap between powder and projectile. When the powder is ignited it could rupture the gun's breech. In short, if you opt for conicals, get into the habit of regularly checking (with your ramrod) the position of the bullet.

As muzzleloading — particularly with an iron-sighted flintlock — is a relatively short-range sport, my preference is to sight in at 60 yards. A 3- to 4-inch group is the goal, more than sufficient for hitting the vital zone of a deer. Of course, this is a personal matter. Some flintlockers are capable of attaining surprising accuracy at 100-yard ranges while others limit their shots to 50 yards.

No matter, a benchrest and sandbags are a must. Consistency is the key to refining the components. Shooter error cannot be a factor when balls or bullets and powder charges are tested.

Fire a three-shot group before adjusting the powder load. If you're not satisfied, change the powder charge five grains at a time until satisfactory accuracy is established.

Manufacturers' manuals list suggested loads for specific rifles and that's the perfect place to start.

Experimentation is the key to finding the best load for your particular rifle. Maintaining consistency is the key to accuracy on the range and in the field.

Cleaning the frontloader

The first lesson of blackpowder shooting is to keep the firearm clean. Even a speck of corrosion or powder caking in a touch hole, for example, can keep a gun from firing.

Detergent and hot water are the basic ingredients for thoroughly cleaning a muzzleloader.

Most touch holes on replica muzzleloaders are housed in a bushing. This bushing can be removed during the cleaning process for maximum flow of hot, soapy water or solvent. However, it's usually necessary to do this only a few times a year, depending on how often the gun is fired. The gun can be cleaned without removing the touch hole.

The area around the touch hole can quickly become fouled with fine powder and the salts remaining from burnt charges. Use an old toothbrush dipped in a blackpowder solvent to get into the crevices and other hard to reach areas on the lock and pan.

The frizzen must also be kept clean but be aware that any oil — even from your hands — on the steel face must be removed before shooting. The slick surface will reduce or eliminate sparking. However, the frizzen is prone to rust and a light coat of oil should be applied when the gun is to be stored.

After determining the proper combination of powder and projectiles, load up and seat the ball. Then, using a pen knife, scar the place on the ramrod where it exits the muzzle. This will not only aid in determining that the gun is loaded but will also verify that you've used the proper powder charge.

Finally, when that deer sneaks up behind you, you don't want to alert it by revealing your presence with a resounding "click" as you cock the hammer. Instead, keep pressure on the hammer with your thumb, pulling it back as far as possible while simultaneously and gently squeezing the trigger. When the cock is in firing position, slowly release the tension on both the trigger and the hammer. The gun will be ready to fire — and you haven't made a sound.

Practice this move on the range before you attempt it in the field.

For the record, flintlock handguns were also made legal by game commissioners in 2000. Most black powder hunters consider them inefficient, however.

Tom's Tips

-The famed Kentucky Rifle should properly be called the Pennsylvania Rifle. This Revolutionary War firearm was fashioned with a grooved barrel that provided spin to the ball and provided welcome accuracy and distance. Over the years, however, the Pennsylvania-made gun became famous as Daniel Boone's "piece." His wanderings may have attributed to the name "Kentucky" instead of maintaining the tag of its proper birthplace.

The Remington Model 7, chambered in 7mm-08, is an excellent flat-shooting choice for youth, women and small-framed shooters.

Chapter 9

GUNS AND LOADS
Pennsylvanians' Favorite Firearms

Like deer camps and deer hunters across Pennsylvania, firearms used for big game have changed over the years.

As a farm-country kid, my first "deer gun" was an old Ithaca double-barrel with which I also tended to pheasants, squirrels and cottontails. I never shot a deer with it but the old "twice-barrel," which a Pennsylvania Dutch neighbor jokingly called it, was confidently carried afield each December, loaded with a pair of "punkin' balls."

Shotguns are now mandated in the state's Special Regulations Areas and available with rifled barrels and scopes that make them surprisingly accurate at 100 yards or more — a long shot from the old smoothbores many deer hunters used in years past. More on them later.

What's on the Gun Rack?

In the mid-1980s *Pennsylvania Game News*, the popular monthly publication of the Pennsylvania Game Commission, surveyed readers on their choices of deer hunting calibers. To no one's surprise, the 30-06 was the most widely used caliber. A nationwide survey would probably have yielded a similar finding.

Today the 30-06, originally a military cartridge, may have slipped a bit in popularity. But not all that much. Now many more calibers and rifles are available. The wide array of guns designed to appeal to whitetail hunters may create some confusion for a fledgling deer hunter wanting to get into the sport or simply seeking to update his or her equipment.

I won't claim for a second to be an authority on rifles, or on any particular type of firearm for that matter. But in making my full-time living as an outdoor writer for two dozen years and having spent countless hours afield with a variety of hunters, I'm always curious as to their choices of guns and loads.

Some will be seen carrying rifles with enough knock-down power to incapacitate a buffalo while others opt for more "tamable" guns and cartridges. "Brush guns," chambered in 30-30 or the old 32 caliber Remingtons and Winchesters, were once the solid (and affordable) choices of most Pennsylvania hunters. I vividly recall those early days at my dad's deer camp. Tall Maples Hunting Lodge in Sullivan County, in the early 60s. Most of the guns lining the rack were pump or lever-action 30-30s and 32s or military converts handed down from one generation to another.

There's nothing wrong with using them today, of course, as my kids all started out with my Remington 32, a Winchester 30-30 or a Winchester 35. My wife killed her first deer with a 30-30 Winchester, preferring it over my Model 700 Remington 30-06 as its size and weight was more to her liking, and made for a more comfortable fit.

Since then she's graduated to the Model 7, Remington 7mm-08 which I doubt she'll ever give up. The former "wildcat" caliber is a relative newcomer to the deer hunting scene and seems to be growing in popularity. Weighing just over six pounds, it's the perfect choice for the young hunter or woman. That's not to say men shouldn't consider it. The 140-grain load traveling at 2,800 feet per second is a dandy flat-shooter and may well be the perfect cartridge for medium game (although Betty Lou also cleanly dropped a 500-pound Colorado cinnamon bear and two Quebec caribou with it).

Choosing a deer gun is foremost a personal matter. Consider that more rifles are produced for deer hunting than any other purpose, yielding a wide choice of new and used guns from which to pick. The only limit may be one's pocketbook.

Excellent choices for Pennsylvania hunting are the aforementioned 7mm-08 and 30-06 calibers. Add to that the 243 Winchester, 270 Winchester (my personal favorite), 300 Savage and the 308 Winchester, among others. Each caliber offers two to five commercial loads from which to choose.

Experienced shooters like nothing more than to spend hours arguing which calibers are best for deer and I have no intention of getting into that scuffle here. Suffice to say there's a big choice of firearms for "up close" shooting as well as reaching out and touching game with their flat trajectories.

As for rifle types, the solid performances of bolt-actions have made them the choice of most whitetail hunters. Lever-actions are steeped in hunting tradition across Pennsylvania but have declined in popularity since WWII. Pump-action rifles are also carried by many hunters, although they can't match the hardiness of a bolt-action. Semi-automatic rifles for deer are not permitted in Pennsylvania.

Shotguns

The growth of deer populations in suburbia and the ban on rifle use in some counties has brought about new interest in shotgunning among both hunters and

Russ Englehart of Berks County downed this 9-pointer on Schuylkill County gamelands using a Winchester Model 70, 30-06 Featherweight and a reload 150-grain Nosler solid base bullet.

Many Special Regulations Area hunters are topping their shotguns with scopes.

rifle/ammo manufacturers. It's a good bet even more localized areas will go the shotgun-only route in years to come.

No longer must a deer hunter shoot an erratic smoothbore, then wonder where a slug is headed beyond 35 yards. Rifled barrels and specialized loads have made shotgunning for whitetails a highly efficient proposition.

During my school teaching days in lower New York in the mid-1960s, I drooled over the flashy Ithaca Deerslayer in the window of a sporting goods store. I'd drop by and shoulder it every so often, but my meager salary kept me from purchasing it for local hunting, which required the use of shotguns then, as today, in the southern tier of the Empire State.

The 12-gauge, Model 87 Deerslayer (Don't you love that name?) is still popular. It's available in both pump and auto-loading models. (Note: While semi-auto rifles are not permitted for Pennsylvania deer hunting, semi-auto shotguns are legal.)

The resurgence of deer shotguns has also brought a cadre of new slug-shooters on the scene. They include the Winchester Model 1300s (including a 20-gauge ladies/youth gun), Mossberg 12-gauge Trophy Slugster, Browning's BPS Deer Special, Remington's Model 870 pumps, SP-10 Magnums and 11-87s, and Harrington & Richardson and New England Firearms slug guns.

The shotgun I carry when heading south of my Northampton County home into the Special Regulations Area north and west of Philadelphia is the Remington 11-87 topped with a Simmons 2X Pro Diamond scope. With a one-in-24-inch bore twist and a slug choke, it maintains super accuracy and plenty of knock-down power from 50 to 100 yards.

Of course, the old "punkin-ball" has been replaced with rifled slugs and newer sabot slugs, in both 2-3/4 inch and 3-inch, 12-gauge loads. Some manufacturers also make .410, 16-gauge and 20-gauge slugs. Velocities reach 1,400 to 1,500 feet per second at the muzzle and deliver 1,600 to 2,300 foot pounds of energy at 50 yards, with variations from one slug type and manufacturer to another.

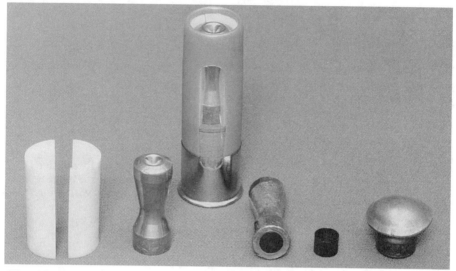

The Winchester Hi-Impact sabot slug expands greatly by virtue of its hollow-point configuration.

I've had good luck with two loads, both capable of punching 3-inch groups off a benchrest at 100 yards with scoped sights: Remington's Copper Solid sabot slug and Winchester's Hi-Impact sabot slug loads. Sabots are plastic, slotted sleeves into which the slug is seated. The slug separates from the tight-fitting sabot upon firing, providing maximum energy retention.

Remington's all-copper load is similarly accurate. The nose sections of the unique non-lead bullet expand more than double upon impact, then separates for additional penetration.

Buckshot is the choice of some, albeit few, shotgun hunters. In the Southeast Special Regulations Area buckshot is permitted but it's banned in Allegheny County, surrounding Pittsburgh. Occasionally, special hunts in suburban parks may require the use of buckshot. It's a short-range load, available in OOO, OO and O sizes (.36, .33. and .32 caliber, respectively). Anyone using buckshot should make certain he or she has patterned several loads before going afield. While some users claim effectiveness out to 50 yards, that seems to be stretching things with injured and lost game the result. Keeping shots below the 35 yard mark is arguably best.

Considerations are currently in the works to expand "special regulations areas" which have rifle restrictions. In 1998, a committee exploring the subject recommended banning the use of center-fire rifles in all or portions of six counties in the Southwest and 11 southeastern counties. The matter is currently a back-burner item. Be aware, however, that it may be brought to the forefront at any time, but not before it's filtered through public hearings and testimony.

Handguns

Handguns are legal for whitetails in Pennsylvania although a special permit is needed to carry one afield. Details are provided in the digest accompanying each year's license.

Don Lewis, *Pennsylvania Game News'* legendary gun columnist, recommends sticking with 41 Magnums or larger for Pennsylvania whitetails. He also cautions against putting too much faith in the popular .38 Specials and .357 Magnums.

"A lot of Pennsylvania handgunners use both cartridges for white-tailed deer," Lewis writes in his book, *The Shooter's Corner* (Pennsylvania Game Commission; 1989), "but success with them requires ultra-precise bullet placement."

He adds: "The most powerful handgun cartridge falls far short of equaling the power output of even the old 30-30 Winchester cartridge. I feel it's utter nonsense to even suggest using a handgun beyond approximately 100 yards."

Certainly there are exceptions. While not a typical "handgun," Remington's XP-100, which I've used on Texas whitetails, is a highly accurate, long-barreled (14-1/2 inches) handgun which has been around for more than 30 years. Holding a handsome laminated, hardwood stock, the bolt-action guns are chambered in eight calibers including the 7mm-08 and 35 Remington. The barrel is tapped for scope mounting.

Similarly popular is the Thompson/Center Arms Encore, a break-open single-shot pistol with interchangeable barrels. Available in 15-inch and 12-inch barrels in a dozen calibers, it's a solid choice for deer hunters graduating to a more challenging type of deer hunting.

Experienced handgunners know their limitations as they've spent many hours on the range. Most top their pistols with scopes and choose their loads carefully.

Handgun hunting for whitetails is not a venture which should be undertaken on a whim.

Other deer guns

While percussion muzzleloaders are not permitted during the special flintlock-only season, they are legal in all other gun seasons. Both sidelock and the newer and phenomenally-accurate in-line frontloaders offer popular options.

Replica sidelocks and in-lines are fired with percussion caps. I've taken big game, including whitetails, with my CVA 50-caliber caplock and the sabot-bullet-shooting 50 caliber Knight Hawk from Modern Muzzleloading (Knight Rifles) in Centreville, Iowa. Looking like a modern rifle but loading like Old Betsy, the "hybrid" in-line muzzleloader is highly accurate well beyond 100 yards. I've shot mule deer and antelope in excess of 150 yards with the Knight Hawk and have also taken whitetails with it, all at ranges under 100 yards. Most recent was an Iowa 9-pointer on my Knight Hawk, topped with a 4x scope and loaded with a .45 caliber, 260-grain, Speer pistol bullet seated in a plastic sabot. It and other in-lines from Markesbery, White, Traditions, CVA and Thompson-Center are the most accurate and reliable of front-stuffing guns.

While scopes are not legal during the flintlock-only seasons, they are permitted — and recommended — in all other seasons.

Scoping your gun

While we won't get into all the details of scope mounting and sighting in (the information is available in most deer hunting books and magazines), suffice it to say that most Pennsylvanians choose either standard 4x scopes or variables in 2-7x or 3-9x powers.

For shotguns and sidelock muzzleloaders, lower power scopes from 2x-4x are most widely used. Check out the lighted "red-dot" scopes which are especially help-

The Knight MK-85 is an excellent choice for shotgun-only areas and is accurate to 150 yards.

Many state gamelands offer shooting ranges for zeroing in.

ful in low-light conditions. The more powerful variable optics used on centerfire rifles are the choices of many hunters who mount them on their in-lines.

Scope costs can run as little as $30 to well over $500. The best advice when shopping for one is to buy the best you can afford. While the low-priced scopes of today are as good or better than the high-priced brands of 30 years ago, you still get what you pay for. There's nothing more frustrating than waiting all year for opening day, then hunkering down in your treestand during a rainstorm and having your optic fog up.

When shopping for a scope pay particular attention to reticle styles. Squint through several types before making a decision as it, like so many facets of choosing deer hunting needs, is purely personal. Check out the scopes with large objective lenses, which permit more efficient light passage, particularly at the edges of the day.

Yet another option is the peculiar-looking but highly effective HOLO-Sight from Bushnell, a high-tech holographic gunsight for mounting on shotguns, handguns, muzzleloaders or rifles. Unlike a conventional sight, the HOLO-Sight projects what appears to be an illuminated crosshair 50 yards in front of the gun on a window-type display. Yet, no forward light is projected. Users benefit from faster target acquisition as both eyes remain on the target. The small sight, also excellent for use on turkey guns, has variable crosshairs in dot and ring-type displays in laser-red.

No matter if you use a rifle, shotgun, handgun or muzzleloader, the recommendation is to scope it. If you've never mounted a scope, take it to a gunsmith and have him do it. Often gun dealers will offer mounting as a service for buying an outfit.

The older a hunter gets, as I've discovered, the more likely it is that eye problems will prevent the efficient use of iron sights. Clean, quick harvests are best made with the aid of magnifying lenses atop your gun.

-An inexpensive police whistle should be a part of every hunter's gear. Not only will it alert others to trouble, should you need help, but it's also a far-ranging signal when you're lost. It has even been known to stop fleeing deer in their tracks — for a clean shot.

-When hunting hilly terrain, morning stands should be on high ground where natural air currents carry scent upward. Conversely, stick to low country stands in the afternoon when scent will shift to a downhill.

A scope with a large objective len permits greater light-gathering power, especially welcome at dawn and dusk.

Tom's Tips

-Hunters typically use their binoculars only when movement or a distant deer is seen. In thick cover or high grasses, and at the edges of the day, scanning with binoculars often turns up hidden deer that would otherwise remain undetected. Establish a slow, methodical grid pattern to cover the entire area every 10-20 minutes or so.

-Hunters who tread off the beaten path rely on map and compass to find their ways. Topographic maps are the most useful of backcountry guides and the knowledgeable hunter will take the time to learn to read them. The U.S. Geological Survey has topo maps for the entire U.S., including your favorite hunting areas. For free information on maps and aerial photographs, call 1-800-USA-MAPS.

-Take a few minutes to stretch leg, back and arm muscles before climbing into a treestand. Do the same before walking after spending a long period cramped in a stand. A couple minutes of stretching exercises can prevent sprains and pulled muscles.

-To get some idea of how heavily a deer trail is used on pre-season scouting trips or in-season hunts, wet a crossing site with a couple quarts of water and smooth it with a concrete worker's trawl. Check the smooth surface 12-24 hours later to see how many deer have passed by.

"Soft" blaze orange garments as worn by outdoor writer George Smith of Luzerne County are more quiet and believed to be less visible to deer than stiffer garments, which tend to glare.

Chapter 10

GEAR FOR DEER
Outfitting Yourself

Visit your favorite sporting goods store or flip the pages in the dozen or so catalogs showing up in the mailbox summer and fall and you'll find the widest selection of deer hunting gear ever available.

Some you'll need. Some you won't. Only you — and your wallet — can decide what's a "must" and what you can do without.

Dress for success

To suggest an "ideal" outfit for hunting in Pennsylvania would be futile — nay, impossible — and we won't even attempt it here. From the October bow opener through the buck and doe seasons and into the January hunts, weather conditions, hunting styles, "legal gear" (orange), necessary gear (camouflage) and how much money's in the checking account will influence what you wear.

The biggest differences in external clothing are found in the bow and gun seasons. Not only do temperatures vary by as much as 60 degrees or more but it's common knowledge that bowhunters don't want to be seen — by deer or by others afield. That's why they wear camouflage.

Gun hunters don't want to be seen by deer either but they do want their presence noted by others in the deer woods. Archers can have it their way the first four weeks of the season but must conform to state law (250 square inches of blaze orange on the head, front and back, visible from 360 degrees while moving) by wearing the safety color when the bow season runs concurrent with the turkey season. The color is not required in the late bow-muzzleloader hunt although many participants wear at least an orange hat or vest.

When fluorescent orange was first mandated in Pennsylvania, grumbles were heard from oldtimers accustomed to donning their dark Woolrich outfits and heading to the woods. But that's all changed as hunters today want to be seen by others, resulting in lower accident rates.

Although it's not easy to remain hidden when dressed in the required clothing, there are a couple of factors to keep in mind when buying blaze orange.

Scientists who have studied the reactions of deer to hunters in orange garb noted that some outerwear is easier for deer to see than others. They advise wearing "soft" orange clothing. The shininess of cheap, orange vests of plastic or vinyl will be brighter and more likely to draw attention. They'll also be noisy. Some orange hats also produce a "shine" and should be replaced with a hat of softer fabric.

The camouflage revolution began in the early 1980s and hasn't seemed to slow down. Two of the most popular are the Realtree and Advantage patterns from Bill Jordan and Mossy Oak's Break-Up.

Deer see orange as white or light gray, not the way we see it. When hunting in snow, blaze orange blends in somewhat with the white countryside, as deer see it. To other hunters it stands out like a neon sign.

In darkened woods and under dull skies the fluorescent orange provides the greatest contrast and is most readily seen. Nevertheless, it's movement of the hunter that most often reveals his presence to deer.

Camouflage-orange, which never seemed to take hold among Pennsylvania hunters despite its wide availability, may be the best bet for eluding a deer's attention. The mottled orange, black, and in some patterns, green, gray or brown, breaks up the human outline and creates a blending effect with the environment. At least deer see it that way. Camo-orange is legal in Pennsylvania as long as the total amount of visible orange meets or exceeds the legal requirement.

Since the early 1980s the choice of camo clothing has gone from the old Viet Nam tiger-striped and military woodland patterns to a wide array of choices from nearly 20 manufacturers. Realtree, Advantage, Trebark, ASAT, Tru-Leaf, Mossy Oak, Bushlan, Hide-N-Tree and others continue to fill shelves and catalogs for the camo-conscious and fashion-conscious hunter. Each year brings new patterns and garments with new features.

As important as choosing a pattern is knowing what it's made of and how well it holds its colors after repeated washings. From cotton to fleece and wool to Cordura, camouflage is the dress of the day, especially in bow season.

Picking a pattern to match the environs in which you plan to hunt is the key to choosing the outdoor wardrobe. Selections have never been greater.

More recent in the marketplace are scent-control systems from head to toe. Look for Scent-Lok and Gore-Tex Supprescent hang-tags on apparel and some footwear.

Georgia Sport & Trail's popular Deer Trekker boots hold 600 grams of insulation, Gore-Tex for waterproofing, oil resistant neoprene soles and Health Shield, which kills foot odor.

The items will be more costly but if you're a serious hunter, they will also be more efficient in minimizing the number one reason deer know you're there — smell.

Footwear

To even attempt to detail the many types of footwear available to hunters and the features included in the modern footwear would take half of this book.

For most gun hunting, leather boots with moderate insulation is preferred. If your feet get cold, choose heavier (600 grams and above) insulation. The type and thickness of socks will also determine how cold-proof a boot you'll need.

Educate yourself on the varied products making up a boot by reading hang-tags. Gore-Tex, Gore-Tex Supprescent, Cordura, HealthShield, Thinsulate, Cambrell and others will all be seen and described.

Also check the soles, eyelets, hooks, orthotic inserts, padded collars, amounts of insulation (measured in grams), camouflage patterns, pull loops and type of leather used.

Serious bowhunters will choose knee-high rubber boots to prevent leaving scent trails as they approach their stands. The standard is the non-insulated boot in green or brown. However, one or two companies also offer camo-pattern rubber boots.

During my pre-Gore-Tex days, foot perspiration was the number one reason for my getting cold feet. I wore wool socks and a second pair of thinner cotton socks (polypropylene wasn't available back then) next to the skin. But I still got cold feet.

Then someone told me to try spraying my feet with an anti-perspirant before slipping on my socks and boots. It worked.

Today I own several pairs of leather and fabric boots, all lined with Gore-Tex which allows the passage of perspiration vapor to escape from around the foot. But for extra insurance, on cold mornings I'll still spray some anti-perspirant on my feet before stepping out.

When shopping for hunting or hiking boots, take with you the same socks you'll be wearing in the field. I require a wide size and on several occasions in years long gone bought boots that fit well with street socks, but not with my standard polypropylene and wool.

While in the store, slip on both boots, then take a short "hike." Check ankle support and protection and stand on your toes to see whether or not they touch the boot tips. Assure a firm fit in the heels and snugness (but not tightness) in the instep and toes. Remember, feet will swell after a couple miles of walking, especially over rugged terrain. Boots that bind at the outset will bring problems in the field.

Daypacks

Important to every hunter is wearing or carrying the proper gear for a day afield. For many years a daypack has been part of my deer hunting gear. No matter if I'm heading only 300 yards from the cabin door or setting out on a cross-country jaunt,

Fieldline's fanny pack (left) and daypack are built of water-resistant Quiet Cloth.

I slip it over my shoulders. It's packed with lunch, a couple candy bars, contact lens fluid, drag rope, two sharp knives, bottled water or juice, flashlight, toilet paper, compass, a large, zip-type plastic bag (for the heart and liver), a small zip-bag with a wet cloth to clean up after field-dressing, extra socks and extra shells. Side and front pockets in the daypack hold a camera, raingear, deer calls and one or two other items.

While it sounds like a bundle, the pack weighs only 5-6 pounds and can be stashed in a treestand or hidden along a trail should I choose to hunt a patch of woods without it.

When conditions turn foul I have rain gear in the daypack. If it gets warm, as Pennsylvania's fall weather often does toward mid-day, I have a place to stuff a sweater or vest. If a cold front is forecast, I'll roll a heavier garment in the bag before heading out.

Often, if the hike to my stand is long and/or arduous, I'll shed my outer garment and stuff it in or hang it on the daypack to prevent a build-up of perspiration. Several minutes after arrival at the stand I'll put it back on, after my skin's had the chance to cool as the sweat evaporates.

While my choice of daypack-stuffers may seem extreme, I find use for all the items at one time or another throughout the season.

My preference is for a mini-backpack in camouflage fleece, which is quiet and rain resistant. Nylon or canvas packs may be durable and waterproof but they're also noisy when scraping brush and limbs. Choose a pack with two or three side pockets for calls and other small items. Also make sure it has wide, comfortable straps and tough zippers.

The fanny-type pack is too small for my needs on all but short jaunts from camp. I like it when hunting near home during the bow season however, when I can return and get whatever else I may need should I kill a deer. The advantage of any pack is that pants and jacket pockets are kept free and don't hinder climbing and walking.

Field-dressing knives

I always chuckle when I meet a hunter in the woods carrying a "pig-sticker" on his belt. Few places I hunt lend themselves to hacking through with machetes and I can't imagine how anyone could field dress a deer with one.

I always carry two knives; one a small, 3- to 4 inch lockback blade and the other a gut-hook knife for slitting the belly skin prior to field dressing. The latter knife is also used as a backup blade, which is sometimes necessary for completing the gutting process.

Most hunters use knives far too big for the job. Sharpness is much more important than size and long sheath-knives just add extra weight to the pack or belt. They're unwieldy when it comes to the precision cutting needed to peel skin or slice tough tissue.

Although I seldom carry it afield (except on western hunts), a small knife sharpener is also a handy item. At day's end, after the knife is cleaned, it's used to restore the finely-honed edge that will be needed for the next job.

When bowhunting I also add a pruning shears to my pack. It comes in handy when snipping troublesome twigs and small branches around the treestand — or from the base of the tree where you plan to sit.

Binoculars

I'm constantly amazed at the number of hunters who don't use a binocular. Mine is a constant companion. It has revealed deer I wouldn't otherwise have seen, as well as identifying whether a distant whitetail is sprouting antlers long before it becomes visible to the unaided eye. To me, a quality binocular is as important as a top-notch riflescope.

Knowing a bit about binoculars before putting down your credit card will help in choosing a suitable optic, no matter if you're spending $50 or $500.

The wise shopper should be armed with basic knowledge of the three numbers shown on all binoculars, no matter what the style or make.

The Imperial-Schrade gut-hook knife aids in slitting the belly skin when field-dressing, without puncturing the intestines.

A binocular should be standard equipment for every hunter.

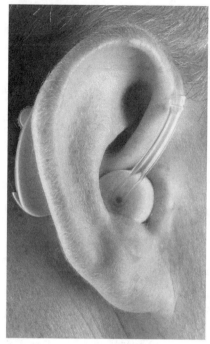

Walker's Game Ear can be worn comfortably while amplifying woodland sounds.

The first number (on a 7x35 binocular, for example) designates that the optic will produce a 7-power magnification. A 10x50 binocular will magnify an object 10 times. An object viewed at 100 yards will appear seven times closer with a 7x and 10 times closer with a 10x binocular. It's that simple.

My personal choice for deer hunting is a 10x.

The second number (in this case 35 or 50) indicates the diameter of the objective (front) lens, measured in millimeters. The larger the objective lens, the more light reaches the eye and the brighter the image. Large objective lenses are blessings when used under low-light conditions, such as viewing game at dusk and dawn.

A third number indicates "field of view at 1000 yards." It designates the width, in feet, that can be seen at a distance of 1000 yards. The stronger the magnification, the less the field of view. Wide-angle lenses increase the view from 35 to 65 percent and are most useful when glassing for big game, as is necessary for mule deer and elk in the West. It is seldom an important factor for Pennsylvania hunters.

The biggest decision in choosing a deer hunting binocular is whether to purchase a compact or full-size model. Full-size binoculars provide the brightest viewing because they're constructed with large lenses. Compact binoculars are less cumbersome when a day's hunting means covering lots of ground. The trade-off of smaller size is smaller objective lenses. When heading out to a treestand for a morning or afternoon hunt I'll take my roof-prism 10x50 Simmons Presidential binocular (best for dim light). When still-hunting and putting on some mileage in a day afield, a compact Bausch & Lomb Elite 10x28 is my choice.

When shopping for a binocular, sight on some distant object — across the showroom or out a window. Check how easily the glass can be focused, remembering you may have to do it while wearing gloves. Also be certain the eye relief is comfortable and provides the full scene. If you wear glasses, fold down the rubber eyecups before testing.

Then make sure these "second eyes" are around your neck whenever you head into whitetail country.

Useful accessories

The hunting industry has flooded the market with "must have" items that many hunters buy — but may only use once or twice. However, some of these aids serve useful purposes when hunting whitetails. Here's a sampling.

• One item I use both for archery deer and turkey hunting is the Walker's Game Ear (phone 800-424-1069) which I like to call "binoculars for your ears." This isn't a gimmick. Try a Game Ear when you're quietly seated on a treestand and suddenly the woods comes alive. Over the years I've used it as much for picking out bird sounds undetected by the "naked ear" as for hearing the footsteps or grunts of deer. On more than one occasion the sound of an errant deer's "crunch" in the leaves — especially in the archery season — has revealed its presence, thanks to the Game Ear.

The hearing aid-type device protects from muzzle blasts by cutting off at noise levels about 110 decibels.

The Pennsylvania product from Bob Walker of Media, Delaware County, is available through most outdoor catalogs and from some sporting goods outlets.

• For the other end of your body are portable seats, which make waiting in the woods more comfortable. The old, spongy "Hot Seats" once served the purpose but they've been replaced by better gear. My favorite is a seat I tried in a recent spring gobbler season. It seemed cumbersome to carry at first but when I used it once, I knew I'd never again leave home without it.

It's called the Turkey & Deer Hunter's Seat By BuckWing (phone 800-555-9908), and is also a Pennsylvania product. Glenn Lindaman's design of the aluminum frame seat includes four short legs and webbing in black or camouflage. Sitting with your butt on the webbing and back against a tree situates your knees in a steady shooting position. Besides, being comfortable, you'll be able to sit still much longer, which is important when hunting either bucks or gobblers.

• D&H Products in Valencia, Pennsylvania makes a compact deer drag — an orange, nylon web strap which fits over the shoulders and attaches to the deer's rack or neck, freeing the hands and arms. It's available in many sporting goods stores. Another is the Tennessee Deer Drag (888-237-1568) which consists of a shoulder strap and a hand-grip to fit any size person or deer. The carcass is pulled with the head off the ground, eliminating snagging on brush or deadfalls. It works as advertised.

• For the bowhunter, a calibrated rangefinder is also an invaluable accessory. It allows hunters to take accurate distance readings of various items in the area — a

An inexpensive calibrated rangefinder verifies short-range distances for bowhunters.

rock, deadfall, stump, nearby path or some other point of interest — while posted or in a treestand. The rangefinder takes the guesswork out of deciding which sight pin to use relative to the distance of some pre-determined spot — near which a buck or doe is feeding.

Laser rangefinders reach out considerably farther. They're most widely used in the open spaces of the West but, depending on where you hunt Pennsylvania whitetails, can also be useful back home. Gun hunters carry them as they reach out from 20 or so yards to 400 and as much as 1,000 yards. One or two models operate in closer ranges and are becoming popular with bowhunters.

Of course you'll find dozens of other items on the shelves at the local sports shop and filling the pages of outdoor catalogs. Only you can decide whether you need another gadget, how much use it will get and whether the cost justifies its purchase.

Tom's Tips

-Wing nuts used on portable treestands are easily dropped, especially when cold weather brings stiff fingers. They can be difficult to find in leaf litter and when stands are being hung or removed in darkness. Spray paint the nuts with fluorescent orange (they show up well in the beam of a flashlight) and carry a couple extras just in case one is lost.

-A single down-feather from a duck, goose or gamebird tied to the end of a 12-to 15-inch piece of thread and hung from the bottom of your bow or a treestand support will signal the direction of the slightest breeze.

-Pack a couple garbage bags before your next trip to deer camp. Camp odors, from tobacco to bacon, will readily penetrate hunting garments. Upon returning from the hunt, take off your clothes and hang them outdoors for an hour or so, then stuff them in a sealed garbage bag overnight. Some hunters also place cotton swabs with a few drops of their favorite cover scent in the bag with the clothing.

-A friend who spends most of his deer season in farm country always makes it a point to look for fresh cow droppings on the way to his stand. He then takes a minute to "refresh" his boots with the "pies." He claims that barnyard bucks are familiar with the odor and it serves to mask both his trail and his body scent while still-hunting.

-The use of 35mm film containers as "scent bombs" is nothing new. Cottonballs are placed inside the film holders, then saturated with cover or attractant scents. The tight fitting caps enable hunters to use and reuse the "bombs," carrying them along when they change locations.

-With electrical or plastic tape, attach a clothespin to the container. Then clip it to a limb or shrub several feet above ground where the scent can more readily catch the wind.

-On cold days, grunt tubes and other deer calls can freeze up after a few breaths are blown through them. Carry the calls in an inside pocket to keep them warm between uses. Also consider packing an extra call in case one fails to perform.

Tom's Tips

-Save those old socks with the worn toes and heels. A pair slipped over the stocks of your guns during storage or transportation will keep them from getting scratched. Of course, you may want to wash them first after they've last been worn, as my wife insists.

-If you stumble when walking and your shotgun or rifle dips into the mud or snow, never continue without first checking the barrel for blockage. Unload the gun and work a thin twig through the muzzle until you're certain all's clear. Not doing so could result in a splintered barrel and serious injury.

-Contrary to the belief of some rifle hunters, the path of a bullet never rises above the line of the barrel, or bore. But it does rise above the shooter's line of sight as both open sights and scopes are adjusted to allow for a bullet's natural drop, or trajectory. Blame the confusion on drawings showing a bullet "rising" through the shooter's sight line. Actually the barrel is tipped slightly upward which accounts for a bullet crossing the line of sight about 25 yards away, then dropping back through the line of sight as gravity pulls it downward anywhere from 50-300 yards away, whichever distance the hunter chooses to be "sighted in."

-Of the four shooting positions — standing, sitting, kneeling and prone — the latter is the steadiest. The sitting position is also steady as long as the hunter's back is against a tree, rock or some other support. Even though most deer are shot while the hunter is standing, the offhand position is the least steady of all. It's recommended that hunters brush up by practicing shots from all positions prior to the deer season.

-One item of constant confusion among hunters is which way to move sights when sighting in a gun. Simply remember to move the rear sight in the same direction (left or right, up or down) you want the impact point to move. The same holds true for sight pins on bows.

-Ever get lost looking for your treestand in the pre-dawn darkness? We all have. An excellent "guideline" can be fashioned from a few dozen wooden clothespins, some reflective tape and orange ribbon. Staple a 6-8 inch length of fluorescent orange ribbon to the pin and wrap a piece of silver reflective tape around one of the flat ends. Clip the pins to trees and bushes at intervals of about 15-20 yards, from which a flashlight's beam will readily reflect off the tape. When stand locations are changed, simply pluck the markers from the trail as you exit the woods.

-Foam pipe-wrap (available at hardware, plumbing and building supply stores) attached to guards, rails and rests on treestands will help muffle sounds that can alert deer.

Shots at fast-moving deer are tempting but should not be tried at long ranges.

Chapter 11

BUCK FEVER AND
ONE-SHOT HUNTS
A Matter of Self-Control

"You shoulda seen the shot my kid made," said the voice on the other end of the phone. "If that buck was 10 yards off it was 200. He emptied his clip on it and got it through the neck — two outa five shots hit it."

"And it was running flat out," he underscored. "I've never seen anything like it. It was unbelievable."

As the outdoors editor of a southeastern Pennsylvania newspaper I cover the hunting scene with editorial policies permitting a cherished free rein in covering this oft-controversial sport. Following the Pennsylvania buck season, I list the names and run photos of hunters and, particularly, their sons and daughters who tied their tags to whitetail bucks — no matter what the size of their "trophies."

I get plenty of letters and calls, among them the one cited above. But that particular tale never made it into print. The caller phoned again a week or so later to question why it hadn't appeared. I patiently explained that I didn't consider the long-shot very ethical and would not add credibility by telling a quarter-million readers about it. The conversation ended quite abruptly when he made a few disparaging comments regarding my ancestry — and hung up.

Had the teenager's running shot have been taken at, say, 20 to 60 yards, I wouldn't have had a problem with it. But a 14-year-old shooting at a deer running flat out at 200 yards is reckless. It's a chance most hunters would not and should not take.

The act of aiming and shooting at a deer takes a matter of seconds. The mere squeeze of the trigger can determine the outcome of a hunting season that encompassed hours, days, even weeks, of a sportsman's time. Most important is the efficient, humane kill of a deer, or any other game for that matter.

The essence of the hunting ethic is to cleanly and quickly kill your quarry with but one shot. No matter if it's a modern high-power rifle, a slug-throwing shotgun, ball-spitting muzzleloader or a well-placed arrow, the one-shot hunt should, and must, be every hunter's ultimate challenge.

With today's plethora of book, magazine and newspaper articles and countless videos on deer and deer hunting available to the hunter, few sportsmen are without the knowledge of where to place the kill shot.

The biggest problem in misplaced shots, many hunters agree, is the hunter's nemesis — buck fever. Long a joke of deer camps, buck fever is, nevertheless, a very realistic affliction.

It may strike the experienced still-hunter as well as the first-timer holding tight to a treestand as a buck approaches. Symptoms are much the same for both hunters, too often resulting in a miss or an injured animal.

In the 48 years I've been hunting whitetails I've experienced buck fever many times. Any hunter who says it's never happened to him or her has (1) never encountered a buck afield or (2) is telling an outright fib. Early on, my buck fever resulted in the predictable missed or lost deer. Later it reared itself when some sizable buck made a surprise appearance and demanded a now-or-never decision.

What can the typical hunter do to lessen the chance of misses or crippling shots and make that "one shot" count?

Ask yourself these four basic questions:

(1) *Are my firearms (bow pins, iron sights, scope) accurate? Might the sights have shifted since the last hunt when the gun fell, was jarred, banged by baggage handlers at the airport or warped from being subject to foul weather or high humidity?*

(2) *Have I done enough preseason shooting? Not just benchrest firing at a target 100 yards off but actually standing, kneeling or bracing myself against a support, as under field situations, and taking aim at targets of varied distances?*

(3) *Given the opportunity to shoot at a deer under differing situations, do I know the proper bullet placement positions?*

(4) *Am I subject to "buck fever" and, if so, can I learn to control it?*

The first two questions have obvious answers and the serious deer hunter will attend to them long before the season opens. Practice, and lots of it, is the key to knowing your gun shoots where it's aimed and that you are actually aiming where it is intended to strike.

The third question shouldn't, but often does, draw a response of "Well, usually!" As for buck fever, we'll taking a closer look later.

One .... and done

Most experienced hunters will agree the "classic" broadside pose demands a lung shot. The lungs make up the largest vital area covering the region from the brisket to a point immediately behind the shoulder. A deer's lung region is about the size of a basketball. It can be hit while the deer is in several positions other than the broadside stance. Whenever I take new hunters afield I stress this aiming point.

Several years back, on hunts in Pennsylvania, New York, Alabama, Georgia and Quebec, I bagged six bucks — four of them with neck shots. Had I not been cock-sure that I could place the bullet exactly where I wanted it I'd have opted for a lower bullet placement. Long ago I was taught that under ideal circumstances neck shots are preferred over all others. I've discovered differently, however, and only take them under special circumstances.

Four of those bucks were less than 70 yards off and looking in my direction (two of them directly at me in high grass). The bullet went through the throat and broke the neck in three of the four situations. One deer was hidden nearly neck-high in a deadfall with the white of its throat exposed. I opted not to take a chance on bullet deflection and aimed high on the neck.

On broadside shots I prefer to place the crosshairs on the rear edge of the foreleg and about a third to a half way up the chest. That should deliver the bullet directly in the center of the lungs. Even a slightly misplaced shot will take out the heart (low), spine (high), esophagus or aortal vessels (front) or, if too far back, the

The broadside lung shot is the surest with both gun and bow.

liver. In all such cases there will be minimal meat loss, another important consideration to most sportsmen.

If the deer is facing you and its chest is visible, the recommended shot placement is immediately above the point where the neck joins the trunk. This will take the bullet directly into the center of the lung area.

On a deer quartering away, the shot should be positioned through the short-ribs so that the bullet enters the lung region. This may be difficult to judge depending on the angle, which varies with each step.

I'm speaking here primarily of situations with firearms. When bowhunting never try a neck shot but always pick the lung-heart area. Mentally isolate a patch of hair and aim for it. After the fact, a clean miss is easier to live with than knowing you drew blood but didn't retrieve the animal. Best of all is letting a buck or doe walk off if it hasn't presented itself with a sure shot at a vital area.

Of course, there are other sure-kill zones, not all of which appeal to gun hunters for one reason or another. Most head shots are devastating and drop deer as if they had stepped into unseen holes. But the head is a small target and a shot may also hit the jaw or nose and result in a merciless, but eventual, death hours or days later. Don't take it.

Another shot that's said to be vital but which I prefer not to take (and have never made) is through or slightly above the anus on a deer moving directly away from the hunter. It's often dubbed the "Texas heart shot." Such a shot, well-placed to the base of the tail, will shock the spinal system and put the deer down. A second shot will be needed to dispatch the animal. Should such a shot miss the mark considerable damage will be done to the hams and severe blood loss will occur. Yet, I'm convinced most rump shots result in lost deer.

The preference of a true heart shot is another subject open to question. The heart is a small target, only slightly bigger than a man's fist, and is often hit by accident when a low lung shot is taken. Then, too, few hunters know the precise location of the heart.

This shot's path will deliver the bullet in the lung area.

The quartering shot will strike the short-ribs and lungs.

Hunters utilizing tree stands must adjust all shots accordingly as the path of the bullet will differ when it's taken from on high. Sometimes the spine will be penetrated on any shots from a severe overhead angle and drop the deer in its tracks. This is also true for bowhunters who typically shoot high when aiming from a tree. Practicing on 3-D targets from treestands will pay off when a similar shot at a live deer presents itself.

Sometimes the aim is right on but the deer seems to duck out of the way in time. Slow-motion videos show what really happens. As the deer tenses and begins to run, it bends its forelegs to spring into action, automatically lowering its back. Many bowhunting videos show the phenomenal reaction time of the deer — and the arrow sailing cleanly over its back. But the speeding arrow is not something of which the deer is aware.

The best way to learn proper bullet or arrow placement is to study photographs of deer in varied poses and visualize kill zones. Better yet, visit a preserve, game park or zoo where live deer are present and visualize the zones.

Overcoming buck fever

My personal battle with the buck fever was overcome with time and experience, which cannot be fabricated.

Most long-time hunters with racks on the wall will tell you buck fever is real and, left unmanaged, can ruin a hunt. I still experience it somewhat today but, given similar situations of 30-40 or more years back, I find myself in complete control.

Mind control and recognizing the onset of the affliction for what it is — a bad case of nerves — will help. Over the years I've learned to talk to myself (silently, of course) when a big buck is sighted. I still get the shakes and have been known to babble and stutter.

But now it happens when a buck is down, not before.

Flinching

One other problem that results in misses may have nothing to do with buck fever, although it may be related, is flinching. Most hunters caught up in the captivating act of taking aim on a deer will not flinch. Indeed, many hunters say they seldom recall feeling the gun's kick or hearing the explosion when afield, even though they may be ultra-sensitive to both when on the range.

Flinching is largely but not solely a nemesis of inexperienced hunters and those who simply do not spend enough time on the range before deer season.

My wife, who started hunting in 1981, missed a mule deer and a whitetail her first times out because she flinched. In the case of the muley, she shot at least 30 yards in front of it (the deer was about 175 yards off) when she tensed her upper torso a mini-second before squeezing the trigger. She claimed she didn't flinch but I watched her do just that as I was looking over her shoulder at the time.

The next morning, on a range, I feigned loading her rifle but, instead, handed her a gun with a spent shell in the chamber. When she squeezed the trigger, she again flinched, even though the gun didn't fire. It was only then that she realized that, indeed, she'd tensed before triggering the shot. Once she understood the problem it was quickly overcome.

Taking the life of a game animal, especially one as majestic as a deer, is not without its responsibilities and spirituality. The flood of emotions, from regret to pride, that command the body when a buck is at your feet are closely mapped by the method in which it was taken.

The one-shot hunt is the essence of such poignant and memorable times. As hunters, we owe it to ourselves, our sport, and especially to our quarry, to abide by it and promote it as an integral part of the Pennsylvania deer hunting ethic.

Tom's Tips

-Dr. Larry Marchinton and his research team at the University of Georgia have identified 13 different audible communications used by whitetailed deer. Only one, the foot-stomp (which every hunter has seen and possibly heard), is non-vocal.

-Some bowhunters refuse to use brightly colored nocks and fletchings because they believe deer will see them more readily than dark colors. That's probably true. But consider that fluorescent yellow, green or orange fletching is more readily detected on the arrows in the quiver, not the arrow nocked for the initial shot. Bright fletchings will enable you to better detect the area of the hit — and find your arrow among the vegetation.

-Misjudging distance may be the number one reason for bowhunters' misses. Most archers spend their opening days in familiar surroundings; stand sites they've visited on pre-season scouting trips. Tying bits of orange ribbon at pre-determined distances on low branches, shrubs or stumps around your stand will help in making precise distance judgments. (Be sure to remove the ribbons when your season's over.)

-When beginning your summer practice for the fall season, first check for subtle bow noises that may spook deer. Have a companion stand a few feet from away in an ultra-quiet room. Draw the bowstring several times to determine if any annoying sounds — like the scrape of the arrow across the rest, cables rubbing or wheels squeaking — need attention.

Despite its size, most of this big buck's body remains unseen in a brushy thicket.

Chapter 12

SEE MORE WHITETAILS
Learning to Look for Deer Parts

The first buck I ever shot, in McKean County back in 1962, showed up broadside at 15 yards. It was plainly seen from nose to tail-tip.

I remember it well.

The first Canadian buck to which I tied my tag was bedded in a thicket of black spruce in an Anticosti Island forest. Had it not been for the attention-getting sight of its left antler, I'd probably have wandered on by.

Deer have a knack for blending in with their habitat, such as this big doe standing next to a deadfall. Or is it a buck?

All or portions of four deer are visible in this winter photograph.

Indeed, in my four-plus decades of pursuing whitetails from Quebec to Arizona, most bucks on which I've centered the crosshairs wouldn't have been seen except for one or two "deer parts" that revealed their presence.

While experienced deer hunters are attuned to looking for tails, ears, legs, noses, eyes, antler segments or the horizontal line of a back or belly, newcomers to the sport often fail to "make the connection" when an entire animal isn't seen.

Novices in the deer woods (and we were all novices at one time) typically take wide-angle views of the terrain, often failing to see deer whose "parts" betray their presence. They expect that any deer in the area — any "whole" deer — will be seen.

Taking a newcomer afield prior to the hunting season is an oft-overlooked facet of his or her training. But it's as important as sighting in a rifle, searching for deer sign, mapping trails, judging shooting distances, locating treestands and practicing gun safety.

Many experienced hunters can also use the practice.

How do you go about teaching such a lesson?

Over the years I've undertaken the satisfying task of training my own sons, several other young relatives and friends, and my wife in the art of finding "deer parts."

First, we reviewed photographs of deer in their natural habitats. Magazine photos clipped for the occasion served the purpose well.

Too elementary? Not at all.

The magazine or book picture lesson is a productive way to spend an evening with a future hunter. Remember, this may be old stuff to a veteran woodsman but, to a first-timer, the information's new and revealing.

Secondly, take a preseason trip to a park, wildlife preserve or research area where deer sightings are guaranteed. Actual sightings of bucks and does in their natural habitat provide the student with first-hand experience in finding "deer parts."

Another effective teaching tool involves a life-size deer target used by bowhunters. Placing the model in brush, high grasses, behind deadfalls and in other situations where only a rump, head, legs, back, belly or other body part is seen at a distance of 30-100 yards or more serves as an excellent teaching tool.

Remember that the novice hunter typically takes a panoramic view of a habitat. He or she expects to see a whole deer, not just a nose or tail.

The veteran knows it's often the small details — the patch of brown among the greenbriar or a smoothly-curved neck or rump that's somehow out of synch with vertical trees or grasses — that yield sightings of deer before they see you.

Yet another lesson involves keeping a ready eye for movement — not the motion of a running buck but rather the twitch of an ear, the flick of a tail or the low sweep of feet and legs through a pine grove.

The experienced hunter will find himself or herself gazing for long minutes at stumps that look like bedded deer, wind-whipped leaves that resemble deer tails or low branches shaped like trophy antlers. Sometimes they're just that. Most times they're not.

Once a "part" is spotted, binoculars should be used to confirm your sighting — or verify that the "bedded doe" is actually a hemlock stump. No hunter should go afield without good optics.

Once a hunter heads out in the frame of mind that anything out of synch might be a whitetail, he knows he's come a long way in picking out the "deer parts" that put venison on the table.

And antlers on the wall.

Tom's Tips

-Small alligator clips come in handy for pinching off the bladder ducts when field-dressing a deer. The ducts can also be tied before removing and discarding the bladder. It prevents urine from tainting the meat.

- Never follow a blood trail by walking atop the deer's escape path. Should you lose the trail and have to retrace your steps, it will be harder to pick it up because you may have obliterated the sign by overturning leaves or kicking dirt and pebbles over it. Always work to one side of the blood trail.

-When it's necessary to drag a buck and you don't have a rope, grasp the antler closest to the ground. This keeps the deer's head and neck up, offering less resistance from the ground, and prevents the antler from hitting your calf on each step.

-In Pennsylvania it's law that you must tag your deer before moving it from the place it was killed. Take special care not to lose your tag. After attaching it to the antler or ear, wrap a handkerchief, scarf or a swatch of cloth around the tag to prevent it from being torn off during dragging.

-The Longhunter Society is an organization providing muzzleloader hunters a record book status like the Boone & Crockett and Pope & Young clubs. Already 600 members have joined the society which has formulated its own big game records program under the auspices of the National Muzzleloading Rifle Association. Any of 28 species of N.A. big game taken with blackpowder guns is eligible.

-For details write: The Longhunter Society, P.O. Box 67, Friendship, IN 47021

SECTION III
TIPS AND TECHNIQUES FOR PENNSYLVANIA WHITETAILS

Craig Krisher's state record non-typical, Lehigh County bow-buck was the reward of intensive scouting.

Chapter 13

SCOUTING
Hunter's Homework

At 5 a.m. on October 1, 1988 Craig Krisher climbed into his portable treestand in northern Lehigh County's farm country.

It was a familiar spot, one in which the then-25-year-old bowhunter had spent other dawns during the previous weeks. That's much of the reason he was filled with confidence that "this will be the day."

Ironically, despite the anticipation, it was no colossal surprise when a monster buck moved down a trail tramped into the nearly impenetrable thicket. Krisher had seen the same buck nearly two dozen times and, along with his lifelong friend and hunting companion Vince Fugazzotto, had captured the velvet-antlered stag on film and video-tape six weeks earlier.

While Krisher awaited sunrise, Fugazzotto sat in another treestand several hundred yards away, also hoping for a shot at the monster buck they'd first seen in mid-June and, later, painstakingly backtracked to its bedding area in a scrub thicket.

Its morning retreat always followed one of several well-worn trails, among them the "apple tree route."

Krisher had arrived at the apple tree, his stand already intact, well before sunrise via a small brook that flowed nearby. On other mornings he and Fugazzotto had patterned the movements of the 23-point whitetail and Krisher was confident it would be passing by to its bedding area between 6:15 and 6:45, as it had on other mornings.

But on this morning — the season opener — the buck was a bit late. At 6:50 Krisher heard something move in the nearby gully and, through a drizzly mist, recognized the magnificent buck that had dominated his thoughts for several months.

The kill was almost anticlimactic. At 12 yards the buck paused to sniff a curiosity scent pad Krisher had placed in the narrow path. The shot was perfect and the buck toppled after only a 30-yard sprint.

At that moment the Pennsylvania non-typical, bow-buck record also fell. Following the mandatory 60-day drying period, it scored 203-3/8 Pope & Young points, providing Krisher and his companion their reward for over 100 hours of preseason scouting.

While not every hunter can spare that kind of time previewing hunting grounds, this success story proves that scouting plays a very definite role in hunting success — even when patterning a specific buck.

Of course, scouting means different things to different hunters.

Some simply want to learn where escape routes, bedding areas and favored feeding sites are located. Time and the distance from their homes to the places they hunt may dictate only cursory preseason visits. Even a day or two of scouting, however, can reap benefits for the effort.

Others search for big bucks and a few — like Krisher and Fugazzotto — pattern specific animals.

Unless you live close by your hunting grounds and can spare mornings before work, then take advantage of daylight remaining after punching the time clock, establishing a dossier on a specific deer may be futile.

Truth is, most hunters can afford only portions of a few preseason days to track their prey.

Scout smart

So what's the recipe for making the most of those scouting hours?

Here are 10 items that should be on every scouter's menu.

(1) The first is simple observation. Krisher and Fugazzotto caught first sight of the record book buck by driving back roads at the edges of the day and observing where deer were feeding and taking inventory of both buck and doe numbers.

They began their quest in mid-June, well ahead of the hunting season. At this time deer are relatively undisturbed. They build their daily schedules on filling their bellies and moving back and forth to their bedding areas.

(2) As food sources change and farm crops mature, deer will expand their feeding areas. The Lehigh County bowhunters first noted whitetail activity in alfalfa and clover fields and later in corn and soybean fields.

Oak ridges provide meager enticement in midsummer but when acorns drop in late summer and early fall, they attract deer like magnets. Locating oak-rich tracts provides a back-up plan as the season progresses.

Krisher also spent considerable time spotlighting, which is legal in Pennsylvania (up until 11 p.m. each night except during the deer hunting seasons when spotlight-

Driving back roads through public lands prior to the season often reveals deer travel routes.

Maggie Power, then 12, had scouted prior to the 1995 season with her father Karl, of Westmoreland County, and their work paid off with this 10-point Indiana County opening day buck.

ing is illegal), revealing nocturnal activity. The men noted the 23-pointer frequented areas as far as 1-1/2 miles apart. But early morning and late afternoon sightings were typically made in the same place, hinting as to the proximity of the buck's bedding area.

(3) "Mock hunts" also provide helpful information on deer activity. Spending time in permanent and portable treestands on back fields or woodlands enables the documentation of deer movements and numbers.

On such outings a binocular and a spotting scope are necessary. Close-up views reveal individual identities. The travel patterns of the same deer seen in several sectors will provide clues to their travels.

(4) Once bucks are located, the next order of business for those with sufficient time is a closer look at the "keeper" bucks observed.

Big bucks sometimes leave distinctive tracks. Krisher and Fugazzotto noted the specific spots where their buck was seen. Close study revealed it had a cleft hoof on its right front foot. The distinctive hoof-print enabled them to backtrack it to its general bedding area over a span of several weeks.

(5) While it's a time-consuming task, tracking one buck or a bachelor group from feeding areas to bedding site often reveals more than one notable trophy. On the morning Krisher made his kill, Fugazzotto spotted a big 9-pointer, one of four or five bucks that traveled together well into September and were still in one another's general company on the season opener.

As the warm days of September yield to October's chill, many of these bachelor groups break up as dominance is established.

(6) Of course, the traditional buck barometers — rubs and scrapes — are among the easiest of signs to locate. Before and during the rut (especially before) fresh scrapes are reliable locaters as they indicate recent use.

Unless specific "new" rubs are seen on follow-up scouting jaunts, their ages are often hard to analyze. Early rubs and scrapes, made during September in most

Some rubs show aggressive antler scraping, hinting that they were probably made during the late pre-rut period.

states, are the result of anxiousness among individuals in bachelor herds. Bucks make them but don't necessarily revisit them.

As fall progresses, sparring is common and small sumacs, pines, cedars and other scrub vegetation will take much of the brunt of such "shadow boxing." As the prime rut period nears, saplings and bigger trees will be attacked.

The adage that only big bucks rub big trees is generally true. They will also spar with small trees but the size of a strafed trunk is a reliable indicator as to the comparative size of a rub's maker.

(7) Merely finding a sizable rub or two is encouraging but locating a rub line demands focused attention.

Problem is, such "lines" may not be quickly recognizable. Field edges, stream banks, skid trails, old logging roads and readily recognized deer trails must be given special attention as that's where more than half of all rubs are often found. Keeping track of fresh rubs and, later in the season, scrapes, on a topographic map, airphoto or a homemade map of an area may piece together prime runs and passages between feeding and bedding areas.

It's here where predictable activity occurs and where tree stands should be hitched.

(8) Scouting involves more than looking for deer, their food or their signs. On public hunting areas it doesn't take long for deer to shift into Plan B or C and abandon the runs and trails, even the bedding areas, to which they became accustomed throughout summer.

For several years I hunted, with moderate success, a Corps of Engineers tract in northeastern Pennsylvania. During the squirrel and grouse seasons I spent more time looking for deer sign than seeking bushytails and ruffs.

But on opening morning and throughout the gun season, places I'd spotted bucks and does casually walking trails yielded little. That's when I bought a topographic map and airphoto of the area and discovered an alternate route into the backcountry. Using a canoe with a 3-horsepower motor, a friend and I cut an hour's walk into a 15-minute boat ride, putting us into the region where hunters pushed deer each morning.

For several years we enjoyed early season success, until others also started using the boat-in passage.

(9) Bowhunters, in particular, like to position stands on the fringes of feeding areas. Traipsing the perimeter of a cornfield or alfalfa patch will readily reveal the deers' approach to a food source. If undisturbed, they'll continue to utilize the same routes, at least up until the transition period when changing foods or rutting activity demands new and more varied wanderings.

With exception, I prefer setting up within a woodlot or forest edge rather than immediately on its rim. Big bucks tend to linger in the shadows until darkness, even though they may accompany the does that often begin feeding well before sunset.

(10) While scouting trips combine knowledge with the welcome enjoyment and anticipation of another season on the horizon, don't let your guard down by "polluting" the area.

Sight and smell, even before the first arrow is released or shot fired, is sufficient to alert wary bucks that something's amiss.

Use reliable cover scents or liquid scent "shields," wear rubber boots and be certain no foreign odors are carried in your clothing. As in an actual hunt, be aware of wind direction and keep breezes in your favor.

Prior to each of their scouting trips, Krisher and Fugazzotto washed their camo clothing in baking soda, then stored it in a plastic bag and applied a scent-block before entering the woods. They were also careful not to leave undue scent in the woods.

As said, scouting and the degree to which it's performed is a personal matter among hunters. Give it as much time as you can afford, even if only for a day or two. The more knowledge gained about your hunting area in preseason, the better your chances of being in that magical "right spot" on opening morning.

Topographic maps and air photos are invaluable in locating deer hideaways and travel routes.

The portable treestand changed the way archers hunt as it became refined over the past 25 or more years.

Chapter 14

TAKING A STAND
Treestand Placement and Safety

When I was a kid it was a treat to hunt deer from a treestand.

Then, "taking a stand" meant climbing onto a wooden platform nailed in a tree and staying there most of the day.

The treestands from which I hunted in Pennsylvania's deer-rich north-country were stationed in places where deer sooner or later wandered by. If deer were seen, great. If not, I often spent long, cold days watching squirrels and listening to distant shots.

Today the portable treestand — like grunt tubes, bow sights, quality camouflage, commercial scents and dozens of other modern whitetail hunting aids — has revolutionized the way hunters seek their prey. In a matter of minutes a stand can be moved to a hotspot, sometimes making the difference between a dinner of venison chops or bean soup.

Of course, many stands are permanent structures, most much better built than the wooden planks hunters nailed up 20 or 30 years ago.

But it's the portables that have revolutionized the way most hunters, particularly archers, today hunt whitetails. Knowing how to read deer sign and figuring out their changing patterns determines just how successful a hunter's treestand techniques may be.

Choosing The "Right" Tree
Follow these tips for choosing the "right spot" for your treestand.

• Find well-used trails between bedding and feeding areas prior to the season. Choose stand locations at the intersections of trails or in natural funnels, such as the convergence of "fingers" along ridges or natural runs where woodlands rim feeding fields.

• In farm country, where treelines, windbreaks or grassy gullies link woodlots, deer like to travel the cover rather than the open spaces. Look for suitable trees to take a stand near the junction of the fencerows and woods.

• When seeking a specific spot to place a stand on a hillside, be aware that deer moving up the hill may see you skylined, particularly in the evening hours when a hunter's silhouette is backed by a western sky. Deer coming over the rise may also be on eye level with a hunter who chooses a tree just under the crest. Move the stand a bit farther down the slope if you and your treestand stand out like the proverbial sore thumb.

• The edges of natural barriers to casual deer movement — such as the ends of sloughs around which deer typically pass or shallow riffle areas in streams and rivers where deer can wade rather than swim, or gentle inclines along an otherwise abrupt-drop-off — are prime spots to set up.

• Stands of oaks, beeches and other mast-producing trees are magnets to whitetails in early season. Late summer brings the nuts to the ground and areas where deer only casually passed through earlier become hotspots, as long as the nuts continue to fall.

• Also consider the ease with which you can enter and exit an area in which a treestand, portable or permanent, has been placed. Shallow streams or tractor paths where man-made odors are found year-around are good choices. Whatever you do, don't plan an approach through thickets or other habitats through which you cannot walk quietly — or through which you expect a deer to travel as it approaches your stand. The scent you leave there may be enough to make a whitetail change its trail.

• If there's the chance of being seen or heard as you approach a bedding area, plan to be in your stand at least an hour before sunrise. Deer can see better than you can in the dark but the cover of darkness will provide an added advantage to remaining unseen. Then, too, if you're near a bedding area or some other travel route, arriving early can put you in position before the deer return from their night's feeding.

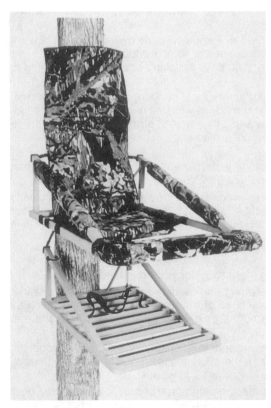

The 27-pound API Super Mag treestand is safe for hunters up to 350 pounds.

• One of the biggest mistakes a hunter can make is choosing a tree on which to hang a stand simply because it has a "nice view." Of course, on the opening day of buck and doe seasons, when deer are pushed, such a stand may be productive. But in bow season or the winter archery-muzzleloader hunt, getting close is the key to success.

The proper balance between cover and open shooting lanes is also an important consideration. Carry a hand clipper to clear troublesome twigs both in the tree and at varied places on the ground, particularly in the bow season.

Potent portables

Like camo and compound bows, portable treestands have come a long way since the first Baker stands were created many years ago. Portables, whether of the bulky ladder type or the small, light climbers, provide the hunter a way to ascend the tree of his or her choice, or move the stand to greener pastures as the seasons progress.

In the market for a portable treestand?

First recognize the four basic stand types: hanging stands, climbers, ladder stands and tripods.

I've used the latter in Texas and have seen them on a couple Pennsylvania hunting club grounds, although it's not as commonly used here as in the South. Tripods are most practical where insufficient choices of climbable trees are unavailable.

Hanging stands are by far the most portable and hold the potential for most danger, particularly while ascending and descending. Ladder stands also pose some danger during set-up as hunters often climb the steps to make strap or rope adjustments before they're secured. Most manufacturers have taken it upon themselves to include detailed instructions (some companies supply videos with their products) and safety devices for customers.

By virtue of their simplicity, hanging stands are easier to carry and can be attached to almost any tree. Their downside is the need for screw-in steps which are illegal on public hunting lands in Pennsylvania, and on private lands, unless written permission is given.

According to one Pennsylvania bow shop owner who sells hundreds of stands each year, archers are getting away from the screw-in steps and going to the strap-on ladders, which are secured vertically against a tree with nylon rope or webbing. The ladders break down into short sections for transport.

Climbing stands have grown in popularity in recent years as technology catches up with the need for safety. Some climbers have devices for ascending and descending which require considerable upper body strength and a bit of athletic prowess. For the uninitiated, they may strain arm and back muscles. The big advantage is they can be set up faster as there's no need to first attach stepping devices to the tree.

Ladder stands are by far the easiest to climb and therefore many hunters, my wife included, consider them the safest. Her Loc-On Titan consists of a fold-away padded seat, a 16-by18-inch grid platform, center-lock bar for attachment to the tree for stability and flat ladder steps which break down into three 40-inch sections. When fastened, the stand reaches 12 feet with a 2-foot addition available.

The climbing stand — as used here by Scott Hoats — enables set-ups anywhere straight-trunked trees can be found.

The Permanent, Portable Treestand

Overhead view of platform support and nailer

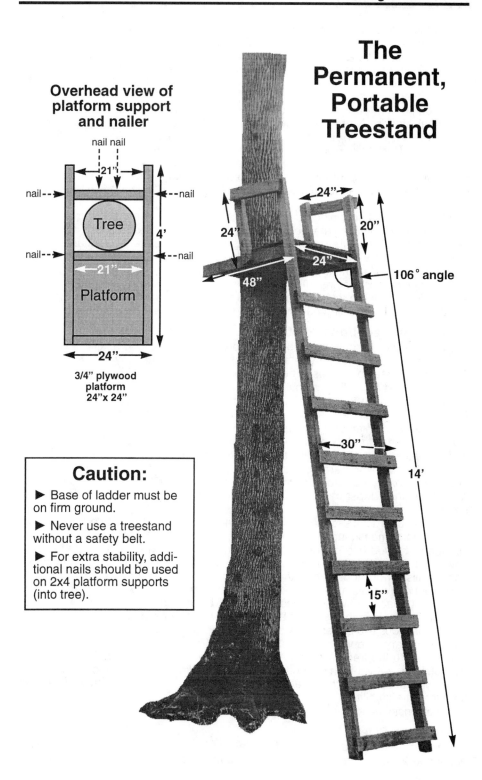

nail nail

21"

nail - - → ← - -nail

Tree

4'

nail - -→ ←- -nail

←21"→

Platform

←24"→

3/4" plywood platform 24"x 24"

24"

48"

24"

24"

20"

106° angle

30"

14'

15"

Caution:

► Base of ladder must be on firm ground.

► Never use a treestand without a safety belt.

► For extra stability, additional nails should be used on 2x4 platform supports (into tree).

A ladder stand can be moved from time to time with relative ease, although it's not one to cart around the woods each day. Hunters with access to private property or members of clubs and lodges often invest in such stands rather than build permanent platforms, which cannot be relocated without considerable work. However, a ladder stand can be easily set up for a day's hunt as it weighs only about 20 pounds, despite its size.

Of course, there are dozens more treestand manufacturers producing safe and functional stands. Names include Amacker, API Outdoors, Big Buck, Loc-On, Loggy Bayou, Lone Wolf, Trax-America, Screaming Eagle, Strongbuilt, Summit Specialties, Trailhawk, Trophy Whitetail and Warren & Sweat, among others.

Expect to pay from $50 to $300 or more for a portable stand with hangers being the least expensive ($50-$75 average). Steps or take-apart climbing poles will add to the cost. A quality ladder stand averages $140-$175 with climbers in the range of $125-$175.

While treestand shopping, also pick up a reliable safety rope. For many years my personal favorite was the Deluxe Safety Belt and Climbing Harness from Game Tracker. It's a polyester strap which fastens around the hunter's waist and a nylon rope with an easily manipulated lock-buckle circling the tree. I use it both in the treestand and while climbing.

Most hunting magazines offer addresses with their ads and will send brochures and catalogs upon request. Or stop by your favorite archery shop and see first hand what's available for scaling new heights — safely — in the deer woods.

The Permanent-Portable Stand

Private landowners and members of sportsmen's clubs, lodges and deer camps usually construct their own treestands. Most are designed as they're being built, utilizing straight trees or mazes of heavy branches in "low-crotch" species.

Few are built according to any blueprint.

Since the early 1980s I've spent time hunting with the Pitman family at White Oak Plantation near Tuskegee, Alabama, a 25,000-acre commercial whitetail haven.

Bo Pitman, White Oak manager, has built more than 500 safe and sturdy wooden, ladder stands which he's able to move, as necessary. I've dubbed the unique, relatively inexpensive stand as the "permanent, portable treestand."

It can be built anywhere and carted on a pick-up or ATV trailer. The Pitmans cut and nail a dozen or more at a time. Of course, on 25,000 acres there's plenty of room for stands. Most of us will get by with from one to three or four as property size demands.

The entire structure is made of 2- by 4-inch treated lumber with a 3/4-inch plywood platform measuring 2- by 2-feet.

When I moved into my new residence in Northampton County in 1997. I built several of Pitman's stands and placed them across the street on a farm my family had permission to hunt. When the land was sold to build a golf course, I merely pulled out a few nails and dragged them back home with my ATV. You won't throw one on your back and walk around the woods, but the safe and inexpensive stands are truly "portable," while serving as permanent high-rises, as well.

The previous two pages show the stand in position and the dimensions of all the cuts necessary to build it. It reaches nearly 14 feet above the ground. The only attachment to the tree is two or three #20 nails which must be driven through the 21-inch long, 2- by 4-inch support on the tree's backside. I also recommend fastening a nylon strap with a "come-along" latch around the tree and the back of the platform for extra stability.

An extension ladder is needed to safely attach and remove the nails.

Treestand Safety

"The earliest record of a treestand fatality in Pennsylvania while bowhunting happened 25 or 30 years ago when a hunter dropped his quiver," according to retired Game Commission Hunter Education Chief Jim Filkosky. "While he was crawling out of the stand to get it he fell on an arrow that had stuck in the ground, with the point upward."

The broadhead severed a leg artery and the victim bled to death.

That, unfortunately, was probably the most unusual treestand-related accident ever.

No one really knows the extent of treestand accidents in Pennsylvania, according to current Hunter Education Chief Keith Snyder.

"Our Game Law specifies that we must investigate, and victims or offenders must report only accidents pertaining to the discharge of a firearm or bow," Snyder explained. "It would take an act of legislation to require that such accidents be reported to us."

Nor does anyone know how many treestand-related injuries and fatalities occur nationwide, but a recent study by *Deer & Deer Hunting* magazine holds some surprises.

A survey of 1,300 hunters revealed that nearly one-third of treestand users have fallen from them during their hunting careers. Most falls (4 in 10) occur while a person is climbing or descending. Another 27 percent of the mishaps happen while the hunter is installing or getting out of or into the stand. Only 15 percent of the accidents take place while the hunter is standing or seated in the stand. Typically, the latter sort of accidents are caused by slipping on moist surfaces, a stand's structural weakness or movements that cause loss of balance.

Accidents just as easily occur on "permanent" stands as on portables.

One of the more surprising revelations in the magazine survey is that 66 percent of all hunters — bow and gun — never use a safety belt or harness while ascending or descending trees. That's when nearly three-fourths of all falls occur.

Dr. Charles Norelli of Allentown demonstrates the lineman's belt and rope he uses to remain secure as he ascends and descends a tree using a climbing stand.

"One sure way to reduce the risks when going aloft is to remain buckled up anytime both feet are off the ground, not just when you have settled in the stand," said *Deer & Deer Hunting* editor Pat Durkin.

He also advises avoiding the use of a tree branch as a step or temporary support. Sooner or later it will break, and the user will go tumbling down.

Safety harnesses

The use of safety belts is also mandatory, from the time you lift your feet off the ground until you return to Mother Earth at the end of the hunting day. The standard nylon web straps fastened around the waist and clipped to a strap or rope around a tree is a thing of the past for wise hunters.

Today, full-body harnesses are the answer. The best harnesses have shoulder, belt and upper leg straps which distribute the shock in the event of a fall. Single-strap harnesses may cause suffocation from pressure being exerted in one place on the body. In October of 1999 an Allentown attorney was found dead in the Monroe County woods, suspended 18 feet above the ground and hanging by his safety strap.

Invest instead in a full-body harness. That $30-$40 investment is a small price to pay for saving your limbs — and your life.

Homemade stands

In a survey of treestand falls in Georgia over a 4-year period it was learned that 75 percent of treestand accidents resulted in moderate to severe injuries. One quarter of those injured suffered permanent paralysis of arms or legs. The study, surprising to many hunters, also revealed that factory-made treestands are much safer than homemade stands.

Of course, not all accidents involve portable stands. Many accidents happen on permanent stands. Hunters get into wooden platforms they haven't checked for a year or find an old stand in the woods and climb into it. Often these stands have loose nails or rotten boards — accidents waiting to happen.

If you use a permanent stand, don't take it for granted that it's in as good shape as it was on your final hunt last year. Wind and weather may have conspired to weaken it. Build and repair damaged stands with new, treated lumber, not scrap material. During pre-season inspections check for rotting wood, broken parts, loose steps or nails, shaky guard rails and screws worked loose by tree movement.

Preparedness and common sense will go a long way to avoiding the nightmare of falling from a treestand.

Permanent treestands should be constructed or repaired well before the season starts.

-When wind direction cooperates, plan your still-hunts and stalks with the sun at your back. Deer show up better when sun and shadows are present and they won't note your movement as readily if they are looking toward the sun.

-A 35mm film container partially filled with old fashioned petroleum jelly (gel) can be a lifesaver when hunting. It serves as a gun lubricant, leather treatment, first aid for a cut, skin cream for chafes and burns and dozens of other uses.

Tom's Tips

-While every target shooter should wear ear protection, donning a muff or using sponge ear plugs is particularly helpful to new shooters for another reason. When practicing or sighting in, the inexperienced shooter will relax a bit more prior to squeezing the trigger if he or she isn't anticipating the loud blast from the muzzle.

-When crossing barbed wire fences, take the low road. Climbing the wire may pull staples from the posts and a slip will tear your clothing or, worse, your flesh. It's best to find a spot where you can crawl under the wire, keeping both the landowner and your seamstress happy.

-Trophy hunters often "take it on the chin" from animal rights crusaders and others who think seeking the biggest and best is contrary to natural selection. Remind them that trophy bucks are older animals who have already distributed their genes throughout the herd's pool. Not only are they passed on by the bucks he's sired but his female offspring will also contribute to the genetic quality in a region. All hunters are "trophy hunters" of sorts, as opportunities warrant. But surely more sportsmen come home with average deer than wall-hangers. It's simply a case of the big ones getting more attention in the press and at the local sporting goods store.

-Windy days are prime times for hunting standing corn. Move into breeze or hunt in a crosswind, moving slowly and carefully studying each row. The rustling of stalks will help hide your movements. Rainy days, or times when heavy rains have softened the leaves, are also good times to visit cornfields.

-One of the heaviest (documented) whitetail bucks ever reported was killed in Maine in 1955. Shot by Harry Hinkley, the deer weighed 355 pounds, field-dressed, three days after it was killed. It was weighed on official scales. Biologists estimated its live weight at 461 pounds. For the record, the buck held a 16-point rack but didn't have the mass of many of Maine's smaller-bodied deer. A 1926 Minnesota deer is said to have field-dressed at 402 pounds; its live weight calculated at 511 pounds.

-Heat from a fireplace or radiator, direct sunlight and cigarette smoke concentration are major enemies of game mounts. Ultraviolet rays and smoke will change hair color and constant dry air will crack the nose and hide. Choose the display area for your trophies with discretion.

-Hairline cracks in your head mounts can be repaired with black model airplane paint. Use a small, artist's brush to touch up the nostril and eyelid areas where cracks often occur.

-If the moon has a halo when you set out in the predawn hours, be sure to pack a rainsuit. The halo is formed by light shining through cirrostratus clouds. These clouds are forerunners of precipitation.

Many archers — including outdoor writer Nick Hromiak of Allentown — wear rubber boots when scouting and hunting so as not to spread human scent across the hunting area, as leather boots may.

Chapter 15

SCENTS AND NONSENSE
Fooling a Deer's Nose

Anyone who's paid his or her dues in the deer woods (interpret that as many hours outdoors and many years of successes and mistakes) can surely relate occurrences which seem to go without explanation.

Take, for instance, that deer clearly out of your scent path which is suddenly alerted to your presence. Or the buck strolling by upwind gazing directly at you perched in a treestand, when you haven't twitched a muscle in 15 minutes. And, perhaps, the doe grazing in an open field 150 yards off obviously smelling your presence when the wind shifts.

Some whitetail phenomena have explanations. Others don't.

Having hunted with hundreds of different companions over the years, it's my belief that many hunters still don't give deer sufficient respect for their abilities in detecting danger in the air. Studies indicate the olfactory senses of a deer may be as much as 10,000 times more sensitive than that of a human. True or not, it's fact that whitetails possess "super noses." Hearing and eyesight are also used to detect other deer as well as hunters. But it's the "chemical lab" — the nose and a portion of the roof of the mouth — that confirms what sort of molecules are drifting in the breeze.

Which brings us to scents — as well as some nonsense — about natural and commercial "deer lures" and cover-ups.

Scent-eliminating and scent-locking sprays, detergents, shampoos and soaps are effective and readily available.

Mock scrapes or actual scrapes treated with doe-in-heat or dominent buck scents are effective as the rut approaches.

Best offense is a defense

The first order of business in the deer woods is to reduce the chances that human odor will betray your presence. While I can recall squirting commercial apple scent around my stand 40 years ago (Yes, the deer scent business, although in its infancy, was present in the 1960s.), then waiting for a buck to come charging in, it's only been in the past dozen years or so that emphasis is being given to blocking tell-tale human odors.

If given only one such item to use while hunting, I'll choose a "scent-locking" liquid or powder as a first line of defense against being detected. At first I thought the pro- liferation of compounds which claimed to minimize human odor — actually locking them in — was a gimmick. Later I became a believer.

One cold night in a "deer camp" (a camping trailer) the toilet stopped up. The odor in the tight quarters was intolerable until Dr. Greg Bambenek, better known as "Dr. Juice" for his line of scent products, sprayed the waste material with his scent-locking solution.

Within minutes the odor was alleviated. And I became a believer.

Don't confuse these items with cover-up scents, such as cedar and pine or essences of fox, raccoon and skunk urines. I no longer use the urine cover-ups as my belief is they, the skunk in particular, are far too revealing to deer. (Besides, my wife frowns on my keeping them in the house.) I'll opt for th fresh-earth and pine (when hunting pinewoods) cover scents.

Most scent companies today market one sort of scent-masking product or another, including sprays for carrying afield, shower soaps, shampoos, scent-free detergents and even powders. Use them on clothing and exposed skin before and during every trip to the deer woods. Clothing should be laundered in the scent-elimi- nating detergents.

Of course, eating an onion sandwich, flavoring your spaghetti with garlic or lac- ing your lunchtime pizza with spices will all work against you. As breathing tends to be a necessity with all of us, avoiding spicy and odoriferous foods for at least 24 hours prior to a hunt is suggested.

Sex scents

The second type of liquid (or solid) that's proven its effectiveness is the sex lure. The one caution here is that improper use can play against a hunter. Rushing the season by using rut lures in early October will probably alarm deer rather than bringing them close. But used properly they can be very effective.

Sex scents, both natural and synthetic, are most effective the last couple weeks of the Pennsylvania bow season. They're even worth a try the first few days of the gun hunt. Remember that even though most does may be bred by the time the buck opener arrives, some aren't, and bucks remain capable of breeding well into January, or later.

Don't confuse estrus scents with pure urine scents, although they are somewhat alike. Common doe urine is more a calming scent than an attracting odor. Of course, considering the number of times does urinate in the woods, another splash of it that soon turns to ammonia will probably do little to bring a buck into your sights. As urine quickly breaks down to ammonia upon contact with air, it soon dissipates on the ground.

Estrus scents, however, hold the magic smell that brings bucks to attention, although does usually react negatively to it. This scent should not be used at any time except in the rut period. For more than 90 percent of the year the odor means absolutely nothing to bucks or does. Timing is the key to its effective use.

I use estrus lures on "drag rags" tied to my rubber boots on the way to a treestand and have watched as bucks nosed their ways up the same paths an hour ro two later. Before climbing into a tree I'll tie the rag to a shrub 10 to 15 yards from my stand. On several occasions both bucks and does were enticed to the rag, although does always seemed uneasy. But on several notable occasions curiosity got the best of them and they had to get a closer smell. Seldom did they hang around to feed afterwards, however.

Among the most effective of scent lures is the tarsal odor of a buck. My late father-in-law, a McKean County native, made an annual collection of buck tarsal glands which he tied to his boot laces each time he went afield. He stored several of the glands, tufts of hairs from the hocks including the skin around the gland, in a mayonnaise jar in the refrigerator between hunts. He even froze fresh tarsals between seasons. His deer tales included stories about bucks that came looking for him after catching the odor of what they thought was another buck.

Buck or doe tarsal glands can also be dragged behind on the way to your hunting area. Bucks moving along or across your path may follow it to your location.

A zip-type bag serves yeoman duty in keeping your clothing and hands from absorbing the smell. After all, you don't want the deer looking at you. Rather, it should be concentrating on the smell emanating from a scent-treated scrape. Never put urine-based or glandular scents on your clothing.

For the record, I've had luck with both synthetic rut scents and natural scents. Given a choice, though, I'll use the real thing.

Finally there's the food scents. Again, I'm sure they've been effective for some hunters but I've never had much faith in them. Acorn, apple, grape and others can be found on sporting goods store shelves. Admittedly, such scents are non-threatening to deer and curious animals may well be drawn to them. A friend from Lycoming County told me of arrowing an 8-pointer that came to his peanut butter scent emanating from a Hunter's Specialties disk three straight afternoons, the fourth evening offering a clear shot.

Of course, food scents can also double as cover scents. But don't use pine scent in an apple orchard.

Scents are today an integral part of hunting, bowhunting and close-range muzzleloader hunting in particular. Using common sense is the key to getting the most from them.

Pennsylvanian Matt Morrett of Hunter's Specialties pins a cedar wafer cover scent to his jacket before heading to a treestand in a cedar grove.

Brad Harris of Lohman Game Calls uses a high-volume grunt tube which is effective in windy weather or when long-range grunting is desirable.

Chapter 16

CALLING ALL WHITETAILS

Understanding Grunts, Bawls and Other Deer Talk

Remember your earliest days of deer hunting?

If your background is like mine, tagging a whitetail may have once seemed the impossible dream. But once a doe was on the ledger, scoring on a buck then became the possible dream.

You studied your prey, read all you could in *Field & Stream* and *Outdoor Life*, and learned a few tricks. After the rack of a spike or forkhorn was on the wall, getting a trophy dominated your mind. That, for most hunters, becomes the dream from which they never awaken.

But over the years you honed a few more techniques, learned a "secret" or two about whitetail hunting and took chances on techniques you'd only read about or heard about at a sports show seminar. Then, one memorable day, it all came together in the taking of a trophy. Or you came close and in so doing developed knowledge which provided confidence whenever you entered the deer woods.

For some hunters the latter plateau — I call it the "confidence plateau" — isn't achieved because hunters, themselves, get into self-imposed "ruts." Many hunters, older hunters in particular, refuse to learn about, then alter, deer hunting tactics. The hoped-for trophy is sought in the same manner as in previous seasons, often by little more than climbing into the same tree stand or posting in the same draw year after year, and hoping "this will be the day" that a monster buck's path, and yours, will cross.

To consistently tip the scales on deer it's necessary to try something new, to enter each year's hunt with a bit more knowledge of the prey and confidence that you're wiser and warier than ever before. Many hunters ignore or refuse to focus their attentions on some tried and true deer hunting methods because of the attitude that "it won't work for me."

Those thoughts came to mind one winter at the Eastern Sports and Outdoor Show in Harrisburg. As I'd been host of an outdoor TV show in the region at the time, I was privileged to be recognized by viewers — many of whom had questions or stories to share about hunting and fishing.

I was especially surprised at a conversation with an older gun hunter whom I'd met previously.

"I don't bother with such things," he muttered as we stood in an aisle listening to a manufacturer of grunt tubes demonstrate his product.

"I've never even a heard a deer make a sound ... I can't imagine that one could actually be called in," he snickered. "It may work some places but here (in Pennsylvania) it's just a gimmick."

We shared a Coke for a few minutes and I told my tale of success on two hunts during the previous months, one in Quebec and the other in Alabama, where 8-pointers came to my calls.

"Sure, but that wasn't in Pennsylvania," the pessimist challenged. "Do you think you could call in a Pennsylvania deer?"

"I've done it," I answered. "What's so different about Pennsylvania whitetails than those that live anywhere else?"

His eyes focused on mine as I continued, telling him of occasions when bleats and grunts meant the difference between venison and an empty freezer.

Bear in mind that all this took place about 1985, when deer calling, at least popularly, was in its infancy.

Why should Pennsylvania bucks be oblivious to sounds that hunters make and deer respond to in other states?

Simply, they're not. More direct is the question: "Will Pennsylvania bucks respond to calling during the bow and gun seasons?"

The answer is an unequivocal "Yes!"

Deer talk

Rut time and the days leading up to the peak, during which bowhunters are afield, is prime time for calling. But that doesn't mean it's the only period deer are responsive. Bucks and does communicate by grunting and other vocalizations throughout the four seasons. We, as hunters, aren't there to hear them except in fall and winter.

I've found that bucks and/or does will respond to at least three types of calls during all the state's hunting periods — particularly the forepart of the bow season and again, although less so, in the initial days of the gun season.

Students of deer lore know these times, respectively, as the pre-rut, full-rut and post-rut periods. Pennsylvania whitetails begin shifting into high gear for the rut during the final half of October, although they technically start when they attain hard antler status in early September. Then they will also make numerous rubs and scrapes, some which they may not visit again.

Bucks do most of their breeding from about November 10-20 although does that go through their 28-day estrus cycle without conceiving will attract bucks through December or longer. Some does are also bred in mid and late October, although that's the exception. Bucks are prepared to breed considerably longer than their mid-November peak rutting time suggests — almost as long as they hold hard antlers and testosterone is produced.

Documented cases in neighboring New York show that matings have taken place between September 22 and February 22. Calling is effective during all Pennsylvania seasons, from the first day of bowhunting to the final day of muzzleloading. After all, deer talk with one another year-around, not only in the fall.

How does the archer or gun-hunter use this information? And what sort of calls among the myriad that have hit the market in the past three years should be used?

First, don't go afield thinking you're turkey hunting and you'll get an answer. Only once in the 15 or so years I've been using calls have I had a deer respond vocally. That was a small Alabama 4-pointer with a "manly," baritone voice. He answered twice, probably out of the frustration of hearing me but not being able to see me.

The best time to call is when you actually see a deer and want to stop it, get a better look and/or bring it close enough for a precise shot.

Secondly, forget the complex information (for now) on deer vocalization that's hit the pages of deer magazines in recent years about the many voices of the whitetail. While interesting and scientifically accurate, it often serves to confuse and intimidate many hunters. Start by mastering a few basic calls, as turkey callers must, then expand your repertoire.

Following are calls that may tip the odds in the Pennsylvania hunter's favor.

The bawl call

The "bawl" (crying) call is considered, along with the bleat and snort, as a distress sound. To the human ear it's a close mimic of a goat or sheep's nasal *maaaaa* sound. However, it's not as prolonged nor is it as loud.

One October morning, while experimenting with a Kelly Cooper call which is capable of adjustments for a variety of sounds, I used the "bawling" mode to entice a button buck to within six yards. I was squirrel hunting at the time, dressed in camo, save for an orange hat, and seated against a tree while holding a .22.

I'd seen the deer at about 75 yards and offered several subdued bawls. Its ears perked and it made a slow, seemingly unconcerned move in my direction. I didn't call again as it headed directly toward my position. It paused on occasion to look for the source of the sound but seemed calm and curious as it advanced. Had I been bowhunting, it would have offered an easy shot.

Dave Hale, half of the Knight & Hale Game Call team, says that bawl calls, although considered mild "distress" sounds, serve as contact calls — particularly among does and young deer of both sexes.

"They have a curiosity effect," says Hale. "A deer will come to investigate the sound or maybe join up with other deer."

On occasion, a bawl call will entice a curious doe and a buck will follow. It's a good vocalization no matter which sex you're after.

Canadians and other north-country hunters have long used a simple rubber band call to simulate the cry. Although its sound is entirely different than that produced by standard calls, it's similar enough to have good results.

Does may also come to grunts and bawl or bleat calls but may show their wariness by stomping the ground with their forefoot.

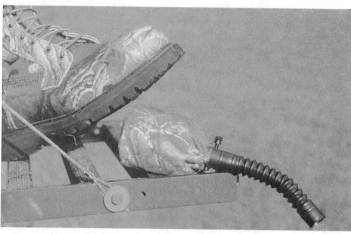

Penn's Woods unique Easy Squeeze Deer Call can be operated with hands or feet.

Pennsylvanian Kelly Cooper, best known for his turkey calling skills, labels the sound as the "doe bawl."

"It's a throatier sound than the bleat," he explained while demonstrating. "It can be used to call to either a doe or a buck. Both will respond."

The bawl call is a good choice for the entire Pennsylvania archery season, not just the pre-rut period. It's also worth a try during the gun seasons.

The contact grunt

Grunting is, by far, the most popular and the easiest call to master. But unlike grunts produced by bucks during the heart of the rut, "contact grunting" is a bit different but just as easy to mimic and, as Hale suggests, is a good pre-rut ploy.

Hale, who studies his herd of penned whitetails throughout the year and records their vocalizations, says unbred does and pre-rut bucks are both susceptible to grunting, which he describes as "a location call."

"It's not as aggressive a grunt as you'd use in the rut," he suggests. "I won't use it unless I first see a deer. Then I might make a loud grunt or two to get its attention. After that I keep it subdued but I'll make 10 or 12 grunts a minute, always making just short, abrupt grunts. Don't be aggressive."

Cooper agrees: "I refer to this as the "trail grunt." I often hear it made by the year-and-a-half old buck who was kicked out of the herd by its mother. Momma doe's getting ready to breed and doesn't want him around so he's out looking — trying to make contact with other deer."

Cooper, like Hale, recommends using the trail (or contact) grunt in short, subdued bursts spaced by 5-10 seconds, then pausing for a minute or two.

Although most deer calls require exhaling or inhaling on a reed-tube, one of the best-sounding calls I've ever heard requires the use of hands. Jerry Peterson of Woods-Wise Products long ago came up with a simple ribbed, hard-plastic amplifying and directional tube — called the Friction Grunt — which is gently scraped with a striker. The volume of the guttural, "hollow" grunts are controlled by the pressure exerted on the ribbed surface. It's one of the only calls capable of duplicating the little-known "clicking" vocalization deep-rut bucks are known to make.

Antler rattling

While seldom referred to as a "call," antler-rattling is another popular, easy-to-master method of communicating with bucks. Indeed, it is a "call" although not done with the mouth.

Considering the period in which Pennsylvania bowhunters are afield, it's most effective during the pre-rut. That's when bucks are just getting into the swing of things and the sound of antlers clashing tells them there's probably a fight going on and does will be about.

A pair of young Pike County bucks test their head gear.

Sparring differs from aggressive rattling in the same way the contact grunt differs from the aggressive grunt.

"I like to use rattle-bags," Hale told me during a hunt several autumns back. "It has the curiosity effect on bucks who will come to investigate. The bag is a lot easier to carry, too."

The sound is similar to that made by gently striking the tips of a pair of antlers against one another. Such sparring in the wild often precedes more serious scraps during the rut period. It's also produced when bucks are entering the aggression stage but not yet in full rut.

"Sort of like checking out one another and maybe pushing and head-shaking a little bit," is the way Hale describes it. "I don't recommend doing any loud clashing early on."

Several manufacturers make rattle bags — composed of a tough, camouflaged, oblong cloth bag housing lengths of hardwoods which, when rolled between the hands, simulate the gentle sparring sounds made by bucks. Lohman Game Calls also has a handy Double Rattling System device consisting of a pair of loose-fitting "strikers" held in a heavy, plastic shell. By manipulating the leaf-like strikers with your fingers, a realistic rattling sound is imitated. It's easy to carry and requires very little hand motion to master.

Of course, real and simulated rattling antlers can also be used. I prefer racks with at least three points each (Cut off the brow tines or you'll end up with scarred fingers.)

Commercial rattling "horns" which are easily carried and duplicate the sounds of the real thing can also be found, such as Primos Game Call's "Fightin' Horns" which come in both natural brown and orange (for safety reasons). The unique design, allowing a mid-point grip with tines on both sides (14 in all) for minimum movement and maximum sound production, allows their fit in a daypack.

"I'll rattle for 10 to 30 seconds at a time," advises Will Primos. "Bring them together sharply and intertwine the points, twisting and grinding them against each other, then jerk them apart."

As a curtain call, Primos strikes the ground with the antlers several times or, if in a treestand, rakes leaves or scrapes the tree trunk. He then waits several minutes before starting the performance anew. If there's no response, Primos moves into the wind a couple hundred yards and starts all over.

As said, the pre-rut period is prime time but rattling can also be effective well into the rut. Biologists agree that in places with low buck-to-doe ratios rattling is most effective. Competition is the key. But that doesn't mean you shouldn't try them in any Pennsylvania landscape, where ratios are typically one buck to 4-5 or more does, a facet of Pennsylvania whitetail history that will hopefully change as attempts are made to bring the buck-to-doe ratio closer to 1:2 or 1:3.

Will Primos uses synthetic antlers to simulate the sound made by sparring bucks.

Much of the fun of spending hours upon hours on treestands is seeing things you might otherwise only experience on someone's video show. Bucks sparring is one of them. I've watched bucks testing one another as early as mid September in southeastern Pennsylvania. The encounters were always brief and never got beyond the point of a head down, antler-tickling and shoving affair. Often the accompanying bucks went back to feeding after a short stint of sparring. On occasion other bucks came in to check out the activity, although does seldom express much interest.

It did prove that bucks, indeed, make rattling noises throughout the entire archery season. Largely, they're testing what it is that's growing from their heads (deer don't have mirrors or hands to otherwise find out). As the season progresses, sparring may become a bit more serious as testosterone flow increases.

Only once have I seen a Pennsylvania buck battle in the gun season. That occurred in Lehigh County on the fourth day of the buck season in the early 90s and lasted a brief minute or so. It was more an aggressive sparring between a 4-pointer and a small 6-pointer than an outright fight. But it was leading to becoming serious when the 4-pointer wisely tucked his tail and ran off, having determined that his foe was a bit more powerful.

Gun season vocalizations

By virtue of a million or so hunters afield on every Pennsylvania buck opener, calling is largely a futile affair on that magic day. Better to find a well-used escape route and sit quietly than to hunker in your stand grunting at spooked deer. After the first couple hours of opening day most deer have encountered hunters and calling, in areas where hunters abound, is probably as useless as whistling in the wind.

Bawls and grunts can be effective during the gun season wherever hunting pressure is minimal or in the second week when hunters have gone back home and things start getting back to normal. On larger tracts of private lands and deep backwoods areas where whitetails haven't been pushed, they'll go about their daily routines relatively undisturbed.

In 1988, on opening morning, I watched a Bradford County forkhorn relentlessly chase does around my treestand. Two bucks, taken by fellow camp members, also showed the swollen necks and heavily-stained metatarsals indicative of a lingering or late rut.

I didn't carry my grunt call with me that morning and the use of one may have been futile, considering the ardor of the 4-pointer. But when things calmed down a couple days later, chances are it would have responded to the call. Every year since, a grunt tube has been carried along with other items in my daypack, just as they are in the fall bow season.

Make no mistake about it. Pennsylvania hunters can increase their chances of filling their tags by using calls and rattling antlers — not only in November's prime time but during fringes of the rut, as well.

On rare occasions bucks come running to check the source of the sound. But usually it's a slow approach, with nose, eyes and ears probing the forest looking for the source of the sound — you.

My wife discovered that on November 8, 1999 when, at about 3:30 p.m., having sat since noon on her treestand about 100 yards west of our front door, she began to feel the boredom from not having seen anything but squirrels and birds. That's when she heard the sound of turkeys. As the season was open, she hoped for a shot at a hen or jake. Problem was, she only had a grunt tube in her pocket. Her turkey calls were back at the house.

For 10 minutes she casually grunted at the three birds, simply to see their reaction, which resulted in stretching their necks, then going back to picking seeds on the wooded hillside. As they approached to within 25 yards she cautiously flicked the safety on her Horton crossbow and was set to aim when she heard the crunch of leaves off to her left.

Slowly turning her head, she quickly forgot about the turkeys. Coming to a stop 15 yards away, its attention directed at the turkeys, was an 8-point buck. Slowly she turned, raised the scoped crossbow and fired a bolt.

It sprinted back down the hill toward the creek, where the 230-pound stag was retrieved a few minutes later, the arrow having hit the heart dead center. The casual, low volume grunting in the thick woods had lured the buck in for a look. Otherwise, it might have easily passed unseen.

Experiences like that convince even the skeptics that it pays to hunt with a grunt.

Wary old bucks will stand and study the source of a grunt or antler rattling before making a commitment.

Tom Neumann of Penn's Woods Game Calls grunted in this 9-pointer near his Westmoreland County home.

CHAPTER 17

BOW SEASON
Deer Hunting's Prime Time

Bowhunters have never had it so good.

Consider this: In 1960 one deer (buck or doe) was taken for every 30 archery licenses sold. By 1970 the success rate grew to one per 25 archery licenses. That number remained fairly constant until 1985 when success rates again started to rise. In 1999, one of every five bowhunters filled a tag.

Bowhunting: The close-to-home quest

Unlike the gun season, when hunters may travel upwards of 250 miles to get to a deer camp, most archery hunting is done within a short drive of home. Many bowhunters hit their treestands for a few hours before work or after, accounting for high harvests in suburbs and nearby farm-country where deer populations have exploded in the past decade.

Ben Moyer, outdoors columnist for the Pittsburgh Post-Gazette, in analyzing the bow harvest numbers for the 1999 season noted that "the percentage of all bucks taken by bowhunters is far higher in suburban and agricultural counties than it is in the central and northern mountain counties."

He cited counties such as Allegheny and Westmoreland in the southwestern part of the state, where 59 percent and 33 percent, respectively, of the total buck harvest (gun seasons included) was made by archers. Compare that to rural mountain counties such as Potter, Lycoming and Warren where bowmen took 12 percent (in each of the three counties) of all bucks harvested. In Elk, McKean and Cameron counties those percentages drop to a dramatic 8, 7 and 5 percent, respectively.

"These numbers tell us that bowhunters take most of their bucks close to home, in populated regions where they live and work," Moyer wrote. "They take those deer on hastily-planned hunts before or after (working) shifts or sandwiched between weekends." Compare figures in other southern counties with high human densities and it will be much the same as those cited by Moyer. For the buck season, many hunters will abide by tradition and head to deer camps in the mountain counties.

But in bow season, they're more likely to hunt near home. That, in part, is the reason bowhunter numbers have continually climbed over the years, and continue to do so.

There's no accounting for when bucks will appear or what they'll do as the deep rut approaches. This 5-pointer was a bit confused by a McKenzie buck target in the author's backyard.

Best bets for bow-bucks

Since 1992, Pennsylvania archers have had the best of all seasons. That's the year bowhunters' dreams of hunting during the rut were satisfied.

With bucks letting down their guard and archers lurking in treestands taking advantage of their errant travels, it was expected harvests during the November portion of the hunt would substantially increase the bag by bowhunters. Indeed, many gun-hunters opposed the season extension claiming archers would get all the good bucks long before their post-Thanksgiving hunt began.

But it didn't happen. In fact, buck harvest figures didn't even climb dramatically although they did continue an upward trend begun in the early 1980s, along with a growing number of archers.

Surprisingly, harvest figures show more bucks are taken early in the season — when vegetation is thick and temperatures may reach into the 80s — than in the November rut hunt. In 1998, for example, a study revealed that opening day was the best buck day and the top day overall for when doe harvests are taken into account.

Other interesting items resulting from a study of when archers are more likely to fill their tags include the following:

• About 5,000 deer, more than half of them bucks, were shot on the season opener.

• The second best day was the season finale in mid-November, 1998, when 3,331 deer (more than 1,800 of them antlered) were killed.

• Understandably, considering that most people have weekend days off from work, more than one-third of the harvest (32,334 bucks and 27,831 antlerless deer) was made on the season's seven Saturdays.

• The season's two best overall harvest weeks were the first and the last, when most hunters are afield. Total kills in both weeks surpassed 10,000.

• The two top buck harvest weeks were the last two, in November.

• The overall success rate in 1998 was one in six, The success rate on bucks was one in 10.

• Archers accounted for only 16 percent of the statewide harvest.

"The harvest numbers illustrate that Pennsylvania's early archery season offers outstanding opportunity from beginning to end," said Game Commission Executive

Standing corn is a sure magnet to whitetail activity.

Director Vern Ross. "It offers less crowded conditions than firearm seasons and deer movements are easier to pattern."

Opening day fervor

Pennsylvania is well-known for its opening day fever — or is it "fervor" — whether it be for trout or turkey, bears or bucks. The bow season is no exception. Deer are on their late summer foods and have gone more than eight months unmolested. Bowmen and women who attend to preseason scouting and locate food sources stand the best chances of tagging a buck or doe.

Nationally known bowhunter Bob Foulkrod of Troy, Bradford County, begins his scouting early, first locating trails leading to and from apple orchards and cornfields. In deep woods, his efforts go to finding oak trees yielding mast.

Throughout Pennsylvania, acorns start dropping about the end of August. Deer, says Foulkrod, will stay in the areas with lots of oaks or even beechnuts into the first weeks of October or longer. That's where a bowhunter should set up early in the season.

Over the years, Foulkrod has noted a tendency for deer in areas of high hunting pressure to shift their feeding patterns as quickly as three or four days into the busy bow season, no matter how much mast is on the ground. That's when he may move his climbing stand to some traditional hotspot, including sites near corn, soybeans, apples or secondary feeding areas.

If you know of a good oak ridge that other hunters haven't found, stick to it, he advises. Places that attracted deer one year will attract them the next. Just give them time.

Foulkrod's pet peeve is hunters who try to get too close to — or actually set stands inside of — bedding areas. You know deer will be there, but they won't stay very long if hunters keep going in, he tells students at his annual bowhunting school. Learn where deer in your hunting region bed, but be aware that they won't stay there if you or others insist on disturbing it.

Treestand placement in or near undisturbed mast-producing areas is a standard opening week practice.

Jody Hugill of State College poses with a Centre County 8-pointer taken on the edge of a woods.

HUNTING THE RUT

I asked four well-known Pennsylvania bow-benders — all of whom hunt the rut in Pennsylvania and other states — to share some advice on their approach to hunting the late season when bucks hit high gear as the peak of the rut approaches.

Non-aggressive doe grunt

Dr. Dave Samuel is a well-known speaker, outdoor writer and retired biology professor from the University of West Virginia, where he taught a course and wrote a book on the anti-hunting movement. At rut time, Samuels has found success with what he calls "the non-aggressive doe grunt."

"If I could choose the two best weeks to bowhunt, the November 2-7 period would be one of them. It's the time you'll get more reaction from rattling, but my favorite technique is to use a doe grunt call. I don't know a time when it's more effective."

I prefer a Wood's Wise doe grunt. I've never had much luck with the aggressive, loud calls with the long tubes. Like most Pennsylvania hunters, I don't hunt many areas with big bucks. Those (loud) calls will chase away the little guys.

I've had a great deal of success in bringing in the smaller bucks that are there. I rarely use the call "blind." That is, I don't call unless I see a deer. If I don't know what it is or, preferably, if it's a buck , I'll use it, especially if it's not coming in my direction.

I don't call to does at that time. They're not ready (to mate) and won't respond. That call seldom gets much reaction from does.

I use a low volume and give two or three calls, then shut up, especially if I know he's heard it. A buck knows exactly where a call comes from. Sometimes he'll start to come in, then hang up. I'll call again and he may do the same thing. It depends on his frame of mind at the time.

One year I called to a buck and he totally ignored it. There was no reaction at all.

The next day I again saw him, called, and he came in immediately and I shot him.

My advice for the first week of November is to use a doe grunt. You have nothing to lose. I've never scared a buck with it.

As I said, that's one of my favorite weeks. Bowhunters who have never hunted that period before will find out they'll see much more deer — and they will respond to calls."

Flee the fields ... hit the hardwoods

Jody Hugill of State College, Centre County, is a frequent lecturer on bowhunting and deer and turkey calling. He's a member of the Hoyt U.S.A., Lohman Game Call and Realtree Camouflage pro-staffs and has does most of his bowhunting in central Pennsylvania. His advice for Pennsylvania's November hunting is "forget the fields — hit the woods."

Most scrape activity takes place at night, with considerable exception as the rut nears.

"The best advice I can give is to get away from the fields and into the woods and the edges of thickets. Deer will still go to fields to feed, usually at night, and the hunter must remember that foliage is down and things have opened up — so detection of a hunter by a buck is enhanced.

After hunting during the first week or two of November in other states, I now realize that Pennsylvania bucks — maybe because of the high buck-to-doe ratio — don't scrape as intently as in states where deer are more in balance. Just finding a scrape doesn't mean the buck will be back. That may not be true for all parts of the state, but it holds in the mountain country where I hunt.

I prefer to first find the route to a scrape area — with several scrapes and lots of rubs — then set up on a trail. I seldom set up on a specific scrape. First you have to find the direction of travel and look for trails that indicate use by bucks. Often these trails aren't pounded down from lots of travel, but they do show big prints. That's where you want to be.

Many hunters will also be rattling during the late season. I also rattle and call but not aggressively or loud. Too many hunters get big rattling antlers and really beat them. A big buck pretty much knows what's in his area because he stays there. No matter if you're trophy hunting or after just any buck, bringing the spikes and 4- and 6-pointers to you will get a big buck's attention, too. Big antlers and aggressive rattling will drive away the smaller bucks. Just light, occasional rattling is recommended.

A hunter not experienced in rattling, but having watched a few videos, must understand that the classic red-eyed buck charging through the woods after someone rattles seldom happens. Bucks will be on their feet more during the rut and will do things they wouldn't do earlier in the season. But they won't let their guard down every minute of the day.

Plan to stay in your stand longer that week. Deer will move all day long. It's the only time when they're up more than they're bedding and hunters must be patient enough to take advantage of it."

In-season scouting .. and scraping

Bob Kirschner of Murrysville, Westmoreland County, has taken six Pennsylvania Pope & Young bucks. He owns his own deer scent company, has done several

Bob Kirschner scouted while hunting and finally ambushed this southwestern Pennsylvania Pope & Young buck in mid-season.

popular videos and is the author of "The Art and Appreciation of Trophy Bowhunting." *He frequently uses the S-words — scout and scrape — in his lectures on the fine art of hunting bucks with a bow.*

"Hunters should use the final days of October to do some scouting for the November hunt. There will be more sign and lots of new sign. It's definitely the best time to get a buck.

Remember that this isn't the first week of the season. Deer will have been hunted for four weeks and will be much more wary than they were a month earlier. Keep your scent level at zero. I can't stress that too much.

This is a good time for an attractant lure. I produce Silver Tip, a dominant doe-based scent collected during the estrus. I've also made a new Buck Crystal scent — actually small crystals that have an extremely long life.

I use them on fake scrapes. The idea is to make a buck think an intruder has invaded his territory. I'll make them close to thickets, as close as I can get to bedding or feeding areas. I want a deer to be able to smell it and see it. Often I'll put the scrape on a mound or some spot where a buck can see it from 20 or 30 yards.

I also make a scent trail, usually in the shape of an inverted question mark, to my tree. Some hunters make such a trail straight to their tree but I'll walk in a circle around it before I get in my treestand.

As for rattling and calling, I simply try to imitate. I only tickle the antlers to make a buck who hears it curious.

But no matter what else you do, keep your own body scent to a minimum. You can do everything else right, but if that buck smells you, he's gone."

Head for the hills

Terry Rohm is a native of Perry County where his brothers and father run a turkey call business and Terry returns to hunt whenever he can. He currently lives in South Carolina where he serves as public relations manager for Wellington Out-

door products, makers of Tink's No. 69 and other deer and turkey hunting products. His advice for late season is to "head for the hills."

"When you think of hunting the extended season, think about turkey hunters." They and other small game hunters will be in the woods at the same time (throughout most of the state) — especially on public lands.

In states where I know fall turkey hunters will be in the woods with me, I'll use them the way some gun hunters have learned to "use" other hunters during the gun season. Deer won't be panicked, but they will sooner or later move uphill if they're disturbed. That's where I'll set up — on ridges and mountain tops. They won't be spooked badly, but that week is also the first full week of the small game season and there will definitely be more hunters walking around the lowlands.

I recommend getting to your stand long before light and staying there as long as you can. Set up in the laurel and near thickets. That's where deer will go to hide. If all you see is does, remember that the prime rut is near and bucks will find them.

Also do some scouting and find out where acorns are dropping. If you can find a white oak ridge, stay on it. Acorns are only available for a short time and there's lots of competition for them — especially the white oaks which they prefer.

I'll use Tink's 69 or a tarsal gland at that time. But even more important, remember to control body odor. You can't overdo it.

Finally, don't hunt one area too much. You're presence will be seen — or even smelled, even if you're not in your stand at the time. If you hunt a place two or three times and saw deer there in the earlier part of the season, but there's not much activity now, move. If you have faith in it you can always come back a few days later when you've given it a chance to rest.

I don't know of a time when Pennsylvania bowhunters have been given a better chance to harvest a buck as during the last two weeks of the season. The closer the peak of the rut — the better."

Pennsylvania native Terry Rohm hangs a tarsal gland from a branch above a scrape.

Jeff Heller of Lehigh County bagged this Columbia County 8-pointer on only his third time out with a bow.

Linda Steiner's Venango County bow-buck was a half rack short of being an 8-pointer.

Barry Haydt of Northampton County wears orange — as required by law when not on stand — as he drags a Carbon County 6-pointer from the October woods.

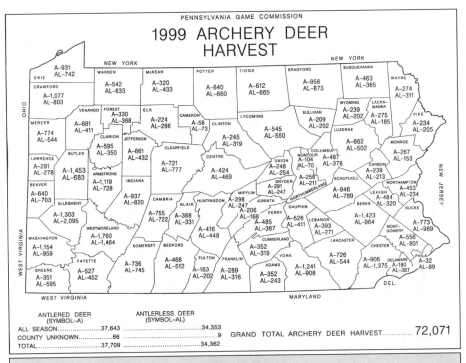

PENNSYLVANIA GAME COMMISSION
1999 ARCHERY DEER HARVEST

ANTLERED DEER (SYMBOL–A)	ANTLERLESS DEER (SYMBOL–AL)	
ALL SEASON..................37,643	34,353	
COUNTY UNKNOWN.........66	9	GRAND TOTAL ARCHERY DEER HARVEST............ 72,071
TOTAL..................37,709	34,362	

Tom's Tips

-Droppings can provide the best clues for deer activity in a specific area. Fresh droppings are black and soft. Within a day or two, depending on the weather, pellets will begin to lighten and become increasingly hard. By comparing droppings along a trail, the relative period of time the animals left them can be determined.

-Early season scouters often find clumped deer droppings rather than the firm, oval or elongated feces commonly seen later in the season. Grasses, forbs, fruits and berries are a deer's prime menu items in summer, accounting for the loose mass of scat which sometimes confuses wandering naturalists.

-Treestand bowhunters, in particular, will find plenty of use for pruning shears tucked into their daypacks. The shears will hasten the chore of clearing twigs and leaves that may hinder a shot.

-A 20-foot length of strong cord with small, spring-type dog leash snaps on each end allows quick and reliable attachment of bows, guns, daypacks and other items when climbing treestands. Latch your gear on one end and snap the other to your belt. Then haul up the gear when you're safely "belted" into your stand.

-Those gritty, adhesive traction strips, sold in building supply and hardware stores for taping onto outside steps, are great for providing sure footing on ladder stands.

Jan Spirat's 1999 opening morning Berks County buck is the largest he's ever harvested on his own property.

Chapter 18

OPENING DAY
Musings and Memories

Precisely one-half hour before sunrise on the first Monday following Thanksgiving I'll be strapped into a treestand some 200 yards west of my office window in upper Northampton County, and three miles south of the Appalachian Trail.

In previous years that special time was spent in Bradford, Carbon, McKean, Potter, Lehigh, Berks and other counties in this beautiful, whitetail-rich state.

My presence is as predictable as tomorrow's sunrise. If I'm alive, I'll be there.

Only once, in 1960, due to a double fracture of my leg in a college soccer game, did I miss the annual opener. I swore then that it would never happen again.

And it hasn't.

It's surprising how many of those hunts I can vividly recall and how few are cherished simply because of racks on the wall.

As I approach 60, it has become springwater-clear that there's plenty more to whitetail hunting than taking a buck, although I'll be the first to admit there's a definite satisfaction in having the Red Gods smile now and again; like the two opening days when my hunting was over minutes after legal shooting time.

Once a Carbon County spike buck caused the shortened hunt and on another occasion it was a Tioga County forkhorn putting a close to my abbreviated season. In both cases I was pleased and disappointed at the same time. The anticipation that builds with the arrival of November and Thanksgiving is suddenly snubbed with the sound of a lone gun blast opening morning.

For that reason I've passed up opening hour bucks on several occasions. In the early 90s in Bradford County, near the New York border, I let a 3-pointer pass at 7 a.m. and ended the day with a spike buck. At the moment of decision, with the crosshairs on the buck's shoulder, I chose not to shoot. But eight hours later a spike with 6-inch prongs fell to my 30-06.

Don't ask why. I don't know. What I do know is that I wasn't a bit sorry that my p.m. buck wasn't a big as my a.m. prey.

In more than four decades of deer hunting, however, I've come to realize that cherished memories don't necessarily focus on the camp meatpole. In Pennsylvania, opening day is rich in ritual and tradition — mostly a matter of just "being there" — as it is a time to bring home venison.

Ask anyone who's ever tossed in his sleep on the eve of the season opener. I did it on my first trip to camp and I still don't sleep soundly today, when there are deer

Hunters freshen their memories of previous opening days with a look at the deer camp's photo wall.

to be hunted tomorrow. When I can sleep deeply on the eve of the opener, perhaps it will signal a time to hang up my gun or bow.

There are always too many big-racked bucks in my dreams; bucks that usually don't materialize but, nevertheless, persist.

Perhaps the fondest memory is a kid's first deer. Maybe it was a buck but probably it was a doe. No matter, if dad was there and the guys at camp shook your hand and patted your shoulder, it was a memory-maker.

To a deer hunter the details of downing one's first buck never dim. Don't try to explain that to a neighbor or fellow worker who doesn't hunt. They'd never understand.

As a kid, I only dreamed of shooting a deer. My first buck was killed in McKean County in 1962, only a couple hundred yards off Barden Brook Road and less than 4-5 miles from the New York state line. I haven't been back for more than 25 years but I'll bet I could find the very tree against which I sat — if it hasn't been cut down or fallen in the meantime.

I first spotted the two deer sprinting across an open valley more than 300 yards away. Then, I didn't have a scoped rifle, nor could I afford binoculars (not on my annual school teacher's salary of $4,100). But my eyes were better a quarter century back and as the deer sprinted up the hillside atop which I was sitting I noted, from a considerable distance, that the lead animal had "horns." I wasted no time getting the .32 slide-action Remington to my shoulder and aiming on the buck that was still 200 yards off, a mere speck in the iron sight.

But for some reason it cut away from its appointed path and dissolved into a stand of oaks and beeches 50 yards or so below the ridge. Foolishly, I dropped the rifle to my waist and stood, hoping to see the buck as it exited the brush.

As luck had it, the buck and doe turned and cut back along the mountain in my direction. When they popped into view both were less than 25 yards away. They continued running, then pulled to a halt less than 20 feet away — the handsome 3-point buck in the lead.

Although the details up to that point are crystal clear, I've never been able to remember raising the gun to my shoulder. In blurred retrospect, I think I fired from the hip, the bullet striking the buck in the neck and killing it instantly.

I do recall that I didn't move for a full minute. I just stared at the deer. My temples pounded and all I could think of was "I finally got one ... I finally got one."

I still have that stunted rack. It hangs near the bigger bucks I've taken since then and appears smaller each time I look at it. But none of the wall-hangers loom larger in my memories than the trophy 3-pointer I killed on that cloudy December afternoon in 1962.

On yet another buck opener, more than 25 years ago in Carbon County, near Francis Walter Dam, I'd canoed across the darkened waters of the reservoir long before first light and was seated against a charred oak tree when the first snowflakes began falling at sun-up.

It was the sort of morning of which deer hunters dream; a fresh tracking snow, quiet walking conditions and good visibility. Hunters moving in via the land route would be a long while in coming, allowing me the comfortable feeling of being alone in the backwoods, knowing that the orange army would be pushing deer my way by 9.

It wasn't long after I heard the first shot ring out near the road, more than a mile away, that I detected a sound — like a deer pawing in the leaves for acorns — just over a hump ridge to my right. I readied myself for a shot, assuming that a buck would soon poke its head over the rise, some 40 yards away.

Five minutes more and the rustling noise continued, but nothing showed. Carefully I pushed away from the tree and crawled toward the rim, just below which I fancied the big-racked buck was feeding.

It was a quiet approach, my shuffling muffled by the cottony snow. As I neared I poked the gun, then my head, over the mound of snow. Nothing was there but the blackened stumps and scarred trunks of trees killed in a fire the previous summer. I dropped back behind the cover of the ridge to regain some composure and again listened for the scratchings. The sounds resumed but the source was a mystery. Again I cautiously peered over the edge.

But this time I was on the receiving end of a stare.

One of the stumps, it seems, was actually the backside of a bear — no more than 30 yards downhill. We locked eyes for what were surely seconds but seemed

Some hunters can only dream of close encounters with big bucks.

like minutes. The last I saw of him he was sprinting up the far hill, his fat buttocks quaking like a vat of Jello with each leap.

The 5-pointer that walked up to me an hour later capped my morning's hunt. But it will always be the memory of the first black bear I'd ever seen in the deer woods that's etched in greatest detail.

Of course, there are dozens, maybe hundreds, of other opening day happenings not soon forgotten: the first deer hunts with my sons; their first bucks; my 6-pointer dropped at 250 yards; the wolf-like coyote that eyed me at 20 steps, then danced off down the ridge; chickadees perched on my gun barrel; the porcupine sniffing my boots; the long-bearded gobbler roosting in the tree above me; a white-footed mouse sharing a sandwich; the Coopers hawk perching on the rail of my treestand; and more, not the least of which are friends to share tales at day's end.

Sure, there are tactics that work on opening day. Like using pre-season scouting knowledge to find escape routes. Or taking advantage of others' presence in the woods to push deer your way. Or simply being patient enough to sit tight and await the deer that will surely be pushed near on the opener.

The real joys of opening days come from the magic in the air, the shots echoing off hills near and far just after daybreak, and the anticipation heightened the night before when stories are told and retold around the fireplace.

I take opening days seriously, but not too seriously. After all, it comes only once a year. But the day is anticipated ever since the close of last year's season.

Most important is that each opening day adds a new page to the memory bank.

On this year's opener, exactly 30 minutes before dawn, I'll be back. My album of memories will be opened as I await the first shot.

Like everyone else I'll hope for a fat buck. But over the years I've discovered that opening day memories aren't ranked according to whether or not a deer was killed or a shot was taken.

The best trophies come from the hunting of memories.

That's what opening days are for.

Tom's Tips

-Hunters using screw-in climbers should always be sure to take an extra one or two with them. Screwing one in above the stand offers a reliable grasp when making that final step up or the first step out. A second step should be fastened just above shoulder height to hold a gun sling or bow.

-When removing screw-in steps from a tree you plan to use later in the season, stick small twigs or wooden matches in the holes. It will aid in quickly re-establishing your "staircase" next time around.

-Two-to five-year-old clearcuts offer excellent whitetail habitat, especially during the hunting seasons. Not only do they have a good supply of grasses, forbs and browse but deer are more difficult to see in the thick growth, thereby holding them when hunters are prowling the surrounding forest. If you find a standing tree amid a clearcut, install a portable stand. It could prove to be an untapped hotspot.

-Lemon oil polish, the type used to dust furniture, restores a faint shine to the antlers on your wall mounts while removing accumulated dust.

Tom's Tips

-Carrying a video camera along on deer hunts is becoming as popular as taking snapshots back at camp. For some hunters in one-deer states, it stretches the hunting time whenever a friend is accompanied and the happenings are recorded on tape. The biggest annoyance in watching such videos is shaky camera movement. For $40-$50, a video tripod with a "floating" head can be purchased. It's the most important accessory for recording those memorable times without triggering "motion sickness" in the eventual audience.

- It's not necessary to cut the scent glands from a deer's legs after it's been killed. There's no way the glands can come in contact with the venison and even if it happens somehow, the lack of blood flow in the meat will prevent it from imparting any disagreeable taste to a steak or roast.

-By studying deer taken by hunters before and after field-dressing, the Tennessee Wildlife Resources Agency released a chart to help hunters estimate the actual live weight of their deer.

Examples are:

Field-dressed Weight	Live Weight
80	105
100	130
130	165
160	205
200	255

-A Pennsylvania State university study revealed, not surprisingly, that venison not only has considerably less fat than farm-bred meats but is also as good a source of protein and iron as beef. A 3.5 ounce cut of venison contains 158 calories and 18 per cent fat while providing 25 per cent of the required daily allotment of iron and 67 per cent of protein. The same-size cut of beef has 222 calories, 42 per cent fat, the same allotment of protein and 18 per cent iron requirements.

-Wound areas in venison tend to become contaminated or start to rot at a surprisingly fast rate, especially in mild weather. After skinning and before hanging, cut away the gelatinous bloody areas. The undamaged parts will glaze over and become dry to the touch, serving as a protective barrier for the carcass.

-Ever stand in a store and scratch your head wondering what length shoelaces are needed to replace the frayed ones on your hunting boots? I have. Here's a way to solve the dilemma. Multiply the number of eyelets on one side of the boot by eight. For example a boot with eight pairs of eyelets will require laces about 64 inches long.

After being pushed during opening week, big bucks remain alert but a bit more reclusive.

Chapter 19

SECOND-WEEK BUCKS
Time For a Change

I heard the rocks tumbling down the steep cliff a full minute before the narrow, high-racked 4-pointer poked through the rhododendron thicket.

It paused near the edge of the Lehigh River, looking back, then across the swift flow as if trying to decide what to do.

It opted to return to the safety of the tangled vegetation rather than become vulnerable while swimming the 60 or so yards to the far bank. In so doing it moved to within 30 yards of the stunted hemlock that somehow managed to maintain a roothold in the infirm riverbed, now at its low-water stage.

I'd backed against the hemlock 30 minutes earlier, the only substantial cover between the rhododendron and the stony, open shoreline. The deer's attention was focused on the rocky, wooded ridgetop from which it had just been pushed by my hunting companion. That year I had the entire second week to hunt and the season still held four more days to seek a trophy.

At 40 yards, I centered the crosshairs on its neck, still debating whether or not to shoot. That's when the buck disappeared from my sights. Seconds later, as the echoes rolled across the far mountain, I realized that Bob Greenbaum, my hunting partner, had made up my mind for me. His 75-yard shot from above had been true. As he inched down the stony slope on elbows and knees, south end first, I straddled the buck.

"I got him," I said. "Good drive."

Bob stopped in his descent to gather his thoughts, then caught the grin on my face.

The scenario took place more than 30 years ago in Carbon County. The previous evening the four of us, including two other camp members, pored over topographic maps and airphotos of our leased hunting area. Several bucks had been taken during the first week, one nearly a mile away, closer to the road. Dozens of others had been shot on the adjacent gameland which was being hunted each day.

As we toasted the evening's planning session, we jokingly agreed to go "where no hunter has gone before."

The point of it all was to find spots that were either unhunted or difficult to access. We figured bucks that encountered orange coats at every turn and scented human intrusion on the breezes for the past week-and-a-half had headed for quieter pastures.

Although not a "pasture," the rocky rhododendron thicket became a safe haven for the wary bucks and does as they could linger away the daylight hours relatively undisturbed.

Bucks don't become voluntarily reclusive during the second half of the hunting season. They're forced into new patterns, untrodden escape routes, night-feeding and days spent scanning their bedding areas.

Unlike some southern states, such as South Carolina, where the gun season stretches across more than four months, north-country hunting is of shorter duration and considerably more hectic.

On Pennsylvania's opening day, for instance, about 60 percent of the total harvest is taken with another 25 percent or more of all bucks tagged the following day and on two subsequent Saturdays. The sheer numbers of hunters in the woods accounts for unnatural activity as deer are pushed here and there.

The quietest time in the woods is the Monday through Friday of the final week when hunters must work for their venison. The savvy hunter will hit new turf and shift gears as time to fill a tag draws to a close.

Here are some suggestions for doing just that.

Scout new country

Late season provides little time for scouting, although investigating out-of-the-way reaches while hunting can pay dividends. With limited hunting time, it's hard to pass a prime location in which you may have bagged bucks on previous openers to set foot in unfamiliar territory. But taking a chance in new terrain can yield dividends.

Deer gathering in a sanctuary atmosphere over a relatively short period will leave obvious fresh sign. Tracks, droppings, upturned leaves, nipped brush and twigs and even recently-scoured scrapes will alert a hunter to whitetail activity.

Scouting with rifle at ready, perhaps still-hunting from dawn to dusk, will more likely yield a shot at a buck than perching in a familiar treestand all day long.

Think post-rut

The peak rut in the Keystone State falls in mid-November. Does which are not bred during that period come into estrus 28 and 56 days later when the rifle seasons are approaching their ends, or winter muzzleloader/bow hunts are about to start.

Where does gather, so will bucks. While a scrape may not guarantee a buck's return visit, finding just one fresh, urine-stained clearing on the ground indicates a buck or two is in the area.

Older dominant bucks may be literally worn out by this time. In one Michigan study a mature buck whose previous 3-4 weeks were spent chasing and breeding does and driving off lesser rivals was observed in a near room-size area for a full 52 hours. It neither drank, fed or bred, only rising from his bed in a dense thicket to urinate and stretch.

The chosen recuperation site for such animals is almost always dense cover in which they can't be seen and where intruders cannot enter readily, at least without making sufficient noise to alert them. But it may be worth a try.

The thicket is the ticket

Thickets come in a variety of sizes and densities. Hemlock and laurel swamps, fields overgrown in briars, sumac and grasses, old orchards and 3-4 year-old clearcuts are all prime havens for deer that don't want to be bothered.

Just because overgrown acreage isn't remote doesn't mean it won't be holding deer. Some of the least likely spots, particularly in suburbs and farm country, are appealing to second week deer. Their proximity to homes and roads is often the reason few hunters tread through them, thereby making them especially enticing as daytime bedding areas.

Outdoor writer
Mike Bleech of
Warren County
hit the thickets
for his late-season
8-pointer.

The mini-drive

High-tailing whitetails were the rule when, during my early hunting years, my dad and as many as a dozen other hunters would get together and perform "concerts," of sorts, as we pushed deer toward standers. Whistles, shouts, smacking sticks against trees and even beating pots and pans alerted every whitetail within earshot that something was amiss.

Most modern-day hunters, however, know that mini-drives are often more productive than all-out warfare. One or two hunters zig-zagging through a thicket with one or two standers at ready is more likely to draw a clean shot at a buck slipping away than an army of drivers and standers pushing high-tailing deer.

"My brother Greg and my dad and I do a lot of drives in small patches of woods .. we've been doing it for years," said Tom Neumann of Penn's Woods Game Calls. "We'll push one little patch then move on."

Neumann said one particular drive in Westmoreland County, where the technique is popular, covers a half-mile and always produces deer, despite the long distance. Over the years deer insist on sticking tight to the ridge, a fact the hunters have noted.

Of course, some drives last only a few minutes. Don't ignore those seemingly inconsequential plots, sometimes only an acre or two in size. Often deer will be as close as 50-100 yards from a feeding area and will stay there throughout the day if in satisfactory cover.

When bucks become nocturnal, particularly older and wiser bucks, it takes effort to move them. Those pushed from one security area will slip into another.

"I love driving," said Neumann. "It's the anticipation of it all ... knowing that a buck could be on its way to you."

Chester County hunters set plans for a slow drive through a woodlot on the edge of suburbia.

No business like snow business

A fresh snowfall always brightens the gleam in a deer hunter's eyes. It also reveals the places deer travel and the relative abundance or lack of whitetails in the area. Add to that easy-to-decipher escape routes and movement patterns.

New snows provide the most obvious clues in that recent passages can be traced. Getting out the morning after a fresh covering provides insight as to where the deer have gone ... and where they've been.

As an option, rather than following tracks entering a feeding area, try backtracking toward a bedding area. Look for prints indicating where deer enter a field late in the day. Then backtrack a bit but don't intrude on the bedding site. Setting up a treestand near heavy-use routes may prove to be a prime evening spot.

Shift gears

Most hunters will agree that the opening day or two of deer season and subsequent Saturdays seldom offer the chance for effective still-hunting. Even painstakingly slow hunting through a woods filled with orange-coated hunters does little more than push whitetails to someone else. The exception, of course, is private land or backcountry where hunter access is limited.

By the second week, deer may continue to linger in untread pockets but, if they've not been spooked in a day or two, they won't be as edgy as they were the previous week.

Still-hunting requires concentration and self-discipline, to which many sportsmen and women are not accustomed. Those who have practiced the technique and respect the visual, auditory and olfactory abilities of whitetails can score on late bucks by covering lots of ground — one slow and methodical step at a time.

Carry your lunch

The final week's hunting hours quickly diminish to a precious few. Cutting out to visit a local diner or heading back home or to camp for lunch may provide a pleasant break — but it can also cost a buck.

On cold days in particular, deer will cut short their dawn and dusk feeding hours. By noon many are again up and around, not traveling far but feeding within or near their sanctuary hideouts.

My preference is to spend the noon hours — from about 10 a.m. through 2 p.m. — in a treestand. Feeding deer move cautiously with their noses to the wind, their eyes constantly scanning the terrain. A moving hunter is more readily detected than one a dozen or more feet above ground in a treestand.

To call or not to call

The grunt tube has become a standard item among most deer hunters. Even the dyed-in-the-Woolrich old-timers who have read enough articles or have seen enough videos in recent years proving the instrument's effectiveness have become believers.

Unlike pre and peak rut-time hunting, when I prefer aggressive calling. I'll opt for more subdued, low volume grunts in late season. Bucks are both physically and psychologically fatigued then and won't come charging out of a thicket to see who's making the sounds. But they will remain curious.

Patience cannot be emphasized enough in late season. Each hunter has his or her own philosophies on deer calling and some won't grunt unless deer are in sight. Others are content to offer 4-5 short grunts every 15-20 minutes or more. I lean toward the latter technique when in a treestand, especially when only a couple days remain in a season.

Be creative

The New York hunters lining the state border not far behind Bradford County's Mountain View Deer Camp each opening day always take a buck or two thanks to our efforts. By the time the Pennsylvania season opens, Empire Staters have already been afield for more than a week. Deer living on the edge of both states soon learn that things are quiet on the Keystone State side.

But that changes a couple weeks later when the Pennsylvania season opens. Hunters have learned that deer return when flushed from the brush on the Pennsylvania opener.

The final Saturday of the season provides the fourth best day to kill a buck, according to Game Commission statistics. If my tag's still unfilled on the season finale and nothing else has proven productive, I'll spend it up a tree near a security area. Weather permitting, I'll spend dawn to dusk there, getting down a time or two, perhaps, to stretch muscles and perhaps return to the truck to warm up.

Other hunters will also be giving the season a final shot and the bucks that detect them may be pushed back into the "refuge" I've previously located.

Starting in 2000, the first day of doe season coincided with the final day of buck season. The change accounts for more hunters in the woods and more bucks on the move. Chances are improved for tying a tag to a last-minute buck.

And if not, there's always the late flintlock or bow season – or next year.

Elaine Young's first-ever buck – an opening day spike – is just as satisfying as her husband Tom's 8-pointer shot on the season's last day. Both deer were taken in Venango County.

In 1999, flintlock hunters harvested 963 bucks and 12,982 antlerless deer.

CHAPTER 20

LAST SHOT
Winter's Blackpowder and Bow Hunts

When deer hunting days dwindle to a precious few, as the hunter's December song goes, thousands of sportsmen with unfilled tags get one more shot at providing some venison for the table.

For archers and flintlockers it's just that — a one-shot affair.

That's why it's important to take time before venturing into the deer woods under cold-weather conditions to make adjustments to bows and front-stuffing guns.

For bowhunters, getting in tune for cold weather hunting means picking up the bow that may not have been used for 5-6 weeks.

Blackpowder hunters should also spend some time on the range before Christmas, even thought they may have been dedicated to muzzleloader shooting every couple weeks during the summer and fall. Unfortunately, many hunters don't take their Hawkens from the rack until a few days prior to the post-Christmas hunt. At least one trip to the range is necessary.

Cold, wind and snow affect not only the hunter but his or her hunting tools, as well.

Cold weather bow tuning

For bowhunters, the October season can be a spoiler. Sitting in a treestand for three or four hours doesn't cramp the muscles nearly as much as in winter when temperatures may dip below freezing in the morning hours and often linger only slightly higher throughout the day. Trying to draw the same 60-pound bow with cold hands and cramped biceps can be a problem.

Deano Farkas of Easton, one of the state's most consistent archers, recommends that bowmen reduce the weights on their compound bows for cold-weather hunting.

"I shoot with a 60 or 65 pound pull in the fall but drop six or eight pounds in the winter season," said Farkas. "I have several bows and I'll use a lighter one when it's cold."

Compound bows are adjustable between varied draw weights with room for adjustment within the 30-45, 45-60 and 60-70 pounds or more ranges. With a minimum of difficulty, and by referring to the instruction book accompanying new bows, every compound's draw can be reduced. If this presents a problem, take it to a pro shop or the sporting goods store where the bow was purchased and seek help.

"I know a lot of guys who fouled up shots at deer because they found they couldn't draw the bow after they sat on stand for several hours in the cold," said Farkas.

He also stresses that bowhunters should visit a range before setting out for a cold weather hunt, preferably wearing the same clothing they'll wear while afield.

The reduced pull not only changes the course of the arrow but also requires sight adjustment. The heavier coat and shirt may also influence the draw and the way a bow is held.

The only way to find out what changes are necessary is to shoot at bale-held targets or 3-Ds and make those necessary adjustments before heading into the cold.

Freeze-time flintlocking

Some adjustment may also be necessary for hunters who try for late-season whitetails with muzzleloaders. The number one reason for missing a deer is that the gun simply doesn't go off. The chances of that occurring are increased by cold and snow.

"Misfires are the most common problems with flintlocks," says Dave Ehrig, arguably the state's best known muzzleloader authority who has taken flintlock bucks in front of video cameras. "There are a variety of reasons why a flintlock won't shoot and most common is that there are problems somewhere in the ignition system."

One snowtime dilemma is a wet pan-powder pan. The spark from the flint won't ignite it. Ehrig recommends changing the fine grain black powder in the pan several times a day, no matter what the weather conditions.

Then, too, shoving a ball down the barrel is always harder (as is everything else done outdoors) when temperatures dip. Forget using a spit patch for second shots. That's like putting your tongue on a frozen pump handle. It will freeze fast.

Clearing the lock mechanism of any grease and lubricating it with a fine oil is also recommended before any winter hunt. From personal experience, I also leave the wooden ramrod at home. Instead I'll carry a fiberglass or metal ball-stuffer which won't break as readily, especially when cold-stiffened muscles impede normal movements.

Another flub can come from cold hands. More than one Pennsylvania muzzleloader shooter has sent an errant shot past a doe because he nudged the trigger too quickly with a glove-covered finger. I've done it myself.

It's much more difficult to gauge pressure on the trigger with a gloved index finger. In the excitement of the moment, I've also known hunters to squeeze the set trigger when they thought they were touching the fore-trigger. Of course, by the time they discovered the mistake their white-tailed target was off and running.

One of my more useful purchases is a pair of heavy hunting gloves with a slit aside the trigger finger. Without removing the glove, the bare finger can be pushed through, providing the delicate feel necessary for timing a shot.

Late season tactics

While one can romanticize the winter hunt as the most challenging of quests, it's far from a prime time experience. If one opportunity presents itself over the course of the December-January late season, consider yourself fortunate.

Altering techniques and taking some chances may be necessary to tip the scales your way. The forkhorn that wandered by your treestand at 15 yards a half-dozen times in October and November you'd now trade your best binoculars to see at 30 paces. In short, it's a new woods out there.

I do most of my late season stalking in the same woodlands in which I stash my treestand in October's bow time or the post-Thanksgiving buck season. But the view from a tree in the depth of winter is notably different than it was under October's Kodachrome setting. Where I could gaze 80 yards one direction, 50 another and maybe no more than 30 yards to yet another trail three months previous, the lack of leaves now makes it possible to watch a band of does slip onto the edge of a pasture 100 yards or more off. Muzzleloader shots of 50 yards or less are preferred with my iron-sighted flintlock and patched ball. I feel confident out to 70-75 yards with a steady rest. With bow in hand that limit drops to 20 yards. No matter what the "weapon," cold weather hunting demands a precise set-up. Positioning is the key to filling a vacant tag, not simply seeing deer.

The author (right) and son Mike make plans for an afternoon hunt with bow and flintlock.

One of the blessings of winter hunting is the possibility of snow. Fresh snowfalls create registers of animals passing in the night. The heavily traveled routes often lead to a buck's or doe's bedroom or kitchen. How close to make your stand poses the dilemma.

Groves of hemlocks, pines and spruces gain new attention, particularly during cold and windy days and when snow is falling. If there's a conifer stand on your hunting grounds, give it special scrutiny.

The best place to start a winter hunt is with food sources. In my part of the country harvested corn and soybean fields and stands of winter wheat continue to lure deer well into winter, even though pickings are often minimal. Bucks which ended their rutting rituals weeks before are now resting and feeding, although no longer having the appetite of three months earlier when ripening corn and acorns dropping like jellybeans made their appearances more predictable.

Now they bed in thickets and eat more browse. Studies at Penn State show deer undergo a biological slow-down in winter. Not only do they rest more but they feed less, requiring and taking in less nutrition than at any other time of the year. Going into the winter in good shape and keeping movement to a minimum to conserve energy is the key to their winter survival. Restoring lost fat and protein must wait until spring and summer. That cuts down on their home territory as the season progresses, a sure advantage to a hunter.

I'm always encouraged to head into the winter hunt when there's snow on the ground. The white cover reveals gouged runs and the recent meanderings of small bands of whitetails. Treestand or ground set-ups are no different for late hunts than they were in October. In each, closing the distance from your position to where you predict a deer will pass, based on evidence in the snow, is vital.

Stalking in the wide open woods is often futile although, in ridge-and-valley country, the skilled bow or blackpowder hunter can do just that after a fresh snowfall, when steps are muffled. If the snow is crusted, forget about still-hunting.

The changing season dictates new strategies and the acceptance of adversities inherent in cold weather hunts. Deer have been pursued for three months, their numbers have been reduced, conditions are tough and the woods are leafless and open.

That's what makes any late season bow or blackpowder deer a trophy.

Most bucks still hold their antlers in the post-Christmas hunt but they're not as active as they were just a couple weeks earlier.

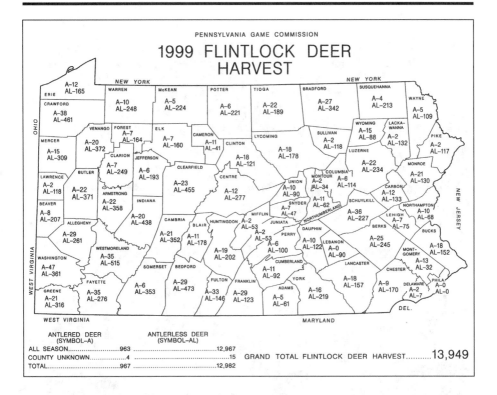

PENNSYLVANIA GAME COMMISSION

1999 FLINTLOCK DEER HARVEST

ANTLERED DEER (SYMBOL-A)	ANTLERLESS DEER (SYMBOL-AL)	
ALL SEASON...............963	12,967	
COUNTY UNKNOWN.........4	15	GRAND TOTAL FLINTLOCK DEER HARVEST..........13,949
TOTAL..............967	12,982	

Tom's Tips

-If you're serious about wildlife photography, consider buying either a 300mm or 400mm telephoto lens. The 300mm equals a 6-power scope; the 400mm an 8-power. With most reasonably "fast" films these lenses can be hand-held, enabling the photographer to get quick shots of deer and other wild animals.

-If you're planning to plant any of the several whitetail clovers now on the market, be sure you first have the soil analyzed. It will tell you whether the soil needs fertilization or lime treatment and save frustration in planting costly seeds that won't grow. Most county agricultural extension offices will analyze samples for a few dollars.

-Blood stains on hunting clothes can be removed by soaking the area in water-diluted meat tenderizer for about an hour, then wiping clean with a wet cloth and washing or dry cleaning as usual.

-Placing antler-supplement blocks or granular licks on your hunting grounds? Most supplements on the market contain phosphorous, calcium and magnesium, the bone and antler basics. But the trace element selenium is also important. It benefits deer indirectly as a catalyst enabling the body's utilization of the minerals.

Norma Laros of Allentown has been hunting for more than 40 years and believes the women's "movement" in hunting will continue to grow.

Chapter 21

KIDS AND WOMEN IN THE DEER WOODS
Hunting's Family Affairs

Kids have always been intrigued by the deer woods.

Some women have, too.

Unfortunately, the number of kids being recruited is today dropping, due largely to urban and suburban upbringing and no one to guide them along the outdoor path that makes a hunter.

In 1976, the Game Commission sold a record 168,546 junior licenses to youngsters ages 12 to 16. Ten years later the sales figures dipped to 131,099. In 1996, junior license sales totaled only 100,851.

Sales to women are more difficult to track but U.S. Fish & Wildlife Service statistics indicate women hunter numbers are growing substantially. Four percent of all license buyers in the late 1980s were women. By century's end it had jumped to 11 percent of America's 17 million hunters, 13 million of whom hunt deer.

Using those figures, it can be assumed that abut 90,000-100,000 women purchase Pennsylvania hunting licenses.

A National Sporting Goods Association report indicates 1,949,000 women hunted in 1999, including 539,000 bowhunters and 317,000 who hunted with muzzleloaders.

"There's definitely an evolution taking place," says Chris Chaffin of the National Shooting Sports Foundation. "Women have become a more stable part of the work force and today have the finances and the opportunity to do things they may always have wanted to do."

Several national organizations have blossomed in recent years, all with an eye to bringing more women into the fold.

"Turkey hunting, deer hunting and archery are the most popular choices at our events," said Trish Berry of the 225,000-member National Wild Turkey Federation's Women in the Outdoors Program. "We get everyone from surgeons to bookkeepers and housewives to lawyers – all women," she said.

Some, such as outdoor writer Shirley Grenoble of Altoona, whose seminars on deer and turkey hunting attract both men and women, took up the sport on their own. Others became interested via interest from a fiancee or spouse.

My wife hadn't done anything but shoot a .22 once or twice when we met in 1981. Now she has several trophy whitetails on the wall and spends many fall

mornings and evenings on her treestand, with bow or gun in hand. She also delivers seminars for women wanting to become part of the outdoor scene, many as deer hunters.

She's often questioned by girlfriends and wives who want to get started in the sport. They ask predictable questions such as which gun or what clothing and footwear to choose along with personal questions (how to cope in men's deer camp, fear of darkness when traveling to a stand and how to handle "potty" duties in the woods).

This isn't to say that all women need a man's assistance but a husband's, son's or boyfriend's interest is reason many distaff hunters decide to become involved in the first place. Most kids are taken hunting by parents, favorite uncles or friends and neighbors willing to share their time and experience.

No matter what their roots in deer hunting, the presence of women and kids in the deer woods is undeniably positive and vital to the future of hunting. Welcoming youngsters and wives or fiancees to deer camps reinforces whitetail hunting as the family sport it's always been.

Bryan Moose of York, then 15, tagged his first buck on the final day of the 1999 bow season on the Tuscarora Mountain in Perry County.

Kids afield

Sometimes it pays to look back, despite Satchel Page's sage advice to the contrary.

I vividly recall my first morning in the whitetail woods, my dad an acorn's toss away beneath a towering oak. It was an exciting time following a sleepless night in which I'd rehearsed exactly what I'd do when a hat-racked buck strolled along the trail 60 yards down the ridge.

It never happened. Save for several does that sprinted by in mid-morning, the action on that inaugural deer hunting morning was minimal.

But the memory is crystal clear.

Taking kids — even a friend or relative — hunting for the first time is a colossal responsibility. With years of experience under my belt I served as mentor to my two sons, two stepsons, several neighborhood kids and, later, a 12-year-old step-daughter. My approach was to recall my first days — first years, actually — in the field along with the naivete and the occasional fears and unknowns with which a youthful mind approaches any new challenge.

Youngsters are not permitted to hunt in Pennsylvania until they reach age 12, although they may accompany an adult afield prior to that. Such pre-hunt training sessions are invaluable. Add to that a few other activities which will help set a kid on the right path.

If there will be a young hunter at your side this year, consider these guidelines and suggestions for leading up to the "first time out."

• Pennsylvania requires the completion of a hunter education course before a junior license (for those 16 and under) can be purchased. After the course, review the lessons and reinforce the safety aspects with the young hunter. Stress the responsibility of carrying a firearm and the importance of a clean, humane harvest.

• Spend time on the range familiarizing the newcomer with his or her firearm's operation and its safe handling. Firmly and promptly inform the rookie whenever he or she makes a mistake, such as waving the muzzle about or, innocently, pointing it at someone or in an unsafe direction.

A rifle or shotgun can be intimidating, with a natural fear inherent in firing it the first few times. Flinching is a common affliction. Problem is, the shooter often doesn't realize he's flinching and therefore shooting inaccurately. Sneak a spent

Andy Fegely, then 12, shot his first buck in central Pennsylvania in 1982.

shell into the chamber if you believe your student is flinching, then watch his reaction when the trigger is squeezed. The lesson can be quite revealing – and effective.

• Take your new partner to the hunting grounds where you'll be on the opening day of the season. Visit the specific tree or treestand where opening morning will be spent. In Pennsylvania it's law that 12 and 13 year olds "must be close enough that verbal guidance can be easily understood" from a nearby adult.

On your preseason trip, point out trails, escape routes, rubs and scrapes and specify distances to various landmarks. Indicate "out of range" shots and unsafe targets (deer on a horizon, for example). The scouting trip will alleviate many fears for the new hunter.

• After that memorable "first time out," discuss the day's activities and encourage questions the new hunter may have. Continue your teachings on subsequent trips including hunter ethics, game laws, safety and responsibility.

Woods-women

Having a wife as a hunting partner has its rewards, as one might imagine. If your spouse (or girlfriend, mother or sister) has expressed a desire to join you in the field, first establish a game plan based on her desire to participate. Nothing succeeds like success when it comes to training and teaching a new partner, no matter if it's a wife, child or friend.

I'd already logged 30 years of hunting experience by the time my wife Betty Lou came along. Frigid mornings trying to remain still on deer stands were second nature. But I knew better than to expect her to enjoy the same sort of discomforts.

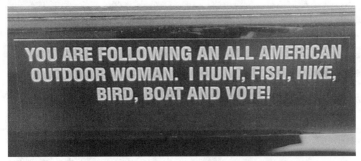

The bumper sticker on this Pennsylvania vehicle says it all.

For every woman afield there are about 10 men. The presumption that hunting is a "man's sport" may not be entirely true but it has basis in fact and it's the way most non-hunters view it. But, thankfully, numbers of women hunters continue to grow, putting a spike in propaganda distributed by animal rights and anti-hunting groups.

My wife and I began her introduction to the sport by studying hunting gear catalogs and taking inventory of the cedar closet where varied clothing items ranging from brilliant orange jackets to camouflage suits hung from racks. While she admits to not being a fashion plate while traipsing the woodlands, she does appreciate a neat-looking and functional outfit. Then, she adopted some suitable small-size men's items, snipping and sewing here and there for a comfortable fit.

Today, more and more hunting garb manufacturers are making women's clothing. It wasn't that way only 10 years back.

Footwear was less of a problem as she was able to find comfortable and insulated leather and pac-boots in sporting goods stores. Whether females inherently get colder than men under similar conditions is beyond the scope of my research. But my wife claims women need additional insulation on chilly mornings. She often appears overdressed when I'm outfitted in just the basics. She's most comfortable with the pac-boots or insulated leather footwear for cold weather hunts, opting for the extra warmth while walking or on stand.

The second item of business, once it was established that hunting, especially big game hunting, was more than a whim, was the purchase of a suitable gun. Her first rifle was my Model 760 Remington. On the shooting bench (we fired several boxes on the range prior to the first outing) she did great for a woman who had only plinked with a .22 previously. But afield, the combination of heavy clothes, pumping adrenalin, and difficulty in finding the target through the scope at moment's notice conspired to assure the deer's clean getaway.

In short, her gun didn't "fit."

Days later we visited a gun shop and picked out a Remington Model 7 chambered in 7mm-08. The 6-pound, 2-ounce rifle topped with a 2-7x Simmons scope was to her liking and has become her favorite firearm.

She also had our gunsmith shorten the stock on one of my Remington 700s chambered in 30-06. Gun fit is a key to confidence afield. A woman's proportions typically demand a short-stocked firearm, one fitting smoothly against the cheek and allowing a quick sight-picture through a scope.

Special care in choosing a deer gun is of utmost importance in the proper introduction of your potential hunting partner (man, woman or youngster) and every bit as important as proper dress and footwear.

Those of us who vividly recall our inaugural trips to the deer woods know the excitement and subtle fear inherent in awaiting first light surrounded only by the sound of our deep breathing and the outstretched arms of barren oaks reaching for the sky. It matters little that one is age 12 or 50 when the experience occurs. At the start, whenever I'd place my wife on a deer stand, pre-season scouting trips had already been taken and a few scenarios of what may occur were provided. It helped alleviate fears and bolstered confidence and independence.

Jeff and Jennifer Detore took their first deer in Venango County in the company of their proud father Mike.

Of course, just because a woman hunts doesn't mean femininity is left behind. In the years we've been traveling afield together, Betty Lou has discovered a few simple, inexpensive items that help make hunting excursions more tolerable. Pre-moistened hand and face towelettes are blessings in the deer woods and at camps lacking running water or modern lavatory facilities. Lipstick is carried in her daypack along with compass and skinning knife. Under her orange or camo cap she always wears earrings. The only items not used are perfume and scented powder.

In the course of our travels, and through a weekly television show I hosted in southcentral Pennsylvania on which Betty Lou was an occasional co-host, she received many queries from mothers, wives and girlfriends. Most letters were from women who were being encouraged to join their men on hunting trips — but hadn't tried it because of a natural fear of the unknown.

She advised them to approach it as she did — with detailed planning and a sense of adventure. The shared experience is one that partners will enjoy, and relive, each time they flash their slides on the screen or page through the family scrapbook.

Another side benefit of women afield is the confusion it brings to animal rights fanatics who love nothing more than to brand male hunters as macho jerks, killers and sexual perverts. She's gone one-to-one with some females in the animal "righteous" crowd and left them babbling in mid-sentence.

For us, hunting is a lifestyle.

The more women and kids encountered afield, the more confident I am about the healthy future of our pursuit.

Pennsylvania women who hunt

Consider the thoughts of these diehard female deer hunters.

• "I see the women's hunting movement continuing to grow," says Norma Laros, an Allentown taxidermist's assistant and lifelong hunter. "My husband Dick and I meet hunters from all over the world and it's very satisfying knowing how many people out there feel the same as you do."

• For Kathy Heller, who runs a Lehigh County fishing tackle shop with her husband Jeff, an interest in hunting came later in life when she visited Jeff's family cabin in Columbia County. In recent years the Hellers became bowhunters with

For Kathy Heller of Lehigh County, the urge to hunt aided her healing process following a mastectomy. She shot her first bow-buck in Columbia County in 1998 and followed with a doe in 1999, exactly two months following surgery.

both of them scoring on bucks. But things didn't look promising when, on August 5, 1999, Kathy had a mastectomy.

"That was a huge challenge but another was that I didn't want to miss the opening of the bow season," Kathy now chuckles. "I explained it to the doctor and he said to try to shoot the bow after six weeks. I never thought I could do it but I did."

On October 5, exactly two months following her surgery, she tied her harvest tag to a doe.

"That meant something very special," said Jeff.

"She had something in her head she really wanted to do and the thought of cancer did not get her down. There's no doubt what hunting means to her ... to us."

• For 15-year-old Sarah Salukas of Northampton County, and her father Larry, bowhunting has served as the bond for bringing them closer as father-daughter and as friends.

"We talk a lot when we're in the car driving to or back from bowhunting and when we're walking out of the woods," said Sarah, who already has a 164-point Boone & Crockett Illinois bow-buck to her credit. "I don't think we'd have all that time together if we didn't hunt."

"I would never be as close to Sarah if we didn't hunt," Larry believes. "Things happen when we're out there that I'll never forget."

• Hunting is not for everybody anymore than childbirth is, anymore than a career in the military is," says Mary Zeiss Stange, author of "Woman the Hunter" and a professor of religion at Skidmore College in New York. "Fewer women will cite getting trophies or exhibiting marksmanship as motivations for hunting ... but that may change over time with more women initiating their daughters."

• "Back when I started hunting I knew only two other women who hunted," said Penny Reinhart Patrick of Schuylkill County. "The difference today is men are more inclined to let women join them and that's good."

Oh yes, as for young girls getting involved in deer hunting, Kelsey Patrick, Penny's then-5-year-old daughter, put in a special order with Santa Claus before Christmas 1999.

"She informed me," said Penny, "that she wants a pink Barbie bow."

Add another female hunter to the growing ranks.

Penny Reinhart Patrick plans to pass on her hunting heritage to her daughter, Kelsey. The Schuylkill County resident shot her biggest buck ever near her home in 1998.

SECTION IV
WHERE TO GO

This autumn scenic (above) of a Clinton County farm and mountains in north-central Pennsylvania differs dramatically from the whitetail habitat in western Lehigh County in the Southeast.

CHAPTER 22

REGIONAL PROFILES
Lands of Big Bucks and Abundant Bucks

Despite its reputation as one of the nation's top whitetail states — with about a million deer hunters and even more deer — Pennsylvania has an image problem.

Like Rodney Dangerfield, the Keystone State too often gets no respect.

While it can't match Saskatchewan in big buck sizes or Texas in whitetail numbers, Pennsylvania enjoys a happy balance of each. Yet, many nonresidents — and a goodly number of residents — never hear about its "book bucks."

"I want to show a true picture of Pennsylvania, right down to the small deer and a hunter behind every tree," a Midwest video producer explained when he sought my scripting services a few years back. "I want to tell it like it is."

I informed him that if he planned to do that, he'd first need an attitude adjustment. And a different script writer.

O.K.! Maybe I overreacted. I'm a native Pennsylvanian and love my state and the outdoor opportunities it has to offer — such as its four million-plus acres of state-owned hunting grounds. And, yes, I do get defensive when someone misrepresents the whitetail potential found here — particularly in terms of the sizes of our bucks.

Of course, there's a basis in truth for some of these beliefs. For one, most bucks don't get the chance to grow beyond 18 months. With exception, few hunters will pass on anything minimally showing the three-inch spikes which make them legal game. It was that way when I experienced my first deer camp 40-something years ago and it's that way today, particularly in the rifle season.

"Selectivity" isn't in the vocabulary of most of the near-million gun hunters afield from the Monday after Thanksgiving and the following two weeks. Of the 160,000-195,000 bucks harvested every year, as many as 80 per cent are 1-1/2-year-old spikes, forkhorns or small 6-pointers.

But enough young bucks survive their initial hunting season hurdle and grow into notable trophies for gun and bow hunters each fall. The little-known truth is, Pennsylvania can match or beat most northeastern states when it comes to trophy racks. And like other states and provinces across the continent, some regions produce consistently better bucks than others — and some produce more bucks than others.

The Pennsylvania Game Commission divides its law enforcement, education and management divisions into six geographic regions made up of 10-13 counties.

Following are thumbnail sketches comparing the most recent harvests and the big buck potential for each of the half-dozen regions.

Many of the state's biggest bucks are found in Pennsylvania's northwestern wetlands.

Northwest

Look to Crawford, Erie and Mercer counties in this region for holding trophy whitetails and to Warren for good deer numbers. Game Commission trophy records over the years show Crawford and its farmlands, woodlots, swamps and marshes as the region's best choice for quality and quantity of deer. In 1999, hunters bagged 4,864 bucks and 4,998 does in Crawford.

Also accounting for more than 4,000 bucks were Venango and Warren counties.

"Diet and refuge," was the short answer from a Game Commission land manager a few years ago when asked to characterize the Northwest, particularly the swampland-farmland of Erie and Crawford counties. Swamps are the nearby refuges into which bucks flee at the opening volley. Some hunters follow, but not as many as stick to the less demanding routes.

Several state gamelands protect these swamps, such as SGLs 277, 122 and 214.

Travel east along the New York border and you'll find big woods country, such as the half-million acres of the Allegheny National Forest in Warren County. The state's only national forest was ravaged by a tornado several years ago and holds numerous deer. Some of them may be hard to hunt in the tangles and thickets. Of course, much of the area rimming Kinzua Dam (Allegheny Reservoir) is readily accessible.

Southwest

What do records show is Pennsylvania's best big buck county in the long term?

Of the state's 67 counties, it's Allegheny, surrounding Pittsburgh, that for nearly four decades has been the most consistent in yielding state record book bucks, largely to archers. More than five dozen Allegheny County bucks have made the Pennsylvania book in the past 25 years. Why? It's because the rolling, hilly, southwestern terrain, urban and suburban, is largely private with numerous wooded holdings closed to hunting. Less pressure equals less of a kill and more bucks making it to maturity.

Only one small state gameland is found in Allegheny county.

Allegheny is unique in that a large proportion of the total harvest is by bowhunters. In 1999, for example, 59 percent of the Allegheny harvest of 2,191 bucks were taken by archers. As in many suburban regions where only bows, muzzleloaders and shotguns are legal, bowhunters often have the edge in gaining access to private property.

Beaver, Butler, Armstrong, Washington and Westmoreland counties have also contributed more than 100 bucks to the state book listing in the past 25 years. Westmoreland has accounted for four of the 10 best non-typicals ever taken by bow and arrow.

While knowing where a big buck lurks during daylight hours and being unable to hunt there offers a certain frustration, it's because of such off-limits hiding places that deer in parts of the region survive and mature. Sooner or later they head to a neighboring soybean patch or cornfield where some lucky hunter awaits. Often it happens in the last two weeks of the season, when bucks are hard into the rut.

Indeed, the Southwest has come on strong in recent times as the state's best area for shooting a buck, replacing the traditional deer hunting counties in the Northcentral region as the tops in "whitetail country."

Somerset and Greene counties, both bordering West Virginia, and Indiana and Armstrong counties all yielded more than 4,000 bucks in 1999. Washington was second in the state with 5,760 bucks trailed by Westmoreland's 5,347 bucks. Westmoreland was tops in the region's harvest of 6,036 antlerless deer.

One report on the region's "personality" referred to it as a land with "urban refuges, fertile land and extensive woodlots," all prime habitat for whitetails.

"There's a lot of private land throughout this section of the state," said Dennis Jones, a land management supervisor for the Game Commission. "The deer have the chance to get older because they're largely inaccessible to most hunters."

Northcentral

It's widely known that this traditional deer camp region holds the fewest trophy bucks. Its claim to fame remains in deer numbers, although that's changed considerably since the heydays of this big woods region. For the past decade and more the Northcentral region has been targeted for herd reductions, which is biologically wise but has caused considerable social frustrations for hunters who recall the way things used to be.

Portions of Tioga and Lycoming counties are known to produce larger deer according to Game Commission biologist Bill Palmer. "Some of the deer living on the remote ridges in the two counties may get to be 3-1/2 or 4-1/2 years old and subsequently hold above-average racks," said Palmer.

Hunters pose with their harvest at the Wolf Run Camp in Centre County.

It was here – where you'll find the lowest human density in the state — that Pennsylvania's reputation as a producer of "mini-deer" was underscored in years past.

It was in the storied deer counties such as Potter, McKean, Tioga, Clearfield, Clinton, Cameron, Centre, Lycoming and others that hunters became increasingly vocal over Game Commission management practices starting in the early 1990s. Predictably, arguments hit their peaks following the annual release of antlerless deer license numbers for each county. Petitions were unsuccessfully filed to stop all doe hunting in some counties to allow the mountain-county herds to "recover." What was needed, however, was for the forest, itself, to recover.

Management goals shoot for anywhere from 16 to 20 deer per square mile of forest within each of the counties. Considering the somewhat dramatic drops in deer numbers the past 15-20 years, it's going to be a difficult sell telling hunters that deer populations will have to continue dropping until the denuded forests – as per Dr. Gary Alt's mission explained at the beginning of this book – can begin to regrow.

In the meantime, the general well-being of deep forest deer is improving.

"Over the past few years I have definitely noticed that our bucks are getting bigger – so have a lot of others," said Bill Haldaman, a Potter County resident and deer guide. "The deer are heavier and healthier and the racks show an improvement."

Thousands of acres of state forests and state gamelands offer hunters an abundance of public hunting grounds. This is big woods country, dotted with oil and gas leases and numerous pulp and paper interests which have cut and regrown untold amounts of timber, all despite being overburdened by voracious whitetails.

No matter, to many hunters this is "deer country" and they pack the truck and head to deer camp here each fall as they've done for a half-century and more.

The "big woods" county leading the pack in 1999 was Clearfield with a whopping 6,048 bucks (and 5,545 does) followed by Potter with 5,138 bucks and Tioga's 5,011 bucks. McKean, Lycoming and Centre all yielded more than 4,200 bucks.

Southcentral

Fertile farmlands and wooded mountain refuges produce some decent bucks here as well as holding substantial numbers of does across its 11-county region. Although it would be misleading to claim that the Southcentral region is trophy buck country, some 140-150 class deer have been recorded over the years.

Private land, some with minimal hunting pressure, provides haven for many bucks – which can grow to be 2-1/2 to 3-1/2 years, when age and nutrition combine for good racks.

The region's public lands, such as Rothrock State Forest encompassing 80,000 acres, give or take, also have both easy access via backwoods roads and off-the-beaten-path sectors, far from roadways. More than 60,000 gamelands acres and plenty of state park and forest holdings make this region inviting.

For the third straight year, Bedford County ranked number one in the region with its yield of 5,177 bucks and 4,512 does in the 1999-2000 seasons. Huntingdon followed with harvests of 4,922 and 3,540 bucks and does, respectively.

Closer to city and suburb near Harrisburg are Perry, Cumberland and Adams counties, which don't yield as many deer as Bedford but are close enough to hunters' homes to be enticing.

Northeast

Bradford is not only the top "big bucks" county in the Northeast but it doubles as the best "abundant bucks" county. Its mountains and rich dairy-land pastures and crop fields account for both honors. Bradford hunters harvested more than 12,000 deer in 1999, 6,056 of them bucks, ranking it the highest in the state.

Other big buck spots in this 13-county region, which attract numerous New York and New Jersey hunters with its abundance of public gamelands and forest lands

Harry Fitser, 80, of Plymouth, a survivor of black lung disease and cancer, says every buck is a trophy. His 4-pointer was shot in Luzerne County.

include the ridge and valley sectors of Montour, Columbia and Northumberland counties. The Poconos (Pike, Carbon, Monroe and Wayne counties) offer plenty of public hunting lands but rank a bit lower in terms of deer numbers when compared to other counties.

The second highest buck kill (3,909) was scored by Luzerne County hunters with Susquehanna (3,743) and Wayne (3,589) following.

Like portions of the Northwest, a sizable chunk of the Poconos is swamp country with numerous lakes. Black bears abound in the rhododendron swamps and deer looking for places to hide will also head into wetland refuges.

Sullivan and Wyoming counties on the western rim of the region are arguably the best bets for trophies, although some relatively good bucks come out of Susquehanna, as well.

The Northeast also offers loads of public hunting in scattered gamelands, parks and diverse tracts of Delaware State Forest.

Southeast

While growing up in this farm country in the 1950s, the sighting of any whitetail caused a stir among local hunters. Today only the big bucks get second glance. Much of the vast farmland region has been swallowed by suburbia, bedroom communities and highways, but enough crop interests exist to maintain overabundant herds. Finding open hunting land is the problem as scattered gamelands and a few other tracts open to the public can be found. The best bet is the mountainous state gamelands on the Blue Mountain — the southern rim of the Appalachians – holding more than 10,000 acres of public hunting grounds from the Delaware River to the Susquehanna River.

Most deer hunting, however, is on private lands.

Farm country and rolling hills along with scattered suburbs characterize the southern portion of this region, which holds both big deer and many deer. However, much of it is today housing developments, industrial centers, office buildings and shopping malls. There's also a good mix of farms and thousands of scattered, rolling woodlots from two to 100 or more acres.

Posted lands in much of the region control hunter access. Keep in mind that just because posters line most property boundaries, it doesn't mean that hunting doesn't take place there. Knocking on a door before the season can still yield a landowner's "yes" when someone seeks permission to hunt. There's plenty of food here and bucks surviving cars and hunters grow big, both in suburbia and farmland.

Consider, as an example, A.J. Muntz's state record typical bow buck shot in Bucks County, north of Philadelphia, where farmland and scattered developments hold numerous deer. In October 1995 the then-28-year-old archer arrowed a

These Pike County deer were photographed on Delaware State Forest land.

long-tined 10-pointer scoring 175-5 Pope & Young points.

Further attesting to the quality of bucks in the state's Southeast, the record non-typical bow-buck was shot in 1988 in Lehigh County, about 30-35 air miles northwest of Muntz's hunting grounds. It broke the then-record 187-2 P&Y buck shot in adjacent Montgomery County in 1985, less than a 30-minute drive north of downtown Philadelphia.

The state record book lists bucks from all southeastern counties, save for Philadelphia. Berks County boasts the most entries in the record book over the past two decades with Chester, Bucks, Montgomery and Delaware (the latter four all considerably smaller counties than Berks and largely within suburbia) also ranked high.

As for quantity, the Pennsylvania Game Commission's annual harvest analysis typically ranks Berks out front. In 1999, hunters harvested 4,046 bucks and 4,089 does in Berks. Schuylkill's 3,871 buck and 3,863 doe kills placed second in the 13-county region of which five counties (Bucks, Chester, Delaware, Montgomery and Philadelphia) are in the Special Regulations Area.

Along with Berks, Northampton and Lehigh

Success came slowly for Dennis Scharadin of Auburn who hunted 18 years before tying his tag to a Berks County 3-pointer.

counties also have high deer densities per square forested mile, running an estimated 50-60 animals.

NOTE: In comparing deer numbers and hunting opportunities across the varied regions and sizing up county harvests, it must be considered that county sizes and accessibility of hunting lands are dramatically different.

More precise are estimated deer numbers and buck and doe harvests based on the square miles of woodlands in each county. These statistics are included in the In Brief information bar in the County Profiles section.

Harvest numbers given are for the 1999 seasons, the most recent statistics available as this is being written.

Taxidermist Bob Danenhower bowhunted near his Lehigh County home for his 1998 8-pointer.

Pennsylvania Game Commission Land Manager Dave Mitchell is also an accomplished bowhunter, as shown here with his big 1999 Lehigh county 10-pointer.

Roadkill pick-ups in Pennsylvania average abut 45,000 a year with some esti-mates of vehicle-related deer fatalities approaching nearly double that figure.

CHAPTER 23

HUNTING WHITETAILS
Town and Country

According to a Penn State study, three-fourths of the Pennsylvania landscape is privately owned.

Game Commission surveys have shown that more than 60 percent of the state's deer hunters pursue their quarry on private lands. That's good news for hunters prowling the more than four million acres of public lands scattered about the state.

Many of the private holdings are farmlands and orchards, ranging from a few dozen acres to vast spreads used to raise cattle, corn, apples, soybeans and much more. Forested hills and checkered woodlots offer havens for farmland deer, providing the best of both worlds — trees and a healthy supply of nutritious crops.

Deer have always been present on Pennsylvania farms, but not in their current numbers. Farmland whitetail numbers have exploded in the past 30-40 years, costing farmers big bucks as the insatiable animals take bites out of their money crops and their profits.

The newest boom areas are lands that, at one time, consisted of forest and farm. Dubbed "urban sprawl," it's eating up once-fertile and productive, wildlife-rich farmland at an alarming rate. From 1985 to 1995 alone, a million acres of Pennsylvania farmland was lost to a dense network of roads connecting rural and suburban residential, commercial and industrial developments.

Beginning in the 1960s and 1970s, the suburbs and city fringes of Pittsburgh, Philadelphia and other cities began being burdened by too many deer. The problem has been growing ever since. People who once welcomed these "cute" brown-eyed animals now curse them, demanding that municipal managers and the Game Commission "do something about it."

The most recent analysis from Game Commission biologists show deer densities ranging from 25-52 deer per square mile of woodland in these areas. In small sectors of the Southeast and Southwest where hunting is taboo, deer densities may jump upwards of 150 per forested square mile.

That's unhealthy for deer and for the lands upon which they live.

Residents of suburbia are beginning to lose their love for whitetails, which not only devour their shrubs and gardens but have caused numerous accidents in recent years. In the summer of 1994 a Montgomery County woman was killed when her bicycle collided with a deer. Other human fatalities caused by vehicles and deer have also occurred.

The change of attitude has animal rightists searching for new arguments as even their own neighbors are becoming weary of protectionist attitudes. However, it

Seeing deer in front and back yards and on roads is no longer a rarity.

must be noted that even though suburban residents are leaning to "our side" (hunting), their simplified reasoning of what it takes to control whitetails isn't always rational or biologically wise.

Nevertheless, the paradox is that the places deer numbers are highest and bucks are biggest are the same spots where open hunting lands are most difficult to find (the cause of the problem in the first place). It's a vicious and problematic circle.

So how does a hunter go about finding private lands — in farm or suburb — on which to hunt? And what techniques are used when your view from the treestand may include a Turkey Hill or 7-11?

Consider the following advice.

Gaining access to suburban deer haunts

For 15 years, Tri-County Bowhunters' co-founder Bob Gabe has been gaining access to the many private lands in southeastern Pennsylvania that serve as buffers between houses and mini-marts. Today, he and the leaders of several other bowhunting organizations have made substantial inroads into opening new hunting grounds by working with landowners who, 10 or 15 years ago, might have slammed doors in their faces. Now, getting one's boot in the door is considerably easier.

"The easiest places (to get access to) are those owned by people whose properties are adjacent to land already enrolled with us," said Gabe. "Our strong point now is that we have references from many property owners, including some key people in the community. Those contacts help tremendously."

"Communication is critical," advises Jody Maddock, founder of Whitetail Associates, another suburban Philadelphia bowhunting group. "When we approach someone willing to work with us, we do whatever that person wants. We dictate nothing. If they don't want us to hunt mornings or Saturdays or they don't want us crossing their lawn, we abide."

In recent years the stereotypical hunter image has changed substantially, according to Gabe. This has fostered a new relationship between hunters and property owners. But the change didn't come overnight. It required plenty of hard work and the slow but steady development of open communication between hunters and homeowners plagued by deer damage.

Once a club member has the chance to explain hunting basics with potential cooperating landowners and provides them with an informational packet, their view of hunting and hunters often shifts dramatically. "In the last 10 to 15 years, the public has come to recognize hunting as a legitimate tool to control deer numbers," Gabe's pleased to report.

So how does a core group dedicated to opening new hunting grounds and serving suburban property set up an organization similar to Pennsylvania's Whitetail Associates and Tri-County Bowhunters?

Following are suggestions offered by Gabe and Maddock, who together have 30 years of suburban hunting politics under their collective belts.

1) When visiting a potential cooperating landowner, don't show up wearing camouflage. Wear a sweater or sport coat and slacks. Image, at the onset, is everything.

2) If other residents in a neighborhood are already working with the hunting group, use them as references. If one homeowner in a cul-de-sac is enrolled, others may eventually join.

3) Prior to seeking cooperators in new areas where the organization may not be known, get a handle on local deer problems. This may involve hiring a wildlife biologist. Then create an informational handout to leave with potential cooperators, including the phone numbers of contact persons. Showing that you're both a hunter and deer manager provides most deer-plagued suburbanites with a new viewpoint.

4) Avoid confrontation. "I can tell when someone answers the door if they're anti-hunting or they just don't want to get involved," said Gabe. "I always leave our pamphlet and thank them for listening, even if only for a minute or two. The handout should explain the local deer problems, the role hunters play in deer management and how the group operates. A homeowner who doesn't want to hear the initial sales pitch may change his mind and call the contact person later."

5) Township officials, council members, police and other influential citizens must also be on the contact list. Ask for time to speak at town meetings or other forums to explain the program or share updates, always emphasizing the service you can provide.

6) Emphasize the members' hunting skills and their concern for the resource. Maddock's group requires members to pass shooting tests and to complete the

These Delaware County bow hunters deep in close contact with the landowner on whose property they hunt.

day-long National Bowhunter Education Foundation course. Also, emphasize the overall biological benefits to having fewer — and healthier — deer.

7) Get involved in local issues involving deer management. Successful hunting organizations have gained respect because they've been able to counter attacks and claims made by anti-hunting groups, whose presence is guaranteed at any public forum involving suburban deer.

8) Have your act together as a group. Selling points of a successful organization may include: liability insurance to protect landowners; a liaison for each area to handle landowners' questions, requests or complaints; placards to place in car or truck windows when a hunter is on land enrolled in the program; information explaining that only safe, downward-angle tree stand shots are taken; removing deer to another location for field-dressing; and processing and sharing venison with charitable groups. Such information should be put in a written report and distributed to each cooperating landowner following the season. The gesture keeps landowners informed and involved.

9) When making your case with a prospective cooperator, always underscore the fact that knowing who is on his or her property provides a sense of security and a true service. Trespassers are quickly evicted and, if necessary, prosecuted. Both Whitetail Associates and Tri-County Bowhunters post and patrol the properties of cooperating landowners.

10) Keep your group small. Maddock's outfit has 30 members who hunt more than two dozen properties totaling 1,200 acres. Gabe's group is a bit smaller.

"As you can imagine, we get many requests to join," said Maddock. "But we can't just take everyone. There's got to be some control, and not everyone may qualify."

And don't make securing land on which to hunt a competitive event. "If anyone from Whitetail Associates knocks on a door and is told that some other group already hunts their land, we back off. We have no intention of competing," Maddock emphasizes.

Bob Walker of Media poses with his mounted 135-class Pope & Young buck shot within a few yards of where this photo was taken in Delaware County. Note the four-lane highway in the background.

"Access has definitely become easier over the years," said Bob Walker of Walker's Game Ear fame, a suburban Philadelphia resident and member of an organized hunting group. In one development where 15 property owners are working with Walker's group, each family has at least one member who has Lyme disease. "Ironically, some of these people years ago wouldn't let us on their land," Walker said. "Now they want us to kill more deer than we possibly can."

The problem of overabundant whitetails roaming suburbia and posing health, safety and ecological threats is a long way from resolution. But thanks to groups such as Whitetail Associates, Tri-County Bowhunters and others, including the Fox Chapel area near Pittsburgh where bowhunters are "registered" with the police department as references, hunters are today enjoying a new respect. Suburban residents are coming to understand that the whitetails must be controlled, for the welfare of both residents and for the deer themselves.

Whitetail Associates has developed a helpful information packet describing the benefits of working with hunters to solve deer management problems. It's available by sending a stamped ($1.50 postage), self-addressed, large manila envelope to Jody Maddock, Whitetail Associates, P.O. Box 596, Bryn Athyn, PA 19009.

Techniques for suburban whitetails

That brings us to the fun part.

Suburban hunting.

As in hunting remote areas, time spent on scouting and familiarization trips before and even during the season is the key to filling a tag in suburbia, suggests Tom Tatum, a Chester County school teacher and outdoor writer who has been hunting suburban whitetails much of his adult life. He suggests looking for small, secluded, semi-accessible pieces of private ground bordering larger, undeveloped tracts or adjacent to county parks. If hunting is done on the larger tracts, deer will soon seek cover in the smaller, posted refuges. Patterning whitetail movements prior to and during the season will often narrow the ideal spot for a portable treestand.

Tatum has discovered one big advantage to suburban whitetails (besides their numbers) is that their travels are predictably restricted. Deer negotiate backyards, skirt the edges

Outdoor writer Tom Tatum has mastered the suburban hunting techniques necessary near his Chester County home.

Newspaper columnist P. J. Reilly patterned this 9-pointer in Chester County and got close enough for a clean shot on the 1999 archery opener.

of woodlots, move within feet of kenneled dogs, trace treeline "funnels" between woodlots and generally stay close to houses. The deer are acclimated to human activity although encountering a hunter in a treestand brings them back to their inherent cautiousness.

"They can sense when bowhunting predators invade their haunts and, if an archer is careless, suburban bucks can make themselves as scarce as an honest politician," Tatum's learned.

Despite the scent of barbecue grills and exhaust in the air, the smell of a human in a woodland setting still perks their noses. Using scent-masking solutions and cover scents is as necessary as when hunting big woods country.

Of course, no one looks forward to following a wounded deer downtown, so setting up as close as possible to where deer make their trails is important. Only sure shots should be taken to avoid the prospect of a long tracking session through suburban backyards.

Tatum warns there's no guarantee that conditions will stay the same and you'll have a place to hunt "forever." One year he discovered a travel route from a woodlot to a cornfield, then patterned and eventually bagged an 8-point bow-buck. The next year the cornfield was gone — and so were the deer's travel lanes.

"Last season's hotspot could turn out to be this year's fast-food parking lot," he cautions. "And it often does."

Surprisingly, Tatum's learned deer here may change their patterns faster than those in forest country. Hunting pressure urges the deer to move on, specifically to posted parcels (of which there are many) where they linger as long as necessary.

In many ways deer here "are like deer everywhere," Tatum says. "They respond to grunting and will go through all the same rituals and routines during the rut."

Another observation he's made over the years is that the first couple days of the buck season are relatively quiet in suburban haunts. The first and second Saturdays, however, "are like opening day is everywhere else. That's when the guys are back from deer camp and they're hunting locally."

"It's not easy to get permission to hunt from landowners but it can be done," Tatum, whose treestand is set up within sight of houses, advises. "It's my experience that landowners are much more inclined to grant permission to a bowhunter than a gun hunter."

However, some landowners who want deer culled are willing to allow the use of shotguns or muzzleloaders as long as they're fired only from treestands, which they consider safer than shooting at ground level.

Despite the burgeoning popularity of hunting the suburbs, deer overpopulation continues. To the dismay of the animal rights crowd, suburbanites are getting a costly lesson on the subject of whitetail management and many are welcoming ethical and responsible hunters in the process.

Hunting farmland whitetails

I was weaned on farm-country deer, although it wasn't until considerably later in my hunting career that buck and doe numbers began to grow in my neck of the woods in the heart of Pennsylvania Dutch farm country.

Places I hunted pheasants as a kid are now turkey and whitetail havens (Today pheasants can no longer be found). I've come to the conclusion that patterning farm-country whitetails is easier than gathering a dossier on big-woods deer.

Although I've never read anything to support or deny my belief, it's my belief that farmland whitetails wander considerably larger ranges than their forest-dwelling cousins. They also travel more specific travel routes, which makes for easier patterning.

As the deer complete their appointed rounds, they revisit food sources and other familiar territory, often hanging in one place for several days before moving on. My pre-season bow scouting may turn up an identifiable buck or two which I often don't see for another few days, until suddenly they reappear. At times I've seen bucks

Andy Sawka's handsome 8-pointer came in Northampton County farmland on opening day of 1996. The farm is now an 18-hole golf course.

Deer pushed from farm-country woods will often break into open fields as they run for the cover of yet another woodlot.

(one an identifiable piebald 6-pointer and his 7-point traveling companion) as far as six miles from previous sightings over two or three days.

The biggest advantage of farmland hunting is that food sources can be pin-pointed. My farmer-friend's corn always starts taking a hit in mid-August. His apple trees lure them by mid-September (along with the unharvested corn) and winter wheat brings predictable visits later in the season. Alfalfa and clover add to the menu selections.

Knowing what's growing on neighboring properties is also important. During the snowy winter of 1993-1994 an unharvested soybean field in northern Lehigh County drew more than 125 deer, like kids to free ice cream. As the farm was posted, hunters were present on adjacent lands where snow-sign readily revealed the animals' travel routes.

Red and white oaks along with beech stands are prime places to set treestands anywhere in whitetail country. On farms, cornfields often rim oak woods, serving as double enticement for deer, especially during bow season.

In their daylight travels or when pushed out of a feeding or bedding area, deer will travel the cover provided by treelines which connect and divide open fields. One treeline in which I place a portable stand each season shows a beaten path leading into the corner of a 50-acre woodlot. Finds like that are prime for starting the bow season as acorns and beechnuts are abundant in the woods and the wind-breaks are used by deer when traveling from one woodlot to another.

Nearly 30 percent of Pennsylvania is covered in agricultural lands with broad diversity from one farm to another. My homeland farms are rolling and hilly with some large, relatively flat tracts. In the Appalachian and Allegheny highlands, how-ever, farmlands are often rimmed by mountains.

In either, deer will take advantage of land breaks forming natural funnels. The cuts and shallow valleys offer deer seclusion while traveling from one salad bar to another. They double as escape routes and often provide bedding areas nearby where a spooked buck can quickly leave without detection.

Funnels linking two or three food sources or adjoining bedding areas are the most productive. One spot I visit each year is a grassy swamp, next to a secondary road with numerous stunted alders and aspens. Next to it is a small grove of wild cedars, a three-acre woodlot and a cornfield. It doesn't take a Sherlock Holmes to wander the area prior to the bow season and find rutted paths and pressed grasses in the thicket where the deer have passed and bedded.

Opening days in farmlands are little different than in forest country. Hunters spook deer from one place and the wise hunter will stay in his or her treestand as long as possible. The hunter who can sit still for the day will always see deer, some within reasonable shooting range.

As the season progresses, however, driving deer may be necessary. I can recall my first days as a deer hunter when I joined my father and his friends on local deer drives. Then, permission to hunt was easier to find than today. We'd spend the morning traveling from one woodlot to another, alternating between standing and posting. When one woods was worked, we'd drive on to another.

Small, 10-75 acre woods dotting farmland can be more easily covered. Deer pushed from small woodlots often break into open pastures or wheat fields as they flee to yet another woodlot or overgrown thicket, offering clear shots to standers.

Then, too, for the early a.m./late p.m. hunter who must work from 8 to 4, a treestand on the edge of a corn or soybean field can make the most of limited hunting time. At one of my hunting plots, I can park my car and be in my treestand in less than five minutes.

The wooded edges of harvested and unharvested crop fields are also prime spots to set stands during the last couple weeks of bow season, when rutting bucks are more likely to show themselves in daylight. Learning their favorite entry points is necessary for close shots with a bow. If a good run is found, I'll set up 30-40 or more yards inside the treeline along their likely entry and exit routes, not directly on the field edge.

Farm-country whitetails are no smarter or dumber than their suburban or big-woods counterparts. The advantage to hunting them is that, unlike big woods deer, they live in proximity to roads and country residences, and they follow their appetite, usually directly to a farmer's cash crops.

Tom's Tips

-On gloomy days when contrast is at a minimum, try looking at the world through amber-colored shooting glasses. Even on dull days when snow covers the ground the yellow lenses will aid in spotting deer and movement by increasing contrast as they seemingly brighten the woods.

-Burdocks, trefoil seeds, beggar's ticks and other cling-ons held tight by fleece-type hunting garments can be removed by scraping them off with a strong pocket comb.

-Velcro is a welcome high-tech fastener for everything from tent flaps to sneakers. But to a deer hunter it can be the item that spoils the day. The sound of a velcro pocket flap being pulled open can alert a deer at 100 yards. Either choose hunting clothes without velcro or sew cloth over those already on your coat or jacket.

Trophy bucks don't come easy but Pennsylvania hunters have bagged some monsters over the years.

Chapter 24

MAKING THE BOOK
How Some of Pennsylvania's Biggest Bucks Were Taken

Looking for a trophy buck?

Head toward town or farm country.

That's what records from the past quarter-century or so show. Big woods country, like the popular "Golden Triangle" of northcentral Pennsylvania, yield lots of deer but chances of finding a trophy are slim. The same holds true for most of Pennsylvania's northeast.

Conversely, the counties holding cities, suburbs and farms in the Southeast, Northwest and Southwest have been providing haven for some wall-hangers in the past couple decades. Here nutritious foods are available and bucks get to grow to 3-1/2 years and more, a time when genetics, diet and age combine to create heart-grabbing racks.

Places like my "backyard" in southeastern Pennsylvania, where even a deer track drew comment in the1950s, now produce some of the heftiest, corn-fed whitetails in the state.

Take, for example, the 23-point, non-typical, Lehigh County stag Craig Krisher of Macungie shot on the opening day of bow season in 1988. It scored a whopping 203-3 Pope & Young points, qualifying it for both state and national record books.

Krisher's trophy in the non-typical bow category surpassed a 187-2 P&Y buck shot by David Krempasky three years earlier. As the proverbial crow flies, both deer fell less than 40 miles from one another. Krempasky's kill was made on a farm in the heart of Montgomery County's suburbia, less than a half-hour drive north of Philadelphia.

Then there's Ralph Stoltenberg's Butler County record typical bow-buck, scoring 174-2. It's followed by second and fourth place bucks shot in nearby Allegheny County, surrounding Pittsburgh.

Farm-country and private-land suburbs may hold the most trophies but some surprises also come from mountain counties. Lycoming, Sullivan, Tioga, Clearfield, Bradford and over three dozen other forest counties sporadically provide bucks in excess of 140 B&C points. Places that held legendary, deep-woods whitetails a half-century ago now produce quantity rather than quality. The areas in proximity to highest human population today yield the biggest racks.

In many parts of the commonwealth, a half-hour drive from the center of town yields excellent habitat, along with fields of corn or soybeans and acorn-studded

Ralph Stoltenberg, Jr. arrowed his 174-2 point typical bow-buck in Butler County in 1972. It ranks third all-time.

woodlots. Places where ringnecks and rabbits were once king have become whitetail country.

A popular video shot in southwestern Pennsylvania shows a respectable whitetail bow-buck shot within a short walk of a major highway. The hunter parked in a Kmart lot.

Surely buck hunting has taken on a new look in the Keystone State since I was a Woolrich-decked kid only dreaming of deer with racks bigger than forks. Yet, it was back then and before that some of the long-standing record book bucks were taken.

Consider the state record 189 Boone & Crockett typical gun-buck shot by Fritz Janowsky in Bradford County in 1943. Or Floyd Reibson's 182-2 B&C buck shot in Sullivan County back in 1930 and Perry Kinley's 177-pointer B&C stag taken in Jefferson County in 1920.

For many years I hunted out of a Bradford County camp within shooting distance of the New York border. It wasn't until a few years after my initial visit that I learned that Janowsky's long-standing state record was shot nearby, possibly only several hundred yards from my treestand.

Then 13, Janowsky hunted a patch of woods about a quarter-mile from his home that memorable day in 1943. He'd heard about a particularly large buck that had been wounded earlier in the season. With luck on his side, he located it hiding in the downed top of an old tree, then sneaked in close and shot it with a shotgun and pumpkin ball.

Fearing that he'd be in trouble with his parents for having gone hunting without permission, he kept the rack but gave the deer away. For many years it lay in a garage loft until Janowsky finally entered it in the state's scoring and records program in 1979.

Other racks eventually scored by the commission were even older. Some, of course, came more recently.

Today, in high (human) population counties, the greater proportion of lands are under private ownership. On many of these acres, such as those bordering Pittsburgh and Philadelphia, whitetails that learn to avoid cars and trucks on the numerous roadways live to ripe old ages. Many of them dwell behind "No Hunting" signs and limit their travels to nocturnal wanderings, especially during the hunting seasons.

It's these bucks, which eat well and develop their full genetic potential, that occasionally make fatal errors and end up immortalized in the record book.

Keystone Book Bucks

Solid information is hard to come by when researching the history of Pennsylvania's biggest bucks. The most reliable source is *Pennsylvania Big Game Records: 1965-1986*," published by the Pennsylvania Game Commission.

For the following accounts, I also referenced more recent records from the commission's tri-annual measuring sessions in 1986, 1989, 1992 and 1995. Measuring days were canceled in 1998 but plans are to restore the sessions again in 2001 and every three years thereafter. Deer taken since 1995 which might qualify for entrance into the cherished realm of "book bucks" have not yet been confirmed and only local hunters may know about them until they're honored by the Game Commission.

Typical bucks measuring 140 Boone & Crockett points and non-typicals with minimum scores of 160 or more were considered as Pennsylvania-style "book bucks." To make the continental Boone & Crockett record book a typical buck must measure 170 points and a non-typical 195

Fritz Janowsky's 1943 Bradford County typical gun buck scored 189 Boone & Crockett points and continues to hold the top spot in the category. The rack was measured in 1979 and the honors presented by former Pennsylvania Game Commission Executive Director Glenn Bowers.

points. For archers, Pope & Young scores (which use the B&C scoring system) must total 125 typical and 170 non-typical.

While most hunters will settle for smaller bucks, few go afield without at least fantasizing about that buck of a lifetime showing up in their sights.

Every year the whitetailer's dream comes true for a few select hunters, either by design or sheer luck. I had the opportunity to interview a few of these "hall of fame" hunters at the past few measuring sessions.

You will note in the listings at the end of this column that the majority of the top 10 bucks in the gun categories were taken many years ago, some as long ago as 1930. Bow-bucks, however, are of more recent vintage, which is to be expected as bowhunting was a rarity 60-70 years ago. The initial Pennsylvania archery season was held in 1951 and it wasn't for another 20 years or so, with the invention of the compound bow, that bowhunter numbers began to grow.

The state's Big Game Awards Program is co-sponsored by the Pennsylvania Game Commission and the Pennsylvania Outdoor Writers Association. Watch your local newspaper and state magazines for the dates and times hunters can bring their racks and mounts to PGC regional offices for free scoring in 2001 and 2004.

In the meantime, Pennsylvania hunters love to hear success stories, especially when they end with monster bucks — as in these deer tales about the most recent entries into the state record book.

HOW THEY DID IT

The Muntz Buck

In 1993, at age 24, Albert Joseph Muntz — better known as A.J. — figured he'd take up bowhunting.

It was a good move for the Havertown hunter.

"I got into bowhunting because I thought I'd stand a better chance of getting a nicer buck," Muntz had theorized.

Two years later — October 28, 1995, to be precise — the 28-year-old novice bowman did just that. He shot his first buck with a bow. But it was more than merely a "nicer buck" than he'd ever killed with a gun; it was a record-breaker.

The 10-point typical bow-buck now officially ranks number one in Pennsylvania and stands 15th all-time in the national Pope & Young Club record book.

Ironically, Muntz almost didn't hunt on that memorable Saturday afternoon, the 26th day of 1995 season. He'd visited a local mall that morning with his fiancee and planned to "take it easy" the rest of the day, enjoying time off from his duties at Philadelphia Electric Company.

"Then my brother called and said the weather was turning; he really had to prod me to go," Muntz recalls with a smile. "We had over an hour's drive and finally I agreed; so we met at 2 (p.m.) at the barn where we always change our clothes."

Joining him were his brother John and best friend Kenny, the only hunt-

Sal Pitera of Montgomery County owns the number three all-time typical gun-buck shot by Chester Allison in Blair County in 1951. It scores 182-5.

Lewis Hajos of Jerman shot his book-buck in 1941 and had entered it for measurement in 1969. The typical buck from Lackawanna County scored 162-4 points and put him in the 44th all-time position up through 1986.

ers permitted on the 150-acre farm in Bucks County, west of Doylestown and north of Philadelphia. As A.J. slipped into his Mossy Oak Tree-stand-pattern garb, the men decided who would hunt where. At 2:30 they parted company with A.J.'s destination a stand about 500 yards from the barn, just inside the edge of a spit of woods funneling into a grass-field. Trailing from his boot was a drag rag saturated with estrus scent.

Before screwing in the steps to reach a Loggy Bayou treestand already hanging in the tall tulip-pop-lar, Muntz hung his drag-rag and scattered several film canisters hold-ing Tink's No. 69 doe-in-heat scent.

The day was overcast with a 10-mph breeze and a light rain, which aided in muffling his steps en route to the stand. Thirty minutes after strap-ping himself in and with the late after-noon sun peeking through clouds, he heard movement behind him — the sound enhanced by a Walker's Game Ear, a specialized hearing-aid-type device he'd plugged into his left ear upon arrival.

Turning, he saw a pair of does leap a creek and dash into the field. They were followed by a 6-point buck and a big 10-pointer; the big-

A.J. Muntz of Havertown had only two years of bowhunting experience under his belt when he bagged the state record 175-5 non-typical bow-buck in 1995.

gest the novice archer had ever seen in the wild.

"They stayed out there 15 or 20 minutes chasing the does," Muntz recalls. "That was the first I'd seen any sign of the rut."

Muntz felt a tingling sensation across his shoulders as he studied the bigger buck pursuing the uncooperative does, which sprinted away open-mouthed and panting each time one of the suitors gave chase.

"They weren't all that far away but too far for a shot," Muntz said. "I estimated them at 45-50 yards much of the time."

Suddenly, however, the does bolted back into the woods, sprinting past Muntz's stand where they stopped in a thicket. The bucks trotted in their paths, issuing audi-ble grunts, then paused side-by-side 20 yards from Muntz's drawn bow.

As they looked for the elusive does and sniffed the air, Muntz aimed his Pro-Line New Wave bow and 125-grain Thunderhead toward the big buck. To his amaze-ment, the 10-pointer dropped in its tracks. Adding to the drama of the moment was the 6-pointer, standing only a few feet away, which only casually glanced at his downed partner.

"It was as if he'd just bedded down," according to Muntz's recollection. "Finally — I don't know how long it was — I whistled and the does took off with the 6-pointer going after them."

Fearing the buck was merely stunned and would get to its feet and run off, he nocked a second arrow. Taking aim, however, he noted blood on the antlers and decided to wait. Ten minutes passed before he descended the stand, still visibly shaking from the course of events fresh in his mind.

"I didn't even go over to look at him," Muntz chuckled. "I really didn't think he was down for good and I didn't want to take a chance at having him run off."

Gathering his partners, they returned to find the buck dead.

"We just couldn't believe what we were looking at," Muntz recalls. "I knew it was big but close up it looked even bigger."

John Muntz immediately knew it was the same deer he'd spotted from another stand, set 75 yards away in the same 25-acre woodlot, two weeks earlier.

The arrow had entered between the upper neck and shoulder, its path clipping an artery. The pass-through Easton Gamegetter exited lower on the buck's right side. Later that evening it field-dressed at 210 pounds. Tooth structure indicated it was 3-1/2 years old. The main beams measured 30-5/8 and 29-5/8 inches with a 23-3/8 inch inside spread and 6-1/8 and 5-5/8 inch basal circumferences.

Following the mandatory 60-day drying period, the rack gross-scored 183 Pope & Young points with deductions for discrepancies in the brow and G-3 tines dropping it to 175-5, according to certified B&C scorers. However, a certified Pennsylvania Game Commission officer tabulated it at 174-7. It wasn't as high as that determined by the other scorers but was still enough to beat the existing state record by a fraction of an inch.

The previous top typical bow-buck, scoring 174-2, was shot by Ralf Stoltenberg, Jr. in Butler County, on the opposite end of the state north of Pittsburgh, in 1986.

The Van Houdt Buck

A 17-year-old hunter took top spot for his 1991 buck in the non-typical gun category during the 1992 measuring session. Daniel Van Houdt of Quakertown bagged the 15-point, drop-tined whitetail near his upper Bucks County home on opening day. The buck scored 189 B&C points, ranking it thirteenth on Pennsylvania's all-time list. The rack held four drop-tines, a fact not unnoticed by Van Houdt and his father in earlier sightings.

"We watched it all summer long," said Van Houdt. "We even have it on video."

But on opening morning of the buck season the big deer was as elusive as ever. At 4 p.m the youngster decided to leave his stand and stalk through a marshy area

Then age 17, Dan Van Houdt shot his 15-point, 189 Boone & Crockett nontypical gun buck in Bucks County in 1991.

into which an 8-pointer he'd fired at earlier that day had run, and where he'd seen an abundance of rubs several weeks before.

"All of a sudden he just stood up — about 30 yards way," said Van Houdt. "I shot and he went right down."

Van Houdt and his father, Dan, Sr., had seen the deer the past two bow seasons but it became elusive as the gun season neared. Dan used a slug-loaded 12-gauge Ithaca Deerslayer to make the one-shot kill.

The McConeghy Buck

Jeff McConeghy of Clairton was honored for an Allegheny County 10-pointer, the largest typical bow-buck (161-3) measured in the 1992 session and the fifth biggest in the commission's all-time record book.

Making the trophy even more unusual, McConeghy shot the deer on December 28 during the winter archery-flintlock season while hunting from the ground "a few miles south of Pittsburgh."

"I saw it 10 or 12 times in the first season but couldn't get close enough," he explained. "I hunted three days straight (in the late season) and about 7:30 I was walking along the edge of a field when I spooked it."

McConeghy couldn't get off a shot so he and a friend wandered across a hillside field to the opposite end of the knoll on which they'd scouted several heavily-used trails. At 11:20 the massive, symmetrical stag appeared on the trail and was shot at by Jeff's hunting partner, who was set up against a tree about 50 yards away. The deer fled toward McConeghy and paused long enough for him to place the arrow in the shoulder area at 20 yards.

The two waited a half hour, then followed the blood trail off the knoll where they easily found the monster deer. McConeghy used a Bear Whitetail II bow, an Easton Gamegetter arrow and Satellite Broadhead.

The Weiser Buck

Paul Weisser of Numedia received a plaque for the largest non-typical gun whitetail entered in the 1992 measuring program. The 15-pointer scored 161-1,

Paul Weisser, Jr. of Numedia (left) shot his 15-point, 161 Pope & Young buck in Westmoreland County in the 1989 archery season. It ranks 7th all-time. Jeff McConeghy of Clairton (right) arrowed his 161-3 typical bow-buck on December 28, 1991 in Allegheny County. It holds the 5th all-time spot in the category.

ranking it sixth in the Keystone State's all-time list. The deer was taken on the third Saturday of the 1989 bow season.

"He was with another big buck when I saw him the week before," a smiling Weisser explained. "I was in a treestand and he came down a trail and just stopped broadside about 20 yards away."

"He was looking straight ahead," Weisser recalls. "He never knew I was there."

Weisser said he passed up a 12-pointer earlier in the season in anticipation of a chance at the 15-pointer. After the shot he waited an hour before blood-trailing the book-buck. During that time he watched six other bucks pass by his treestand, set only 400 yards from his Columbia County home.

Weisser used a PSE Laser Mag bow, Easton arrows and a 160-grain Thunderhead broadhead.

The Walker Buck

Paul Walker of Somerset made news in the 1995 measuring session with a typical gun-buck he shot more than a half-century earlier. On December 6, 1941 a friend convinced Walker to go hunting. The pair traveled to an old homestead in the Laurel Hill Mountains of western Pennsylvania where, as they were making up their minds where to park, Walker spotted a large buck in a distant field.

He stalked it under the cover of an adjacent Somerset County woods, moving each time the deer dropped its head to feed. Closing to within 100 yards, he leveled his iron-sighted, 30-40 Krag and dropped the 210-pound stag. It was a 15-pointer with a 28-1/4 inch spread. Nearly 54 years later Game Commission measurers determined its B&C score of 171-6.

"I didn't even plan on going hunting that day," Walker recalled with a grin. "But I guess it was good I did or I'd never be here to get this award."

The Brumgard Buck

Topping the non-typical whitetail-with-a-gun category in the 1995 session was a 24-point York County buck shot by Kevin Brumgard of Mt. Wolf on the first Friday of the 1992 buck season.

Brumgard had asked his boss for the afternoon off, then traveled to county land near his parents' home where he said he likes to hunt "at least once every season." Upon entering the woods he spooked what he believes was the same buck he would encounter an hour later.

Paul Walker's 171-6 typical Somerset County gun-buck was measured more than 50 years after it was shot in 1941.

"I saw the glare off the antlers as it ran off but I had no idea how big it was," Brumgard explained. "I continued on to the top of the hill and stood on a stump and watched, hoping he'd come back."

At 3:15 p.m. the buck did just that. Brumgard shot straight on the magnificent deer which measured 197-6 B&C points. He used a Ruger Model 77, 7mm magnum topped with a 3-9x Simmons scope.

The buck ranks sixth all-time in the non-typical category.

The Epprecht Buck

Donald Epprecht of Mont Clare, Montgomery County, hunted about five miles from home on Nov. 3, 1993 when he got a bow-shot at a buck he'd been after for the previous two years. But the shot went awry and the then-38-year-old hunter chalked it up as "experience."

"I left the woods dejected (but) still had a whole week of hunting ahead of me," said Epprecht, who had taken vacation time to spend time in the autumn woods. Two days later he was back in the same area which was pock-marked with numerous scrapes. Before ascending into his permanent treestand, he hung a tarsal gland and created a mock scrape within shooting distance.

"I was kind of giving up hope by 9 when all of a sudden he showed up," said Epprecht. "I shot him broadside at 15 yards and retrieved him a half hour later about 100 yards away."

The 10-pointer holds the number three all-time ranking in the typical bow-and-

Kevin Brumgard's 24-point York County buck was taken in 1992, measuring 197-6 and ranking 6th all-time in the non-typical/gun category.

Donald Epprecht's Montgomery County archery buck shot in 1993 holds 6th place in the all-time typical category with 163-3 points.

arrow category. The rack is only 17 inches wide but that's made up for with mass and high tines which gives it a score of 163-3 points.

He used an Oneida Screaming Eagle bow with pin sights.

The Funk Buck

In the non-typical bow-buck category, David Funk of Newtown, Bucks County copped top spot in the 1995 awards program, slipping into the number five all-time listing with his 1993 trophy, scoring 163-7 inches.

On the cold, windy afternoon of October 30 — Halloween eve — Funk and two friends checked out a patch of Bucks County woods in which he'd shot video of a monster buck during the previous two summers. The three hunters decided to conduct a mini-drive, each walking slowly in hopes of crossing paths with the buck should it be bedded in the brushy, 5-acre woodlot.

As the trio of camouflaged hunters moved through the

Another Bucks County non-typical buck killed by David Funk of Newtown currently holds 5th place in the category. The 14-pointer scored 163-7.

The 1989 measuring program included entries by (left to right): Wayne Edwards of New Castle (10th all-time typical bow-buck; 153 points from Lawrence County in 1981); Lewis Black (typical gun category; 174-1 from Beaver County in 1979): and Richard Carl of Shamokin (7th non-typical gun-buck all-time; 197 points from Northumberland County in 1982).

dense undergrowth about 40 yards apart, one of them spooked the buck as he hastily shot and missed. Seconds later the second hunter also made an errant, rushed shot. Hesitating to leave the heavy cover, the buck slipped along a creek-bed with its head to the ground, eventually passing by Funk at only 15 yards.

"I led him a little bit and shot," he recalls. "I knew I hit him. We waited about 20 minutes and just couldn't take it anymore so we went looking for it. We found him 20 yards away in the underbrush.

For accounts of other Pennsylvania book-bucks, check out Pennsylvania's Big Game Records: 1965-1986. Get it from the Game Commission for $10 postpaid (state tax included) by calling 1-888-888-3459.

PENNSYLVANIA'S ALL-TIME RECORD BOOK BUCKS

TOP 10 TYPICAL GUN BUCKS

NAME	HOMETOWN	COUNTY TAKEN	YEAR	SCORE
Fritz Janowsky	Wellsburg, NY	Bradford	1943	189-0
Ivan Parry	Graysville	Greene	1974	184-6
Chester Allison	Roaring	Spring Blair	1951	182-5
Floyd Reibson	N/A	Sullivan	1931	180-4
Raymond E. Miller	Bedford	Bedford	1957	177-5
Perry Kinley	N/A	Jefferson	1920	177-0
John Zerbe	N/A	Mifflin	1936	176-5
Clyde Rinehuls	Sayre	Bradford	1944	176-0
Arthur Young	N/A	McKean	1930	175-4
Robert Hoffman	Mt. Pleasant	Westmoreland	1949	174-6

TOP 10 NON-TYPICAL GUN BUCKS

Edward Dodge	Knox	Erie	1942	238-6
A.L. Prouty	Tampa, FL	Lycoming	1949	214-0
Ralph Landis	N/A	Juniata	1951	207-7
Robert W. Rozetar	Pottsville	Schuylkill	1948	207-4
R.K. Mellon	Ligonier	Westmoreland	1966	200-1
Kevin Brumgard	Mt. Wolf	York	1992	197-6
Richard Carl	Shamokin	Northumberland	1982	197-0
Kenneth Resinger	Ickesburg	Perry	1949	196-6
Edward G. Ligus	Greensburg	Westmoreland	1956	196-0
C.K. Bero	Hopwood	Fayette	1949	195-4

TOP 10 TYPICAL BOW BUCKS

A.J. Muntz	Havertown	Bucks	1993	175-5
Ralph Stoltenberg, Jr.	Butler	Butler	1986	174-2
Christopher Joyce	Pittsburgh	Allegheny	1985	167-6
Donald Epprecht	Mont Clare	Montgomery	1993	163-3
Jeff McConeghy	Clairton	Allegheny	1991	161-3
Gregory Sarvey	Alliquippa	Beaver	1990	155-2
Andrew Getsy	Patton	Cambria	1965	155-1
Brian Jones	N/A	Somerset	1988	153-7
Jodi Korff	Gibsonia	Allegheny	1985	153-0
Wayne Edwards	New Castle	Lawrence	1981	153-0

TOP 10 NON-TYPICAL BOW BUCKS

Craig Krisher	Allentown	Lehigh	1988	203-3
Robert Mertiff	Tyrone	Northumberland	N/A	192-5
David Krempasky	Ambler	Montgomery	1985	187-2
Timothy Hunyady	Roncoe	Fayette	1988	178-0
David Funk	Newtown	Bucks	1994	163-7
Willis S. Kuhns	Ligonier	Westmoreland	1970	161-2
Paul Weisser Jr.	Numedia	Westmoreland	1989	161-1
Thomas Cammarota	Media	Delaware	1986	158-7
George Hendricks	Ligonier	Westmoreland	1977	152-5
Thomas Griffith	Apollo	Westmoreland	1990	143-2

Antlerless deer permits are available only through county fiscal offices.

CHAPTER 25

PENNSYLVANIA PROFILES
A County-by-County Reference Guide

Public hunting lands scattered across Pennsylvania total nearly four million acres, ranging from gamelands, Game Commission cooperative programs and state forests to federal acreage and local watershed and municipal lands.

Few, if any, states in the East offer the range and variety of public access landscape as found in Pennsylvania. Open hunting lands can be had in almost every county with the widest choices in the more remote areas of the state.

Detailed on the following pages are the most extensive and concise listings of deer hunting information ever published under one cover. Information was gathered from a variety of private and government agencies.

The county listings are as accurate as possible, considering the many changes (such as acreage added to gamelands) continually taking place. Figures are as precise as possible, considering that public recreation lands are under the jurisdictions of more than a half-dozen government agencies and dozens of local and regional bureaus.

Profiles of Pennsylvania's 67 counties are given as a guide to choosing the best hunting lands based on deer numbers, public hunting opportunities, available food and lodging and, of course, deer hunting potential. The most recent harvests and deer population estimates are included for comparison.

Maps show the relative locations of gamelands, state forests, state parks and roads in each county. Precise locations and major and secondary roads leading to the hunting lands are shown on official Pennsylvania Dept. of Transportation highway maps.

However, co-op agreements and other private land-use programs change annually. Lands may be shifted in and out of the program for varied reasons or acreage will be reduced or expanded from time to time.

Anyone wanting updated information on specific tracts should contact the Game Commission, forest and parks departments, federal agencies or individual cooperators for details. Sources of information are provided along with addresses and telephone numbers.

State Game Lands

Nearly 1.4 million acres of gamelands on more than 300 tracts are owned and managed by the Pennsylvania Game Commission. These properties were purchased at $400 per acre or less, beginning in 1920 when the first gameland was bought in Elk County for $2.50 per acre. Most of the funds for setting aside these

Nearly 1.4 million acres of gamelands bought by hunters' license dollars also benefits non-game species, such as this meadowlark singing atop a post at the Middle Creek Wildlife Management Area in southeastern Pennsylvania.

properties, open to the general public, were funded through hunting license dollars. No tax money was involved in this massive land conservation program.

Detailed maps of individual gamelands are available (cost: $1 postpaid) through the Pennsylvania Game Commission's regional offices and the Harrisburg headquarters. The 9x15-inch Sportsmen's Recreation Maps show streams, roads and towns in the surrounding area plus trails, roads, parking lots and prominent natural land features within each gameland.

Of value to every hunter seeking open lands is the set of six Outdoor Recreation Maps, one for each of the commission's half-dozen regions, depicting public and leased lands open for hunting. In addition, each map shows municipalities, roads, drainage areas, contour intervals and other physical features to help the user become familiar with the region. The 24x36-inch maps can be purchased at or mail-ordered through commission offices (see addresses in regional listings). Each map folds to a convenient 6x9-inch size. The maps are printed on spun-bonded stock which resists fraying and tearing.

In recent years, portions of 88 roads on gamelands have been opened to all-terrain vehicles (ATVs) by qualified holders of "disabled person permits." The vehicles may be used as hunting blinds. Contact your Game Commission regional office for details.

State Parks and Forests

The Dept. of Conservation and Natural Resources owns and manages Pennsylvania's state forests and parklands. The Bureau of State Parks is in charge of the latter; the Bureau of Forestry handles the former. Some parks are located within or adjacent to state forests.

Pennsylvania has 114 state parks, many offering camping, fishing, hiking and hunting, although hunting is not available at all parks. In the larger parklands, however, hunting land is available with Safety Zone areas strictly enforced. In some suburban parks, controlled deer hunts are conducted every year or two.

The parks also offer camping and several have modern cabins for rent throughout the four seasons.

Maps and information on specific state parks are available by writing: Pennsylvania Dept. of Conservation and Natural Resources, Bureau of State Parks, P.O. Box 8551, Harrisburg, PA 17105-8551. Or call 1-888-PA-PARKS.

More than 2.2 million acres of state forests in 44 counties are under the auspices of 20 offices across the state. The lands are managed to provide sustained yields of timber, protect watersheds, conserve water and afford recreational opportunities. More than 2,600 miles of roads and 2,500 miles of hiking trails penetrate these lands.

More than two million acres, most open to hunting, are available in state parks and forests.

In most regions, forest lands are not contiguous. Rather, they're scattered across a region in specific tracts. Highway maps clearly show access and borders of all public forest lands.

For specific information on hunting state forest lands, contact the following offices.

FOREST DISTRICT OFFICES

Forest District	Address	Telephone
Michaux S.F.	10099 Lincoln Way East, Fayetteville, PA 17222	(717) 352-2211
Buchanan S.F.	RD 2, Box 3, McConnellsburg, PA 17233	(717) 485-3148
Tuscarora S.F.	RD 1, Box 42A, Blain, PA 17006	(717) 536-3191
Forbes S.F.	POB 519, Laughlintown, PA 15655	(724) 238-1200
Rothrock S.F.	Box 403, Rothrock Lane, Smithfield, Huntingdon, PA 16652	(814)643-2340
Gallitzin S.F.	131 Hillcrest Dr., Ebensburg, PA 15031	(814) 472-1862

Forest District	Address	Telephone
Bald Eagle S.F.	POB 147, Laurelton, PA 17835	(570) 922-3344
Kittanning S.F.	RD 3, Box 705, Clarion, PA 16214	(814) 226-1901
Moshannon S.F.	Box 952, Clearfield, PA 16830	(814) 765-0821
Sproul S.F.	HCR 62, Box 90, Renovo, PA 17764	(570) 923-6011
Lackawanna S.F.	Rm. 401, 100 Lackawanna Ave., Scranton, PA 18503	(570) 963-4561
Tiadaghton S.F.	423 E. Central Ave., S. Williamsport, PA 17701	(570) 327-3450
Elk S.F.	RD 1, Route 155, Box 327, Emporium, PA 15834	(814) 486-3353
Cornplanter S.F.	323 N. State St., North Warren, PA 16365	(814) 723-0262
Susquehannock S.F.	P.O. Box 673, Coudersport, PA 16915	(814) 274-3600
Tioga S.F.	Box 94, Route 287 S, Wellsboro, PA 16901	(570) 724-2868
Valley Forge S.F.	RD 2, Route 23, Pottstown, PA 19464	(610) 582-9660
Weiser S.F.	Box 99, Cressona, PA 17929	(570) 385-7800
Delaware S.F.	POB 150, 474 Clearview Lane, Stroudsburg, PA 18360	(570) 895-4000
Wyoming S.F.	POB 439, Bloomsburg, PA 17815	(570) 387-4255

Farm-Game and Safety Zone Co-ops

Some 4.7 million acres of Farm-Game, Forest-Game and Safety Zone Cooperatives are available to hunters. The lands are privately owned with certain landowner benefits afforded participants. The Game Commission does not publish specific listings of these properties but information is available through regional offices. Keep your eyes peeled while cruising backroads as most co-ops have special signs on the property borders.

The general location of co-op lands are shown on the Regional Outdoor Recreation Maps previously mentioned.

Forest-Game Co-ops

More than 600,000 Forest-Game Co-ops are scattered across the state, courtesy of more than 50 owners of large tracts of private woodlands. They're most abundant in big-woods and mountain country where timber and pulpwood, oil, gas, coal, water authority and other companies and individuals open all or portions of their holdings for public hunting. However, some of them are close to larger towns and cities.

Again, the properties are not detailed on Game Commission maps as they're in a near-constant state of change. However, the Outdoor Recreation Maps do show general areas where such properties are located.

As of this writing, the following Forest-Game Cooperators were offering open recreation lands.

Forest-Game Cooperatives

• Adobe Mining Co., Grove City: 1,434 acres; Butler and Venango counties.
• Bailey Estates, Clearfield: 1,276 acres; Clearfield County.

Longtime Pennsylvania Deer Association President Jim Seitz is a regular on Potter County forest co-op lands.

- Blythe Twp. Municipal Authority, New Philadelphia: 2,757 acres; Schuylkill County.
- Bradford City Water Authority, Bradford; 12,000 acres; McKean County.
- E.M. Brown Inc., Clearfield: 5,625 acres; Clearfield County.
- James & Shirley Burke, Weedville: 1,000 acres; Elk County.
- Camp Mack Boy Scout Camp, Lancaster: 1,600 acres; Lancaster and Lebanon counties.
- Chatham Water Co., Woolrich: 5,200 acres; Clinton and Lycoming counties.
- Matson Lumber, Inc., Brookville: 20,000 acres; Clarion, Crawford, Forest, Indiana, Venango and Warren counties.
- Minersville Borough Municipal Authority, Minersville: 4,500 acres; Schuylkill county.
- National Fuel Gas Supply Corp, Erie: 1,709 acres; Elk, Forest, McKean and Warren counties.
- Nesquehoning Borough Water Auth., Nesquehoning: 2,553 acres; Carbon County.
- New Holland Borough, New Holland: 2,500 acres; Lancaster County.
- Northern Forests Co., Smethport: 5,000 acres; Cameron and Elk counties.
- P&N Coal Co., Punxsutawney: 1,807 acres; Armstrong, Clearfield, Elk, Indiana and Jefferson counties.
- Pennsylvania Electric Co., Johnstown: 1,350 acres; Wyoming County.
- Collins Pine Co., Kane: 104,108 acres; Cameron, Clarion, Elk, Forest, Jefferson, McKean, Potter and Warren counties.
- Cooney Bros. Coal Co., Cresson: 9,321 acres; Blair and Cambria counties.
- Curtin Real Estate, Bellefonte: 6,455 acres; Centre County.
- City of Dubois, Dubois: 4,684 acres; Clearfield County.
- East Broadtop Railroad, Rockhill Furnace: 5,000 acres; Huntingdon County.
- Elk Lick Reserve, Smethport: 1,500 acres; McKean County.
- Girard Estate, Girardville: 1,367 acres; Schuylkill County.

- Glatfelter Pulp Wood Co., Spring Grove: 24,385 acres; Bedford, Cumberland, Franklin, Fulton, Huntingdon, Juniata, Mifflin, Perry and Snyder counties.
- Borough of Hamburg, Hamburg: 4,300 acres; Berks County.
- Hauto Estates, Nesquehoning: 3,258 acres; Carbon County.
- HEJ Corp., Mt. Pocono: 1,763 acres; Clinton County.
- International Paper Co., Erie: 22,500 acres; Cameron, Forest, McKean, Potter, Venango and Warren counties.
- Larimer & Norton Inc., Warren: 1,078 acres; Warren county.
- M.A. Lawson, Warren: 1,200 acres; Warren County.
- City of Lock Haven, Lock Haven: 5,200 acres; Clinton County.
- Mahanoy Township Authority, Mahanoy City: 1,784 acres; Schuylkill County.
- Mallery Lumber Corp., Emporium: 59,220 acres; Cameron, Elk, Jefferson and McKean counties.
- Mansfield Water Co., Mansfield: 1,100 acres; Tioga County.
- Pine Grove Borough, Pine Grove: 2,036 acres; Schuylkill County.
- Quaker State Oil Refining Corp., Titusville: 12,546 acres; Crawford, Forest, McKean, Warren and Venango counties.
- Ram Forest Products Inc., Shinglehouse: 11,823 acres; Elk, McKean and Potter counties.
- Roaring Spring Borough, Roaring Springs: 1,400 acres; Blair County.
- Rochester & Pittsburgh Coal Co., Indiana: 30,285 acres; Armstrong, Clearfield, Clinton, Indiana and Jefferson counties.
- Schuylkill County Commissioners, Pottsville: 3,292 acres; Schuylkill County.
- Schuylkill Haven Borough, Schuylkill: 4,500 acres; Schuylkill County.
- Seneca Resources Corp., Erie: 75,591 acres; Armstrong, Cameron, Clarion, Elk, Forest, Jefferson, McKean, Mercer and Venango counties.
- S.F. Properties Inc., Coudersport: 26,210 acres; Potter and Tioga counties.
- St. Mary's Area Joint Water Auth. St. Marys: 1,860 in Elk County.
- Stone Valley Exp. Forest, University Park: 6,182 acres in Huntingdon County.
- Borough of Tyrone, Tyrone: 3,634 acres in Blair County.
- West Penn Power Co., Greensburg: 2,300 acres; Armstrong County.
- West Penn Power/Allegheny-Pittsburgh Coal Co., Greensburg: 4,235 acres; Washington County.
- Westmoreland Co., Greensburg: 4,182 acres; Westmoreland and Fayette counties.

Harvest/Density Information

In addition to available hunting lands, information provided under each county's "In Brief" listing includes the most recent (1999) buck and doe harvests (totals from all seasons), archery and muzzleloader season harvests, estimated deer densities, density goals and buck harvests based on the amount of forested square miles (designated as FSM). Of course, these figures change each year but remain proportionately similar.

The information is provided as ready reference and for the reader to make comparisons of deer hunting opportunities in each of the state's 67 "management units."

Food, Lodging and Services

An address and telephone number for requesting information on food, lodging and services is included in each county profile.

Federal Lands

In addition to state and co-op lands, many federal lands are also open to hunters. National forest, military, Corps of Engineers, National Wildlife Refuge and National Recreation Area lands are detailed at the end of the county information section.

Although Pennsylvania can't match the immensity of Bureau of Land Management, U.S. Forest Service, National Monument and other federal lands in the West open to hunting, the Keystone State does have a variety of scattered, federal properties open to public recreation, including hunting.

For specifics on deer hunting opportunities on the following sites, contact the management offices via the addresses and phone numbers provided.

Allegheny National Forest

The most notable federal parcel in the state is Allegheny National Forest, spanning more than a half-million acres south of the New York border in Warren, McKean, Elk and Forest counties. The multiple-use, 512,000-acre forest is a whitetail, small game and turkey hunter's delight.

The focal point for anglers, boaters and some hunters, who gain access to the backwoods via boats and canoes, is the Allegheny Reservoir, completed in 1965 by the U.S. Corps of Engineers as a flood control project. The high-walled Kinzua Dam blocks the waters of the Allegheny River, backing the lake 27 miles into New York's Allegany State Park and the Seneca Indian Reservation.

Black bear, deer, grouse, squirrel, snowshoe hare and waterfowl abound in the region and many hunters utilize the numerous motels and bed-and-breakfast operations nearby (see individual county listings for information sources).

More than 65 million board feet of timber is harvested from the Allegheny N. F. each year, creating a diverse array of clearcuts and second growth habitat, prime for whitetails. The forest stands include red and white oak, black cherry, yellow poplar, white ash, red maple, sugar maple and scatterings of softwoods.

It should be noted that numerous in-holdings are found within the federal property. Free maps, available from the forest service, designate the private lands as do signs and other markers along backwoods roads and within the woodlands.

Many miles of well-maintained forest roads lead to scenic overlooks and picnic areas throughout the playground, although most are not plowed in winter. Nearby towns of Warren, Bradford, Kane and Ridgway offer food, lodging and shopping. Numerous private campgrounds are also located within or adjacent to the national forest. A few national forest campgrounds stay open through the deer season.

For hunting information and maps, write: Allegheny National Forest, P.O. Box 847, Warren, PA 16365. Phone: (814) 723-5150.

U.S. Army Corps of Engineers

The U.S. Army Corps of Engineers owns and manages 23 facilities in Pennsylvania open to recreational use. While fishing is the main attraction on corps' impoundments, some also offer hunting lands surrounding the lakes and dams. Many of the properties adjoin or are within state forests, parks and gamelands.

Federal properties open to hunting include: Raystown Lake (Huntingdon County), Francis Walter Dam (Carbon-Luzerne), Crooked Creek Lake (Armstrong), Blue Marsh Lake (Berks), Cowanesque Lake (Tioga), Loyalhanna Lake (Westmoreland), Mahoning Creek Lake (Armstrong, Jefferson and Indiana), Shenango River lake (Mercer), Tioga-Hammond Lakes (Tioga), Tionesta Lake (Forest), Woodcock Creek Lake (Crawford) and Youghiogheny Lake (Somerset and Fayette).

For additional information and brochures, call or write the office closest to the specific facility.

- *U.S. Army Engineer Dist., POB Box 1715, Baltimore, MD 21203-1715. Phone: (301) 962-3693.*
- *U.S. Army Engineer Dist., Wanamaker Bldg., 1001 Penn Square East, Philadelphia, PA 19107-3390. Phone: (215) 656-6515.*
- *U.S. Army Engineer Dist., Wm. S. Moorhead Federal Bldg., 1000 Liberty Ave., Pittsburgh, PA 15222-4186. Phone: (412) 644-6924.*

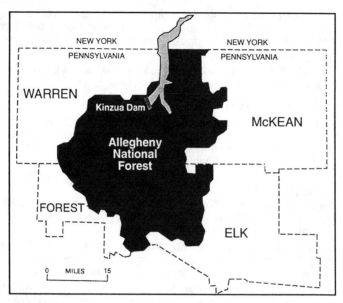

Military Installations

Several military installations in the state permit hunting, with restrictions. Officers may also conduct controlled hunts to reduce deer numbers within the federal lands. These are not "public" lands in the true sense of the word, rather restricted grounds with access by permit.

Beginning in 1994, the Pennsylvania Game Commission issued "deer control permits" to military bases. This allows the bases to conduct deer hunts without requiring participating hunters to have doe licenses from the counties in which the facilities are located.

Posts draw up management plans and, along with the commission, determine how many permits are needed to cull specific numbers of antlerless deer. The Dept. of Defense pays the commission $5 for each permit. Licensed Pennsylvania hunters must apply directly to the installations. Drawings are conducted whenever applications exceed available permits. If applicants are fewer than the license allotment, individuals are allowed more than one permit.

By law, military installations may set their own seasons, typically for limited periods between October and February.

Military bases offering hunting opportunities include:

• *Fort Indiantown Gap, USAG, Annville, PA 17003-5011. Phone (717) 865-5444 or (717) 865-2362. (18,000 acres in Lebanon County)*
• *Letterkenny Army Depot, Chambersburg, PA 17201-4150. Phone (717) 267-8300. (19,000 acres in Franklin County)*

National Wildlife Refuges

Two National Wildlife Refuges are found within Pennsylvania borders. John Heinz (Tinicum) N.W.R. is an urban sanctuary in Philadelphia. Hunting is not permitted.

Erie National Wildlife Refuge in Guys Mills, Crawford County, east of Meadville, permits hunting on much of its 8,516 acres. The refuge is divided into the Seneca Division and Sugar Lake Division, each with different ecological attributes.

For information write: Erie N.W.R., RD 1, Wood Duck Lane, Guys Mills, PA 16327. Phone: (814) 789-3585.

Delaware Water Gap National Recreation Area

The Delaware Water Gap National Recreation includes the Delaware River in Monroe and Pike counties and New Jersey. Under jurisdiction of the National Park

Service, hunting is permitted on portions of the 70,000-acre facility, about half of which is in Pennsylvania's Pike and Monroe counties.

For information, write: Delaware Water Gap N.R.A., Bushkill, PA 18324. Phone: (570) 588-2435.

County Treasurers

In Pennsylvania, County Fiscal Offices (a.k.a. County Treasurers) handle all doe license applications and sales. Each year hunters apply to counties for regular and leftover permits. Hunters applying for doe permits after the initial application days, or non-residents who must apply at a later date, are advised to call the fiscal offices to check on license availability prior to sending their applications. Regular hunting and fishing licenses and permits are also sold by county treasurers.

Potter and Philadelphia counties' doe tag sales are handled through the respective regional offices of the Game Commission.

COUNTY TREASURERS' OFFICES

Adams (717) 334-6781
Allegheny (412) 350-4103
Armstrong (724) 548-3260
Beaver (724) 728-5700
Bedford (814) 623-4846
Berks (610) 478-6643
Blair (814) 695-5541
Bradford (570) 265-1700
Bucks (215) 348-6244
Butler (724) 284-5151
Cambria (814) 472-5440
Cameron (814) 486-3348
Carbon (570) 325-2251
Centre (814) 355-6810
Chester (610) 344-6370
Clarion (814) 226-4000
Clearfield (814) 765-2641
Clinton (570) 893-4004
Columbia (570) 389-5626
Crawford (814) 336-1151
Cumberland (717) 240-6380
Dauphin (717) 255-2677
Delaware (610) 891-4000
Elk (814) 776-1161
Erie (814) 451-6203
Fayette (724) 430-1256
Forest (814) 755-3536
Franklin (717) 261-3119
Fulton (717) 485-4454
Greene (724) 852-5225
Huntingdon (814) 643-3523
Indiana (724) 465-3845
Jefferson (814) 849-1608
Juniata (717) 436-8991

Lackawanna (570) 963-6731
Lancaster (717) 299-8222
Lawrence (724) 658-2541
Lebanon (717) 274-2801
Lehigh (610) 782-3112
Luzerne (570) 825-1764
Lycoming (570) 327-2249
McKean (814) 887-5571
Mercer (724) 662-3800
Mifflin (717) 248-8439
Monroe (570) 420-3515
Montgomery (610) 278-3070
Montour (570) 271-3016
Northampton (610) 559-3000
Northumberland (717) 988-4161
Perry (717) 582-8984
Philadelphia (610) 926-3136
Pike (570) 296-3441
Potter (717) 398-4744
Schuylkill (570) 628-1433
Snyder (570) 837-4221
Somerset (814) 445-2071
Sullivan (570) 946-7331
Susquehanna (570) 278-3579
Tioga (717) 724-9213
Union (570) 524-8781
Vernango (814) 437-9500
Warren (814) 728-3415
Washington (724) 228-6780
Wayne (570) 253-5970
Westmoreland (724) 830-3167
Wyoming (570) 836-3200
York (717) 771-9603

NORTHWEST REGION

"The Northwest" is comprised of two geographic areas. The line representing the southern extent of the Wisconsin Glacier, here some 70,000 years ago, runs diagonally from the northeast to the southwest, cutting the region in half. Land in the glacial zone, north of the line, is characterized by small ponds, swampy depressions and knob-like mounds of sand and gravel. The glaciated part tends to be damper, flatter and more suited to agriculture than the more hilly and forested land to the south. The land not affected by the glacier is characterized by the "big woods" of Warren, Forest, Jefferson and Clarion counties. The terrain is marked by deep river valleys and steep hills and mountains. "For big game hunters, deer, turkey and bear are getting more plentiful and widespread with each passing year."

Bob MacWilliams, Pennsylvania Game Commission

Pennsylvania Game Commission
Northwest Region
P.O. Box 31
Franklin, PA 16323
Phone: Toll free 1 (877) 877-0299; (814) 432-3187; (814) 432-3188
Butler, Clarion, Crawford, Erie, Forest, Jefferson, Lawrence, Mercer, Venango and Warren

BUTLER COUNTY

Situated north of Pittsburgh, Butler County ranks high on the list of counties with trophy whitetail potential. Covering 789 square miles, Butler's landscape is largely hills and broad sandstone and shale ridges along with mountainous country composing the Allegheny Plateau. Elevations range from 740 to 1,580 feet.

Fifty-one percent of the county is forested with another 30 percent in farmland (half in harvested cropland). The primary crops are oats and corn.

Butler holds two state gamelands tracts, the largest SGL No. 95 near Old Annandale with 8,536 acres. Much of the 13,600-acre Moraine State Park is also open to deer hunters. A scattering of mature oak woodlots bordering crop farms make this a prime whitetail spot.

Food, lodging and services, contact: Butler County Tourist Promotion Agency, 201 South Main St., Butler, PA 16003. Phone: (888) 741-6772 or (724) 283-2222.

IN BRIEF:

State Gamelands: 8,935 acres

State Parks & Forests: 13,640 acres

Farm-Game Co-op: 13,500 acres (126 farms)

Forest-Game Co-op: 77 acres

Safety Zone Lands: 59,000 acres (500 tracts)

1999 Buck/Doe Harvest: 4,617/4,317

1999 Archery Buck/Doe Harvest: 1,453/683

1999 Muzzleloader Buck/Doe Harvest: 22/371

Forested Square Miles (FSM): 397

1999 Buck Harvest/FSM: 11.6

Winter Deer Density/FSM: 47

Desired Winter Deer Density/FSM: 23

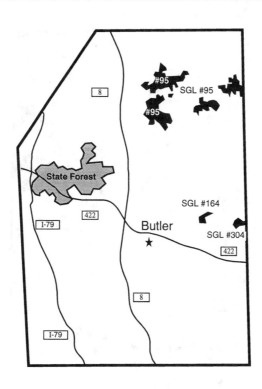

CLARION COUNTY

Farmland makes up one-fourth of Clarion's 607 square miles of landscape, about three-fourths of that in livestock production. Hay, corn, oats and wheat are its primarily crops.

Mountainous with rolling hills and steep ridges, the plentiful second and third growth hardwood forests are home to numerous whitetails. About 60 percent of the county is forested with elevations ranging from 740 to 1,580 feet. Reclaimed strip-mines have also improved wildlife habitat here.

Three large gamelands tracts hold deer: SGL No. 65 near Shippenville (3,413 acres); SGL No. 72 near Clarion (2,025 acres); and SGL No. 74 near Strattanville (6,320 acres).

Cook Forest State Park near Cooksburg has 4,000 acres open to hunters.

Food, lodging and services, contact: Northern Pennsylvania's Great Outdoors Visitors Bureau, 175 Main St., Brookville, PA 15825. Phone: (800) 348-9393 or (814) 849-5197.

IN BRIEF:

State Gamelands: 11,758 acres

State Parks & Forests: 4,000 acres

Farm-Game Co-op: 40,000 acres (377 farms)

Forest-Game Co-op: 4,884 acres

Safety Zone Lands: 20,424 acres (140 tracts)

1999 Buck/Doe Harvest: 3,197/3,028

1999 Archery Buck/Doe Harvest: 595/350

1999 Muzzleloader Buck/Doe Harvest: 7/249

Forested Square Miles (FSM): 370

1999 Buck Harvest/FSM: 8.6

Winter Deer Density/FSM: 41

Desired Winter Deer Density/FSM: 26

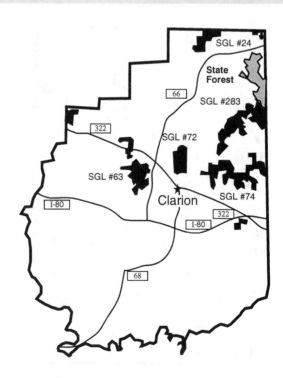

CRAWFORD COUNTY

South of Lake Erie on the Ohio border, Crawford may be best known for its great fishing potential and its attraction for waterfowl but it's also one of the state's top trophy whitetail counties.

Its 1,011 square miles are hilly and mountainous in some places with an abundance of low wetland and riparian areas. Woodlots and forests make up 48 percent of the county.

A dozen separate gamelands tracts are scattered across Crawford, many in wetlands and all with woodlands. Gamelands acreage ranges from 154 to 5,555, with some new additions in the early 1990s. Erie National Wildlife Refuge, one of two such federal refuges in Pennsylvania and the only one on which hunting is permitted, is located at Guys Mills.

Most of Pymatuning State Park's 18,275 acres are open to hunters.

It's here and in other farmland-wetland areas where hunters stand the chance of encountering big bucks, for which Crawford is known. The sector from Meadville north for a couple dozen miles or more into neighboring Erie County draws considerable hunter attention.

Food, lodging and services, contact: Crawford County Convention and Visitors Bureau, 211 Chestnut St., Meadville, PA 16335. Phone: (800) 332-2338 or (814) 333-1258.

IN BRIEF:

State Gamelands: 22,380 acres
State Parks & Forests: 18,275 acres
Farm-Game Co-op: 72,000 acres (725 farms)
Forest-Game Co-op: 3,585 acres
Safety Zone Lands: 43,000 acres (319 tracts)

1999 Buck/Doe Harvest: 4,864/4,998
1999 Archery Buck/Doe Harvest: 1,077/803
1999 Muzzleloader Buck/Doe Harvest: 38/461
Forested Square Miles (FSM): 485
1999 Buck Harvest/FSM: 10.0
Winter Deer Density/FSM: 39
Desired Winter Deer Density/FSM: 19

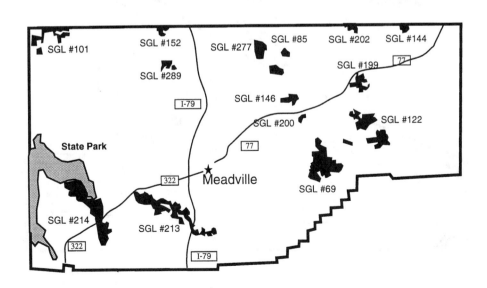

ERIE COUNTY

The only county touching a Great Lake, Erie County's deer hunting takes a back seat to its fishing potential. However, Erie regularly produces trophy-class bucks on its 804 square miles of terrain.

As part of the glaciated region, its rich soils support 47 percent of the county that's forested. The terrain is rolling with swampy valley floors and occasional wet uplands. Elevations span 573 to 1,900 feet.

Farms occupy 39 percent of the county, providing potatoes, oats, corn and apples, all to the liking of hungry deer.

Erie has more gamelands (13) than any other Northwest Region county, with nearly 14,000 acres. Similar to neighboring Crawford County, many gamelands tracts are composed of wetland and woodland habitat. It's in this mix of marshlands and farmlands that the biggest deer make their homes.

Food, lodging and services, contact: Erie Area Convention and Visitors Bureau, 109 Boston Store Place, Erie, PA 16501. Phone: (814) 454-7191.

IN BRIEF:

State Gamelands: 13,885 acres

State Parks & Forests: None

Farm-Game Co-op: 31,000 acres (295 farms)

Forest-Game Co-op: None

Safety Zone Lands: 46,000 acres (338 tracts)

1999 Buck/Doe Harvest: 3,203/3,248

1999 Archery Buck/Doe Harvest: 931/742

1999 Muzzleloader Buck/Doe Harvest: 12/165

Forested Square Miles (FSM): 373

1999 Buck Harvest/FSM: 8.6

Winter Deer Density/FSM: 36

Desired Winter Deer Density/FSM: 29

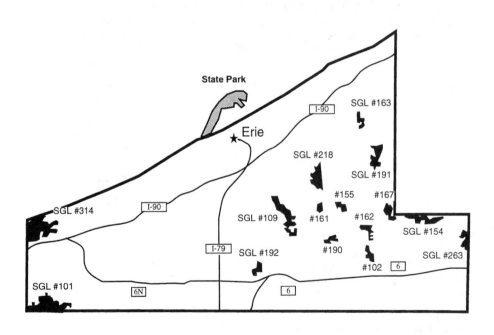

FOREST COUNTY

Covering only 428 square miles, Forest County lies within the Allegheny Plateau region with elevations from 1,040 to 1,944 feet. As with most other northwestern counties, its topography is hilly and mountainous in some regions, with deep stream valleys.

However, as its name implies, 93 percent of the county is covered in woodland. Farms here occupy only three percent of the land, placing it in the bottom four in the state in agricultural importance. The county is also the least populous in the state with only a dozen people per square mile.

Two sizable public hunting tracts are available including 2,247-acres of Kittanning State Forest and SGL No. 24 near Newmanville with 8,390 wooded acres.

Flavoring the entire county's scenery and recreational opportunities is Allegheny National Forest, composing more wildlands than a hunter could cover in a lifetime. All national forest land, save for inholdings and safety zone areas, is open to hunting.

Food, lodging and services, contact: Northwest Pennsylvania's Great Outdoors Visitors Bureau, 175 Main St., Brookville, PA 15825. Phone: (800) 348-9393 or (814) 849-5197.

IN BRIEF:

State Gamelands: 8,390 acres

State Parks & Forests: 2,247 acres

Farm-Game Co-op: None

Forest-Game Co-op: 53,081 acres

Safety Zone Lands: 16,236 acres (80 tracts)

1999 Buck/Doe Harvest: 2,764/2,724

1999 Archery Buck/Doe Harvest: 330/368

1999 Muzzleloader Buck/Doe Harvest: 7/164

Forested Square Miles (FSM): 397

1999 Buck Harvest/FSM: 7.0

Winter Deer Density/FSM: 39

Desired Winter Deer Density/FSM: 23

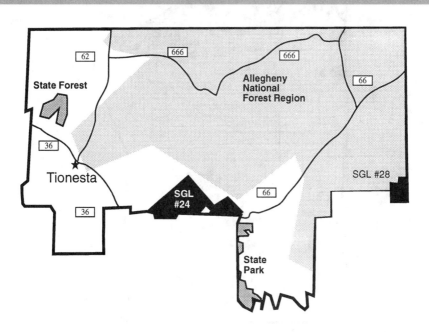

JEFFERSON COUNTY

Like most counties in this region, the hilly countryside ranges in elevation from 1,100 to 2,220 feet with some steep mountains and broad ridges. Some 61 percent of Jefferson's 657 square miles is forested.

Topography is rugged and reclaimed strip mines now covered with grass and planted trees are obvious, and beneficial to deer. Cattle pastures and croplands cover 21 percent of the county, the latter producing alfalfa, corn and grains.

Kittanning State Forest, northeast of Munderf, offers 9,380 acres of public hunting lands with five gamelands providing another 39,723 acres. The biggest is mountainous SGL No. 54 near Brockway with 22,049 acres followed by 6,564-acre SGL No. 283 near Cooksburg's oil well country and hilly SGL No. 31 (5,176 acres) near Punxsutawney.

Food, lodging and services, contact: Northwest Pennsylvania's Great Outdoors Visitors Bureau, 175 Main St., Brookville, PA 15825. Phone: (800) 348-9393 or (814) 849-5197.

IN BRIEF:

State Gamelands: 39,951
State Parks & Forests: 9,590 acres
Farm-Game Co-op: 67,145 acres (401 farms)
Forest-Game Co-op: 11,315 acres
Safety Zone Lands: 24,196 acres (162 tracts)

1999 Buck/Doe Harvest: 3,305/3,651
1999 Archery Buck/Doe Harvest: 661/432
1999 Muzzleloader Buck/Doe Harvest: 6/193
Forested Square Miles (FSM): 403
1999 Buck Harvest/FSM: 8.2
Winter Deer Density/FSM: 37
Desired Winter Deer Density/FSM: 19

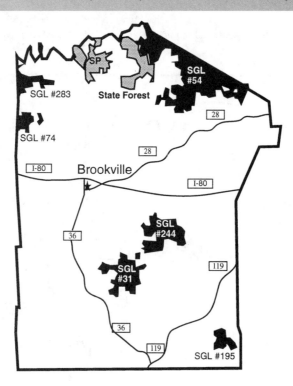

LAWRENCE COUNTY

Typical of most of the Allegheny Plateau, Lawrence County's landscape is characterized by hills and mountains ranging in elevation from 760 to 1,440 feet. Swampy valleys and moist uplands are typical of the region, which borders Ohio on the west.

Forty-two percent of the county is wooded with an equal amount of acreage in farmland. Livestock farming exceeds crop production, the latter primarily alfalfa, corn, oats and wheat.

Five sizable gamelands tracts are open to hunters. The biggest is 21,821-acre SGL No. 54 near Brockway followed by 6,564-acre SGL No. 283 near Cooksburg.

The average deer harvest numbers slightly over 2,000.

Food, lodging and services, contact: Lawrence County Tourist Promotion Agency, 229 South Jefferson St., New Castle, PA 16101. Phone: (888) 284-7599 or (724) 654-7599.

IN BRIEF:

State Gamelands: 2,574 acres

State Parks & Forests: 2,000 acres

Farm-Game Co-op: 74,000 acres (770 farms)

Forest-Game Co-op: None

Safety Zone Lands: 4,900 acres (56 tracts)

1999 Buck/Doe Harvest: 844/1,150

1999 Archery Buck/Doe Harvest: 291/278

1999 Muzzleloader Buck/Doe Harvest: 2/118

Forested Square Miles (FSM): 151

1999 Buck Harvest/FSM: 5.6

Winter Deer Density/FSM:28

Desired Winter Deer Density/FSM: 22

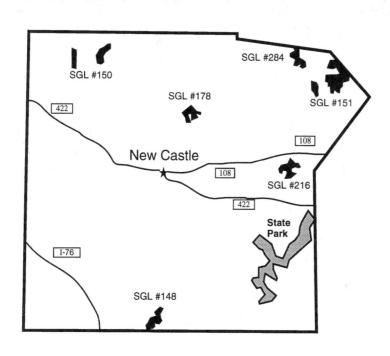

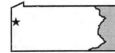

MERCER COUNTY

Set on the Ohio border, 672-square mile Mercer County is covered in hardwoods on 39 percent of the county's landscape.

Hills and mountains ranging from elevations of 822 to 1,620 feet and farms, composing 41 percent of the county, offer varied game habitat. Dairy farming dominates although oats, corn, hay and wheat also benefit whitetails throughout the county.

Mercer's three gamelands all hold deer, the biggest being SGL No. 130 at Sandy Lake with 2,356 acres. Close by, Maurice Goddard State Park offers another 1,316 acres. Add to that 84,000 acres on farm-game holdings and 43,000 acres under Safety Zone projects.

Like Erie and Crawford, Mercer County boasts an abundance of marshlands rich in game. The buck harvest here averages between 9-11 per square forested mile.

Food, lodging and services, contact: Mercer County Convention and Visitors Bureau, 50 North Water St., Sharon, PA 16146. Phone: (800) 637-2370 or (724) 346-3771.

IN BRIEF:

State Gamelands: 4,196 acres

State Parks & Forests: 1,316 acres

Farm-Game Co-op: 84,000 acres (947 farms)

Forest-Game Co-op: 199 acres

Safety Zone Lands: 43,000 acres (371 tracts)

1999 Buck/Doe Harvest: 2,750/3,245

1999 Archery Buck/Doe Harvest: 774/544

1999 Muzzleloader Buck/Doe Harvest: 15/309

Forested Square Miles (FSM): 263

1999 Buck Harvest/FSM: 10.5

Winter Deer Density/FSM: 40

Desired Winter Deer Density/FSM: 22

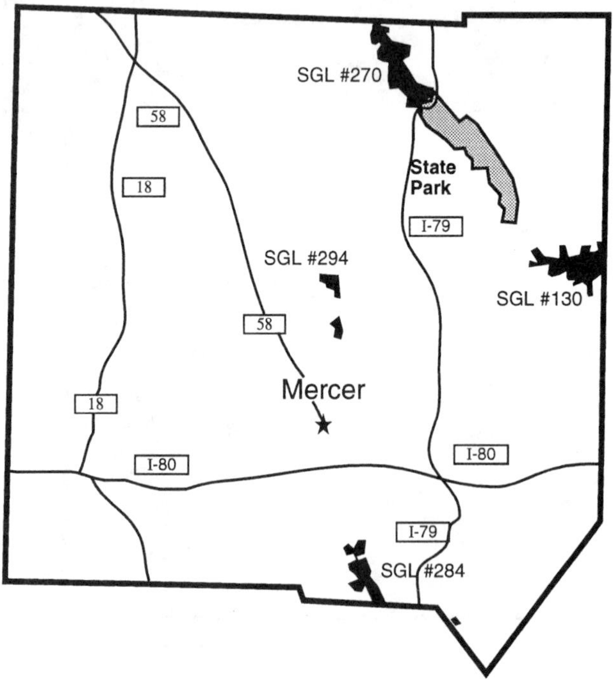

SGL #270

58

18

State Park

I-79

SGL #294

58

SGL #130

18

Mercer

I-80

I-80

I-79

SGL #284

VENANGO COUNTY

Mixed hardwoods characterize this 679 square mile county of hills and steep mountains. Topography consists of irregular woodlands sliced by steep stream valleys.

Fully 72 percent of Venango is forest land with only 15 percent farmland, the latter primarily cattle country with the remainder yielding corn, oats and wheat. Elevations span 860 to 1,725 feet.

Venango's Oil Creek State Park near Oil City offers hunters access to 6,500 acres with five gamelands tracts providing more than 22,000 public acres. The largest is SGL No. 39 near Franklin (9,635 acres) followed by SGL No. 45 at Van (5,170 acres) and SGL No. 96 near Dempseytown (4,973 acres).

Of special note is the sale and transfer to gamelands of the 11,116-acre President Oil Tract costing $3.3 million.

Food, lodging and services, contact: Oil Heritage Region Tourist Promotion Agency, P.O. Box 128, 206 Seneca St., Oil City, PA 16301. Phone: (800) 483-6264 or (814) 677-3152.

IN BRIEF:

State Gamelands: 22,659 acres

State Parks & Forests: 6,500 acres

Farm-Game Co-op: 54,000 acres (farms)

Forest-Game Co-op: 13,127 acres

Safety Zone Lands: 24,711 acres (203 tracts)

1999 Buck/Doe Harvest: 4,129/3,618

1999 Archery Buck/Doe Harvest: 681/411

1999 Muzzleloader Buck/Doe Harvest:20/372

Forested Square Miles (FSM): 485

1999 Buck Harvest/FSM: 8.5

Winter Deer Density/FSM: 34

Desired Winter Deer Density/FSM: 19

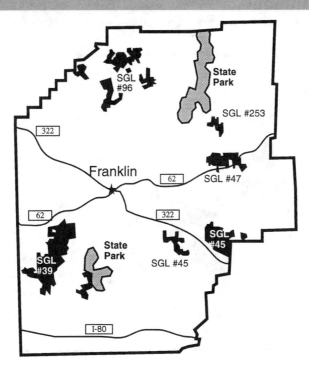

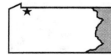

WARREN COUNTY

On the state's northern border, Warren County is well-known as a whitetail haven with an abundance of public hunting grounds. Best known is the 512,000-acre Allegheny National Forest which is shared with McKean, Forest and Elk counties.

Most of the county (79 percent) is in forest. Topography varies from 1,080 to 2,220 feet across the rugged mountains and steep riverine valleys.

Only 15 percent of Warren is farmland, primarily cattle raising land. Hay, corn and oats grow on the five percent of the county devoted to crop farms.

In addition to national forest land, Warren also holds six gamelands, three exceeding 8,000 acres. SGL No. 86 at Tidioute is 14,227 acres, SGL No. 29 near Warren has 9,363 acres and SGL No. 143 near garland, 8,177 acres.

Some hunters use boats to access their deer hunting grounds on the shores of 12,000-acre Allegheny Reservoir (Kinzua Dam) which separates Warren and McKean counties.

Food, lodging and services, contact: Northern Alleghenies Vacation Region, 315 Second Ave., P.O. Box 804, Warren, PA 16365. Phone: (800) 624-7802 or (814) 726-1222.

IN BRIEF:

State Gamelands: 33,768 acres

State Parks & Forests: 360 acres

Farm-Game Co-op: 31,578 acres (239 farms)

Forest-Game Co-op: 18,125 acres

Safety Zone Lands: 44,329 acres (275 tracts)

1999 Buck/Doe Harvest: 4,326/4,848

1999 Archery Buck/Doe Harvest:542/633

1999 Muzzleloader Buck/Doe Harvest: 10/248

Forested Square Miles (FSM): 698

1999 Buck Harvest/FSM: 6.2

Winter Deer Density/FSM: 31

Desired Winter Deer Density/FSM: 21

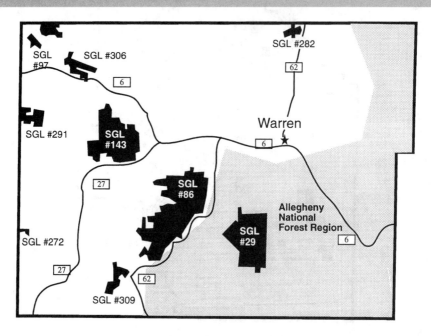

SOUTHWEST REGION

"Grouse and squirrel are thriving in the reverting farmlands and woodlands in this corner of the state. The small timber operations typifying this area further enhance the abundance of many desirable game species. The same habitat diversity and an abundance of foods also mean many deer. Deer hunting is excellent, particularly in certain areas of Armstrong, Beaver, Cambria, Greene, Indiana, Somerset, Washington and Westmoreland counties. Deer in these counties are often heavier and produce larger racks than those found in the highly publicized, more mountainous regions."
**Barry Moore,
Pennsylvania Game Commission**

Pennsylvania Game Commission
Southwest Region
P.O. Box A
Ligonier, PA 15658
Phone: Toll free 1 (877) 877-7137; (724) 238-9523; (724) 238-9524
Allegheny, Armstrong, Beaver, Cambria, Fayette, Greene, Indiana, Somerset, Washington and Westmoreland

ALLEGHENY COUNTY

Despite its urban-suburban personality, the rugged rolling hills and valleys surrounding Pittsburgh annually yield some of the state's biggest bucks.

Woodlands rise 400-500 feet from valley floor to summit, in places quite abruptly. Forests comprise 37 percent of the county. Farmland composes only eight percent of the county's 728 square miles with apples, corn and grains the chief crops.

As in much of Pennsylvania's suburbia, finding public hunting lands here is a problem — which accounts for the higher age structure of whitetails which find haven on private lands and other "no hunting" areas. Only one gameland – SGL No. 203 near Armitage with 1,245 acres — is available and no state park or forest lands are present.

Deer density here approaches about five times the carrying capacity — and many more times beyond the tolerance levels of most suburban homeowners. Some of the bucks found in Allegheny are monsters, serving well its reputation as a trophy producer.

Allegheny County composes the Southwest's Special Regulations Area with liberal doe hunting opportunities.

Food, lodging and services, contact: Greater Pittsburgh Convention and Visitors Bureau, Inc., 425 Sixth Avenue, Pittsburgh, PA 15219. Phone: (800) 366-0093 or (412) 281-7711.

IN BRIEF:

State Gamelands: 1,245 acres
State Parks & Forests: None
Farm-Game Co-op: 16,333 acres (118 farms)
Forest-Game Co-op: None
Safety Zone Lands: 5,597 acres (62 tracts)

1999 Buck/Doe Harvest: 2,191/5,405
1999 Archery Buck/Doe Harvest: 1,303/2,095
1999 Muzzleloader Buck/Doe Harvest:29/261
Forested Square Miles (FSM): 260
1999 Buck Harvest/FSM: 8.4
Winter Deer Density/FSM: N/A
Desired Winter Deer Density/FSM: 5

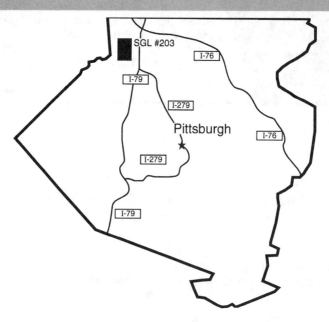

ARMSTRONG COUNTY

Covering 646 square miles, Armstrong is hill-country interspersed with high mountainous plateaus. Its rolling terrain is flat in few places with hilltops rising several hundred feet above flood plains.

Elevations span 740 to 1,720 feet.

Thirty-one percent of the county is in farmland, primarily in crop production. Corn, cabbage and grains are the chief harvest products. Well over 100,000 acres of Game Commission co-op and Safety Zone lands are available to sportsmen exploring access opportunities, mostly on these farms. Look to the region in Armstrong's northwest, on the Butler border, as holding good bucks.

The county offers five gamelands tracts, the largest SGL No.105 with 2,613 acres near East Brady. A portion of the 3,300-acre Mahoning Flood Control Area, shared with Indiana County, is also open for hunting.

Food, lodging and services, contact: Armstrong County Tourist Bureau, 402 East Market St., Kittanning, PA 16201. Phone: (888) 265-9954 or (724) 548-3226.

IN BRIEF:

State Gamelands: 5,217 acres
State Parks & Forests: None
Farm-Game Co-op: 76,129 acres (589 farms)
Forest-Game Co-op: 5,981 acres
Safety Zone Lands: 27,799 acres (196 tracts)

1999 Buck/Doe Harvest: 4,199/4,590
1999 Archery Buck/Doe Harvest: 1,119/728
1999 Muzzleloader Buck/Doe Harvest: 22/358
Forested Square Miles (FSM): 355
1999 Buck Harvest/FSM: 11.8
Winter Deer Density/FSM: 52
Desired Winter Deer Density/FSM: 29

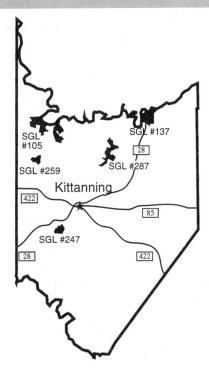

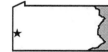

BEAVER COUNTY

Bordering Ohio, Beaver County's share of the Allegheny Plateau is 48 percent forested with 21 percent of the county in farmland, mainly used for cattle raising. Less than half is croplands of corn, grains, beans and apples.

Topography is hilly with spacious plateaus. Elevations vary from 660 to 1,380 feet throughout its 436 square miles. Glacial soils cover the county's northwest region.

Like many counties, most deer hunting here takes place on private lands. Hunting pressure on public lands is relatively light.

Three gamelands are available to Beaver County hunters, the biggest SGL No. 285 near Darlington with 2,169 acres. Two state parks — Hillman (3,780 acres) and Raccoon Creek (3,647 acres) — also permit hunting.

Each year the Raccoon Creek region in the southern part of the county yields some hefty bucks.

Food, lodging and services, contact: Beaver County Tourist Promotion Agency, 215B Ninth St., Monaca, PA 15061. Phone: (800) 342-8192 or (724) 728-0212.

IN BRIEF:

State Gamelands: 1,478 acres

State Parks & Forests: 8,663 acres

Farm-Game Co-op: 50,362 acres (590 farms)

Forest-Game Co-op: None

Safety Zone Lands: 364 acres (5 tracts)

1999 Buck/Doe Harvest: 1,913/2,493

1999 Archery Buck/Doe Harvest: 640/703

1999 Muzzleloader Buck/Doe Harvest: 8/207

Forested Square Miles (FSM): 210

1999 Buck Harvest/FSM: 9.1

Winter Deer Density/FSM: 36

Desired Winter Deer Density/FSM: 22

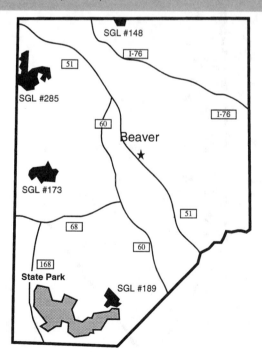

CAMBRIA COUNTY

Covering 691 square miles, Cambria's land is hilly, mountainous in some areas, with 64 percent of the county in forest habitat. Elevations run from 1,120 to 2,880 feet.

Farms cover another 19 percent of the county with just over half attributed to livestock and the rest in potatoes, oats, hay and apples.

Cambria's seven gamelands all hold whitetails. The largest tracts include 20,443-acre SGL No. 108 near Frugality and 15,632-acre SGL No. 158 near Blandburg.

Add to that Prince Gallitzin State Park with 3,440 acres and Gallitzin State Forest in White, Jackson and Reade townships, totaling 1,470 acres. Shared with three adjacent counties, a portion of 13,625-acre Laurel Ridge State Park is also a popular Cambria hunting area.

Food, lodging and services, contact: Greater Johnstown/Cambria County CVB, 111 Market St., Johnston, PA 15901. Phone: (800) 237-8590 or (814) 536-7993.

IN BRIEF:

State Gamelands: 51,399 acres
State Parks & Forests: 4,910 acres
Farm-Game Co-op: 64,517 acres (471 farms)
Forest-Game Co-op: None
Safety Zone Lands: 14,626 acres (117 tracts)

1999 Buck/Doe Harvest: 2,989/2,820
1999 Archery Buck/Doe Harvest: 755/722
1999 Muzzleloader Buck/Doe Harvest: 21/352
Forested Square Miles (FSM): 439
1999 Buck Harvest/FSM: 6.8
Winter Deer Density/FSM: 33
Desired Winter Deer Density/FSM: 21

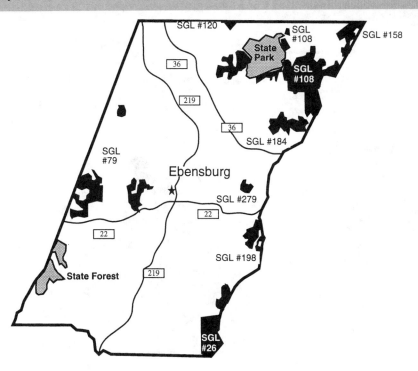

FAYETTE COUNTY

Sixty-one percent of the county's 794 square miles are composed of woodlands. Topography ranges from elevations as low as 740 feet to 3,000 feet.

Cattle, poultry and field crops share the farmland regions across 24 percent of the county. Corn, grains and apples are raised on about a quarter of the agricultural acreage with livestock dominating the remainder.

Five gamelands are scattered across Fayette, the largest SGL No. 51 near Uniontown with 15,498 acres. South of Uniontown is the Braddock Unit of Forbes State Forest providing another 15,792 acres. Included on the public hunting grounds list is 18,719-acre Ohiopyle State Park, overlapping into Somerset County, and a portion of Laurel Ridge State Park in the eastern end of the county.

Most of the little coal towns provide good hunting little more than a short walk away. The Laurel Mountains offer plenty of public and private (permission needed) deer country.

Food, lodging and services, contact: Laurel Highlands Visitors Bureau, Town Hall, 120 East Main St., Ligonier, PA 15658. Phone: (800) 925-7669 or (724) 238-5661.

IN BRIEF:

State Gamelands: 21,464 acres
State Parks & Forests: 34,792 acres
Farm-Game Co-op: 27,597 acres (243 farms)
Forest-Game Co-op: 2,036 acres
Safety Zone Lands: 21,618 acres (123 tracts)

1999 Buck/Doe Harvest: 3,262/2,500
1999 Archery Buck/Doe Harvest: 527/452
1999 Muzzleloader Buck/Doe Harvest: 35/276
Forested Square Miles (FSM): 480
1999 Buck Harvest/FSM: 6.8
Winter Deer Density/FSM: 33
Desired Winter Deer Density/FSM: 23

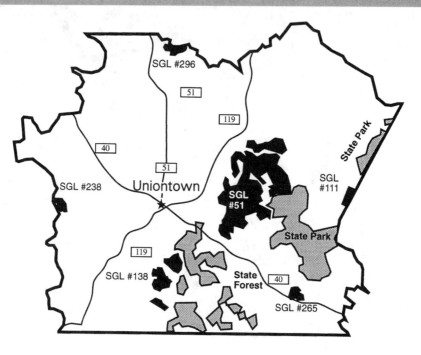

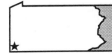

GREENE COUNTY

Bordering West Virginia on its western and southern borders (the county is set squarely in the far southeast corner of the state), Greene County's 577 square miles meander over hill and valley landscape with elevations from 760 to 1,660 feet.

Forests cover 56 percent of the county with farms on another 40 percent of the landscape. Cattle and sheep occupy nearly three-fourths of the farmland with hay, corn, wheat and oats raised on the remainder.

Greene's two gamelands are sizable. SGL No. 223 near Dunkard and Daviston is 6,972 acres while SGL No. 179 near Aleppo and Nettle Hill covers 5,329 acres.

Ryerson Station State Park west of Waynesburg offers another 900 acres of hunting grounds.

This county ranks among Pennsylvania's highest in terms of buck harvests per square mile of forest. Thanks to farmland vegetation and a considerable abandoned farms, Greene's deer are typically heavier than those dwelling in the more mountainous portions of the region.

Greene lays claim to the second biggest typical Pennsylvania record book buck shot in 1974.

Food, lodging and services, contact: Greene County Tourist Promotion Agency, 19 South Washington St., Waynesburg, PA 15370. Phone: (724) 627-8687.

IN BRIEF:

State Gamelands: 12,301 acres
State Parks & Forests: 900 acres
Farm-Game Co-op: 63,672 acres (471 farms)
Forest-Game Co-op: None
Safety Zone Lands: 6,316 acres (48 tracts)

1999 Buck/Doe Harvest: 4,176/4,522
1999 Archery Buck/Doe Harvest: 351/595
1999 Muzzleloader Buck/Doe Harvest: 21/316
Forested Square Miles (FSM): 324
1999 Buck Harvest/FSM: 12.9
Winter Deer Density/FSM: 59
Desired Winter Deer Density/FSM: 20

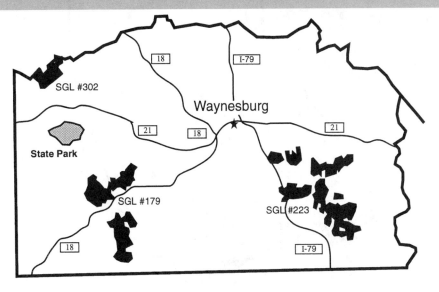

INDIANA COUNTY

Hilly, mountainous and with broad ridges and plateaus, Indiana's elevations range from 830 to 2,160 feet across its 829 square miles.

Forests compose 61 percent of the land with 32 percent in cattle, poultry and crops. Oats, corn, alfalfa and apples can be found in the latter areas.

The larger of Indiana's seven gamelands are SGL No. 276 near Coral (3,942 acres), SGL No. 174 near McGees Mills (3,125 acres) and SGL No. 153 near Bolivar and Robinson (2,812 acres).

Other state hunting lands can be found at 2,000-acre Yellow Creek State Park, east of Indiana, and 384-acre Gallitzin State Forest, east of Cramer.

Conemaugh Flood Control Reservoir, shared with Westmoreland County, accounts for another 6,000 wild acres.

An average of about 9,000-10,000 whitetails are harvested here annually.

Food, lodging and services, contact: Indiana County Tourist Bureau, Indiana Mall 2090, Route 286 South, Indiana, PA 15701. Phone: (877) 746-3426 or (724) 463-7505.

IN BRIEF:

State Gamelands: 12,743 acres
State Parks & Forests: 2,384 acres
Farm-Game Co-op: 69,949 acres (586 farms)
Forest-Game Co-op: 21,039 acres
Safety Zone Lands: 50,635 acres (203 tracts)

1999 Buck/Doe Harvest: 4,517/5,919
1999 Archery Buck/Doe Harvest: 937/820
1999 Muzzleloader Buck/Doe Harvest: 20/438
Forested Square Miles (FSM): 503
1999 Buck Harvest/FSM: 9.0
Winter Deer Density/FSM: 39
Desired Winter Deer Density/FSM: 23

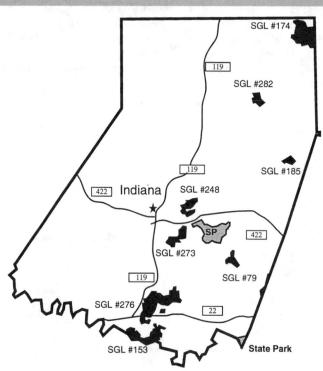

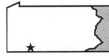

SOMERSET COUNTY

Bordering Maryland, 64 percent of Somerset County is wooded. Another 34 percent is in farmland characterized largely by livestock with just under half in farm crops, including oats, corn, potatoes and apples.

It's hilly and, in some places, mountainous landscape covers 1,073 square miles with elevations running 1,040 to 3,213 feet.

Six gamelands set aside more than 12,000 acres specifically for hunters, all with notable deer populations. The biggest include SGL No. 111 near Confluence with 10,520 acres, SGL No. 82 at Wittenberg with 6,708 acres, 3,158-acre SGL No. 50 near Somerset and 3,029-acre SGL No. 228 near Central City.

State holdings on Forbes State Forest tracts (Babcock, Blue Hole and Negro Mountain) total 26,231 acres with nearly 25,000 additional acres of Forbes State Forest tracts shared with Westmoreland County. Portions of Laurel Ridge and Kooser state parks are also within the county.

Pennsylvania's highest point, Mount Davis, is located in southern Somerset. It peaks at 3,213 feet.

Food, lodging and services, contact: Laurel Highlands Visitors Bureau, Town Hall, 120 East Main St., Ligonier, PA 15658. Phone: (800) 925-7669 or (724) 238-5661.

IN BRIEF:

State Gamelands: 25,699 acres
State Parks & Forests: 37,668 acres
Farm-Game Co-op: 138,431 acres (749 farms)
Forest-Game Co-op: None
Safety Zone Lands: 45,881 acres (257 tracts)

1999 Buck/Doe Harvest: 4,763/4,546
1999 Archery Buck/Doe Harvest: 736/745
1999 Muzzleloader Buck/Doe Harvest: 6/353
Forested Square Miles (FSM): 689
1999 Buck Harvest/FSM: 6.9
Winter Deer Density/FSM: 29
Desired Winter Deer Density/FSM: 24

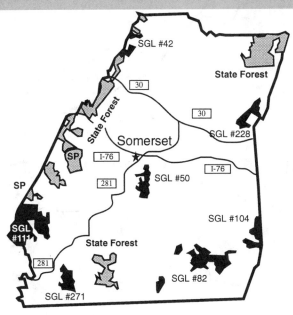

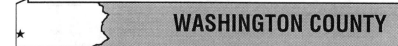

WASHINGTON COUNTY

Bordered by Ohio on its west, Washington County's woodland covers one-half of its 858 square miles. Elevations range from 720 to 1,540 square feet across the hilly and often mountainous terrain.

Farms occupy 40 percent of the county with just over one-third planted in alfalfa, hay, corn and other crops. Cattle and sheep graze throughout the region.

A half-dozen gameland tracts offer hunters more than 11,000 acres.

The biggest is SGL No. 245 near Prosperity (3,653 acres) seconded by SGL No. 117 at Burgettstown with 2,932 acres.

No state forest or park lands are located inside Washington County. In 1992, West Penn Power Company opened some 4,000 acres to hunters in the Buffalo Creek area.

In terms of buck harvests per square woodland mile, averaging 10-14, Washington annually ranks in the state's top 10.

Food, lodging and services, contact: Washington County Tourism Promotion Agency, Franklin Mall, 1500 Chestnut St., Washington, PA 15301. Phone: (800) 531-4114 or (724) 228-5520.

IN BRIEF:

State Gamelands: 9,250 acres
State Parks & Forests: None
Farm-Game Co-op: 57,848 acres (312 farms)
Forest-Game Co-op: 4,235 acres
Safety Zone Lands: 26,663 acres (205 tracts)

1999 Buck/Doe Harvest: 5,760/5,467
1999 Archery Buck/Doe Harvest: 1,154/959
1999 Muzzleloader Buck/Doe Harvest: 47/361
Forested Square Miles (FSM): 427
1999 Buck Harvest/FSM: 13.5
Winter Deer Density/FSM: 67
Desired Winter Deer Density/FSM: 28

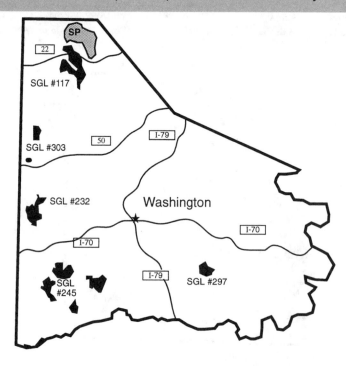

WESTMORELAND COUNTY

Fifty-one percent of this 1,033 square mile county is forested. As is typical of the vast, hilly, mountainous region, elevations span 740 to 2,960 feet.

Farms cover one-quarter of the total acreage with about 46 percent in crops and the remainder dedicated to sheep, cattle and poultry production. Alfalfa, corn, oats and wheat are the main money-crops.

Only one gameland, albeit a sizable one, is found in Westmoreland. SGL No. 42 spans 12,745 acres near Johnstown.

Also open to hunters is 656 acres of Keystone State Park, north of Latrobe, and 350-acres of Linn State Park near Rector.

The county shares two units of Forbes State Forest with neighboring Somerset, totaling nearly 25,000 acres, along with a portion of 13,625-acre Laurel Ridge State Parka lapping into Cambria, Somerset and Fayette.

The Conemaugh and Loyalhanna flood control areas add another several thousand acres to Westmoreland's public deer hunting options.

Food, lodging and services, contact: Laurel Highlands Visitors Bureau, Town Hall, 120 East Main St., Ligonier, PA 15658. Phone: (800) 925-7669 or (724) 238-5661.

IN BRIEF:

State Gamelands: 12,745 acres

State Parks & Forests: 20,141 acres

Farm-Game Co-op: 59,645 acres (625 farms)

Forest-Game Co-op: 2,146 acres

Safety Zone Lands: 11,468 acres (100 tracts)

1999 Buck/Doe Harvest: 5,347/6,036

1999 Archery Buck/Doe Harvest: 1,760/1,464

1999 Muzzleloader Buck/Doe Harvest: 35/515

Forested Square Miles (FSM): 518

1999 Buck Harvest/FSM: 10.3

Winter Deer Density/FSM: 48

Desired Winter Deer Density/FSM: 28

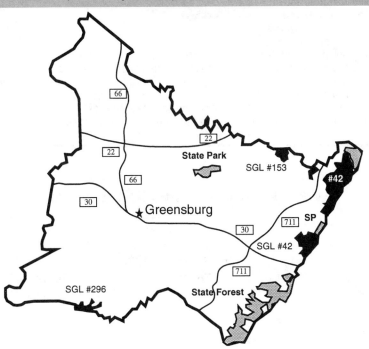

NORTHCENTRAL REGION

"Steep mountains, deep canyons, sycamores reaching ghostly from meandering stream bottoms, secluded wooded valleys and ice cold streams characterize northcentral Pennsylvania. Nowhere else in the commonwealth can one find so much wild land. The changes that occur in many of the towns when deer season arrives are almost unbelievable. At that time of the year one subject is on everybody's tongue — deer hunting. Ten top-notch big game counties make up the Northcentral Region. These counties annually account for 25 to 30 percent of our state's deer harvest (with) Potter, Tioga and Clearfield recording exceptionally large harvests."

Harry Merz, Pennsylvania Game Commission

Pennsylvania Game Commission

Northcentral Region
1566 S RT 44 Hwy.
Post Office Box 5038
Jersey Shore, PA 17740
Phone: Toll free 1 (877) 877-7674; (570) 398-4744; (570) 398-4745
Cameron, Centre, Clearfield, Clinton, Elk, Lycoming, McKean, Potter, Tioga and Union

CAMERON COUNTY

Ninety-four percent of the land is forested within Cameron's 398 square miles. As suggested by the vast mount of woodland, Cameron is one of the state's most sparsely populated counties. Deep, narrow v-shaped valleys and steep slopes make accessing the backcountry a challenge. Cameron is reputed by some to be the "roughest" country anywhere in the northern tier.

In spite of, or perhaps, because of its wild landscape, numerous deer camps are located along most every backwoods road and hunters can gain access to whitetails throughout the region.

Hay, wheat and corn can be found although most farms raise cattle and poultry. Timbering is important throughout the region with numerous clearcuts and second growth areas offering prime deer habitat.

Despite its vast woodlands, Cameron holds only one gameland tract. But it's a big one, spanning 12,963 acres on SGL No. 14 near Emporium.

No matter, as Elk State Forest's 118,466 acres offer unlimited hunting opportunities. Add to that 1,150 acres at Sizerville State Park, northeast of Emporium.

The large amount of forest land, in part, accounts for one of the lowest buck harvest rates per wooded square mile in Cameron.

Food, lodging and services, contact: Cameron County Tourist Promotion Agency, Croffwoos Mills Bldg., P.O. Box 118, Driftwood, PA 15832. Phone: (888) 252-2872 or (814) 546-2665.

IN BRIEF:

State Gamelands: 12,963 acres

State Parks & Forests: 119,616 acres

Farm-Game Co-op: None

Forest-Game Co-op: 27,592 acres

Safety Zone Lands: 7,154 acres (48 tracts)

1999 Buck/Doe Harvest: 1,083/408

1999 Archery Buck/Doe Harvest: 58/73

1999 Muzzleloader Buck/Doe Harvest: 11/14

Forested Square Miles (FSM): 372

1999 Buck Harvest/FSM: 2.9

Winter Deer Density/FSM: 15

Desired Winter Deer Density/FSM: 19

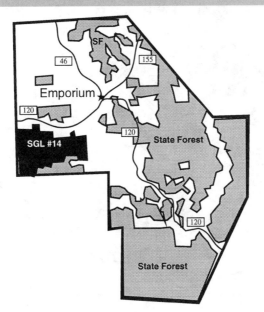

CENTRE COUNTY

As its name implies, this is the central-most county in the state, covering 1,106 square miles. Forests compose 76 percent of the landscape with farms supported on 22 percent.

Just over half of the farms grow alfalfa, corn, oats and wheat, the remainder in apple orchards or cattle. Long, narrow, mountain ridges dominate the southeast with hilly, broad-ridged topography to the northwest.

Hunters can choose from a plethora of state parks and forests or seven gamelands. Of the former, 47,000 acres of Sproul State Forest, north of Snow Shoe, 38,000 acres in Bald Eagle State Forest, east of Potters Mills, 34,900 acres in Moshannon State Forest, east of Philipsburg, and Rothrock State Forest's 20,645 acres southeast of State College offer unlimited choices.

The largest gamelands can be found on SGL No. 100 at Pine Glen (17,019 acres), SGL No. 33 near Philipsburg (16,585 acres) and SGL No. 103 near Snow Shoe (8,993).

Food, lodging and services, contact: Centre County Convention and Visitors Bureau, 1402 South Atherton St., State College, PA 16801. Phone: (800) 358-5466 or (814) 231-8123.

IN BRIEF:

State Gamelands: 64,277 acres
State Parks & Forests: 142,935 acres
Farm-Game Co-op: 32,783 acres (202 farms)
Forest-Game Co-op: 6,455 acres
Safety Zone Lands: 28,522 acres (170 tracts)

1999 Buck/Doe Harvest: 4,898/3,387
1999 Archery Buck/Doe Harvest: 424/469
1999 Muzzleloader Buck/Doe Harvest: 12/277
Forested Square Miles (FSM): 837
1999 Buck Harvest/FSM: 5.8
Winter Deer Density/FSM: 30
Desired Winter Deer Density/FSM: 20

CLEARFIELD COUNTY

Clearfield always ranks near the top in annual whitetail harvests with 74 percent of its 1,149 square miles in forest. Elevations range from 780 to 2,380 feet.

Less than 10 percent of the county is farmland, primarily cattle operations with some corn, grains and apple orchards. Stripmines, mostly reclaimed and of benefit to deer and other game, are abundant. Steep hills and mountains of second and third growth woodlands rising from valleys characterize this popular deer hunting county.

Clearfield's hunters take more than 13,000 whitetails each year.

Eight gamelands areas are scattered across the county. The larger tracts include 4,876-acre SGL No. 93 near Sabula and SGL No. 90 with 3,957 acres near Goshen.

Clearfield County is also home to 97,460 acres of Moshannon State Forest north and west of Clearfield. S.B. Elliott and Parker Dam state parks combine for another 780 acres.

Food, lodging and services, contact: Northwest PA's Great Outdoors Visitors Bureau, 175 Main St., Brookville, PA 15825. Phone: (800) 348-9393 or (814) 849-5197.

IN BRIEF:

State Gamelands: 20,972 acres
State Parks & Forests: 98,240 acres
Farm-Game Co-op: 24,950 acres (263 farms)
Forest-Game Co-op: 18,957 acres
Safety Zone Lands: 18,509 acres (125 tracts)

1999 Buck/Doe Harvest: 6,048/5,545
1999 Archery Buck/Doe Harvest: 721/777
1999 Muzzleloader Buck/Doe Harvest: 23/455
Forested Square Miles (FSM): 848
1999 Buck Harvest/FSM: 7.1
Winter Deer Density/FSM: 37
Desired Winter Deer Density/FSM: 21

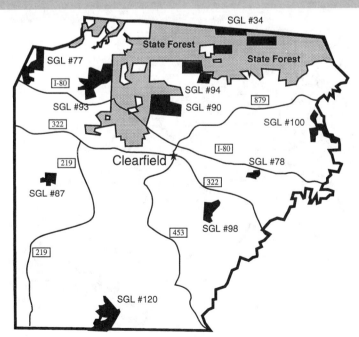

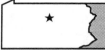

CLINTON COUNTY

Known as "Black Forest County" by many sportsmen, Clinton's seemingly endless mountains, broad river valleys and steep gorges provide unlimited whitetail hunting opportunities.

The land in the southeast is characterized by long, narrow ridges. The northwest is hilly with broader ridges and dissected plateaus.

Covering 891 square miles with 87 percent supporting forests, Clinton's farmland is minimal. However, eight percent of the land base supports harvested cropland (corn, alfalfa, oats and soybeans) and livestock.

Public land is everywhere. Sproul State Forest, around Renovo, covers 190,964 acres, Bald Eagle State Forest near Mill Hall is 53,083 acres and Tiadaghton State Forest, north of Rauchtown, adds another 6,047 acres.

If that's not enough, look to three gamelands tracts. SGL No. 89 near Farrandville covers 10,571 acres and SGL No. 295, near Lamar, offers 10,072 acres.

It must be considered that Clinton's seemingly low rate of 3.3 bucks taken per square mile of forest land must be factored against the tremendous amount of woodland, much of it lightly hunted due to its ruggedness.

Food, lodging and services, contact: Clinton County Economic Partnership, 212 North Jay St., Lock Haven, PA 17745. Phone: (570) 748-5782.

IN BRIEF:

State Gamelands: 22,726 acres

State Parks & Forests: 250,794 acres

Farm-Game Co-op: 56,520 acres (401 farms)

Forest-Game Co-op: 11,835 acres

Safety Zone Lands: 2,136 acres (18 tracts)

1999 Buck/Doe Harvest: 2,573/1,427

1999 Archery Buck/Doe Harvest: 245/319

1999 Muzzleloader Buck/Doe Harvest: 18/121

Forested Square Miles (FSM): 772

1999 Buck Harvest/FSM: 3.3

Winter Deer Density/FSM: 18

Desired Winter Deer Density/FSM: 1

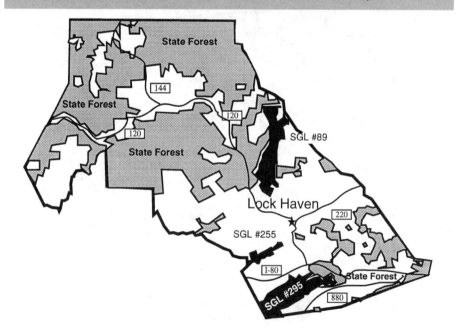

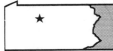

ELK COUNTY

Elk, as its name implies, is the home of Pennsylvania's "other" deer — the Rocky Mountain elk. Tourists flock to the county during the September bugling season to watch and photograph the herd, which now numbers in excess of 400.

But whitetails are also abundant, as are public lands on which to hunt them. Fully 91 percent of the county's 830 square miles hold trees. Elevations here run from 900 to 2,376 feet.

Agricultural holdings cover only four percent of the county with cattle and poultry production dominating although some hay, corn and oats can be found.

Elk County holds 36,115 acres of Elk State Forest, north of Johnsonburg, and 37,129 acres of Moshannon State Forest, southeast of Medix Run.

In addition, 23,148-acre SGL No. 25 near Johnsonburg and 23,995-acre SGL No. 44 at Portland Mills entice whitetail hunters as do three other gamelands tracts totaling more than 14,000 acres.

Like neighboring Cameron County, Elk County can be described as "rugged" with high mountains and steep slopes leading to narrow, V-shaped valleys.

Food, lodging and services, contact: Northwest PA's Great Outdoors Visitors Bureau, 175 Main St., Brookville, PA 15825. Phone: (800) 348-9393 or (814) 849-5197.

IN BRIEF:

State Gamelands: 61,343 acres
State Parks & Forests: 73,244 acres
Farm-Game Co-op: None
Forest-Game Co-op: 55,924 acres
Safety Zone Lands: 6,599 acres (36 tracts)

1999 Buck/Doe Harvest: 2,970/2,100
1999 Archery Buck/Doe Harvest: 224/286
1999 Muzzleloader Buck/Doe Harvest: 7/160
Forested Square Miles (FSM): 753
1999 Buck Harvest/FSM: 3.9
Winter Deer Density/FSM: 24
Desired Winter Deer Density/FSM: 21

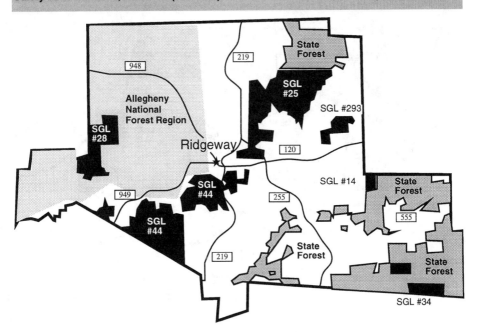

LYCOMING COUNTY

Lycoming often leads the state in black bear harvests and its whitetail numbers and popularity among hunters also rank it high on the deer harvest list.

The northern portion of the 1,237 square mile county is hilly with scattered mountains. To the south, mountains are more prevalent with numerous, narrow sandstone ridges. Elevations range from 460 to 2,403 feet.

Fully 77 percent of the county is forested. Farms compose 20 percent of the landscape with diversified interests ranging from corn, alfalfa, oats, wheat and soybeans to apple and cherry orchards and cattle operations.

Much of Tiadaghton State Forest, covering 172,313 acres near Jersey Mills and Ralston, draws deer hunters. Eight gamelands, including 25,447-acre SGL No. 75 near English Center, add to the unbroken forest.

Food, lodging and services, contact: Lycoming County Tourist Promotion Agency, 454 Pine St., Williamsport, PA 17701. Phone: (800) 358-9900 or (570) 326-1971.

IN BRIEF:

State Gamelands: 42,769 acres
State Parks & Forests: 172,313 acres
Farm-Game Co-op: 15,481 acres (152 farms)
Forest-Game Co-op: 341 acres
Safety Zone Lands: 15,975 acres (107 tracts)

1999 Buck/Doe Harvest: 4,361/2,895
1999 Archery Buck/Doe Harvest: 545/550
1999 Muzzleloader Buck/Doe Harvest: 18/178
Forested Square Miles (FSM): 954
1999 Buck Harvest/FSM: 4.5
Winter Deer Density/FSM: 24
Desired Winter Deer Density/FSM: 19

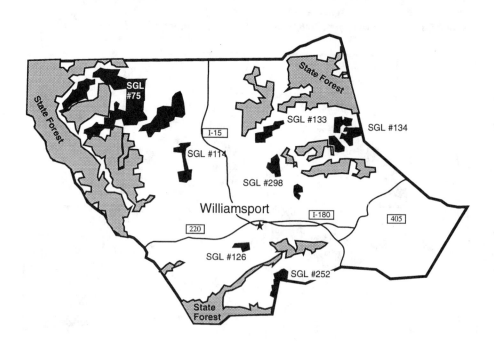

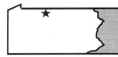

McKEAN COUNTY

Bordering New York, 81 percent of McKean's 979 square miles is forest-covered. Elevations range from 1,260 to 2,460 feet.

Farms occupy only eight percent of the county with cattle ranching predominating. Sparse croplands offer hay, wheat, oats and corn.

Angular ridgetops, sloping valleys and undulating hills describe McKean, which, along with Potter County, contributes to the headwaters of the Allegheny River.

Four gamelands and 5,619 acres of Susquehannock State Forest are within McKean's borders. SGL No. 30 near Betula sets aside 11,572 acres for hunters followed by 8,195-acre SGL No. 61 near Port Allegany.

Like many counties rimming New York, McKean annually produces harvests in excess of 4,000 bucks and as many as 5,000 or more antlerless deer.

Food, lodging and services, contact: Allegheny National Forest Vacation Bureau, Box 371, Bradford, PA 16701. Phone: (814) 368-9370.

IN BRIEF:

State Gamelands: 21,682 acres

State Parks & Forests: 5,619 acres

Farm-Game Co-op: None

Forest-Game Co-op: 126,686 acres

Safety Zone Lands: 51,027 acres (268 tracts)

1999 Buck/Doe Harvest: 4,295/3,522

1999 Archery Buck/Doe Harvest: 320/433

1999 Muzzleloader Buck/Doe Harvest: 5/224

Forested Square Miles (FSM): 812

1999 Buck Harvest/FSM: 5.3

Winter Deer Density/FSM: 30

Desired Winter Deer Density/FSM: 20

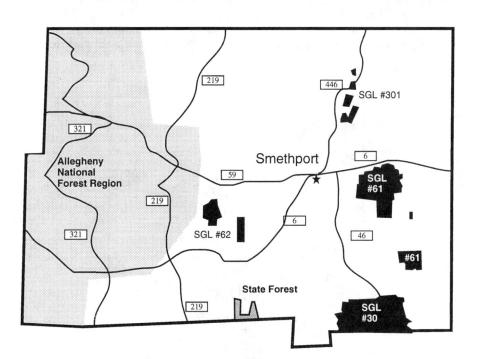

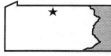

POTTER COUNTY

Appropriately dubbed "God's Country," Potter — and its county seat, Coudersport — is arguably the state's most widely known deer hunting county. For many years it produced the biggest buck and doe harvests and it still seesaws with several other northcentral counties for the annual honor.

In the heart of the Alleghenies on the New York border, much of Potter's steep slopes and broad ridges are far off the beaten path. Covering 1,801 square miles, its elevations range from 1,000 to 2,5687. The county hosts an abundance of black cherry trees, their fruits especially attractive to bears and whitetails in high production years.

Forests cover 86 percent of the county with numerous commercial holdings, much of which is leased to hunt groups and clubs. Farms cover 16 percent of Potter with potatoes, wheat, corn and oats grown on about one-third of the croplands. Cattle production dominates.

Visiting hunters frequent the 266,599 acres of Susquehanna State Forest within Potter's borders or any of three gamelands offering 4,028, 8,221 and 6,786 acres — the biggest SGL No. 64 near Galeton.

In a recent year Potter County hunters harvested more than 9,000 whitetails.

Food, lodging and services, contact: Potter County Visitors Association, Rt. 6, P.O. Box 245, Coudersport, PA 16915. Phone: (888) POTTER2 or (814) 435-2290.

IN BRIEF:

State Gamelands: 19,035 acres

State Parks & Forests: 267,199 acres

Farm-Game Co-op: 64,509 acres (357 farms)

Forest-Game Co-op: 41,262 acres

Safety Zone Lands: 3,563 acres (24 tracts)

1999 Buck/Doe Harvest: 5,138/3,883

1999 Archery Buck/Doe Harvest: 640/660

1999 Muzzleloader Buck/Doe Harvest: 6/221

Forested Square Miles (FSM): 927

1999 Buck Harvest/FSM: 5.5

Winter Deer Density/FSM: 31

Desired Winter Deer Density/FSM: 20

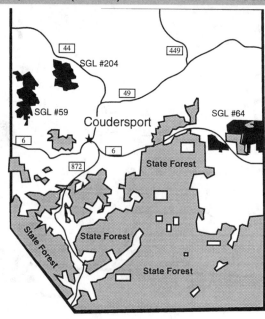

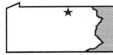

TIOGA COUNTY

Bordering Potter, Tioga is truly "big woods" country with an abundance of public hunting areas for everything from bucks and bears to gobblers and grouse. Elevations across its 1,131 square miles span 840 to 2,543 feet. Two-thirds of the county is wooded.

Much of the remainder is in cattle, dairy, poultry and sheep production with hay, corn, oats and barley growing on tilled farmlands.

As one of the "big woods" counties, thousands of hunters migrate to the rugged and scenic woods every fall. They find an abundance of public land in 148,940-acre Tioga State Forest at Wellsboro and Blossburg with another 1,000 acres at Colton Point and Leonard Harrison state parks, between Wellsboro and Galeton.

Three big gamelands include 13,232-acre SGL No. 37 at Tioga and 8,861-acre SGL No. 208 near Gaines.

Food, lodging and services, contact: Tioga County Visitors Bureau, 114 Main St. Ste. 203, Wellsboro, PA 16901. Phone: (888) 846-4228 or (570) 724-0635.

IN BRIEF:

State Gamelands: 24,487 acres

State Parks & Forests: 150,085 acres

Farm-Game Co-op: 20,605 acres (143 farms)

Forest-Game Co-op: 1,300 acres

Safety Zone Lands: 29,211 acres (122 tracts)

1999 Buck/Doe Harvest: 5,011/4,143

1999 Archery Buck/Doe Harvest: 612/665

1999 Muzzleloader Buck/Doe Harvest: 22/189

Forested Square Miles (FSM): 760

1999 Buck Harvest/FSM: 6.6

Winter Deer Density/FSM: 39

Desired Winter Deer Density/FSM: 19

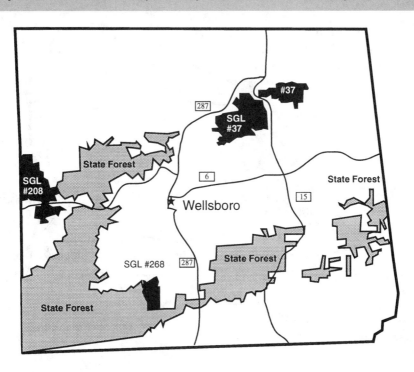

UNION COUNTY

Covering 317 square miles, Union County's elevations range from 440 to 2,160 feet across the north Appalachian ridge and valley landform. Forests cover 68 percent of the county.

Farms occupy much of the remainder with most in harvested crops, including corn, alfalfa, wheat and oats.

A vast stretch of Bald Eagle State Forest — 57,766 acres — can be found in the Laurelton region with only three small gamelands available in the remainder of the county. One is a 682-acre gameland transfer from the Dept. of Agriculture in Hartley Township in mid-1994.

Food, lodging and services, contact: Susquehanna Valley Visitors Bureau, RR 2, 219D Hafer Rd., Lewisburg, PA 17837. Phone: (800) 525-7320 or (570) 524-7234.

IN BRIEF:

State Gamelands: 1,274 acres

State Parks & Forests: 57,766 acres

Farm-Game Co-op: 33,242 acres (337 farms)

Forest-Game Co-op: None

Safety Zone Lands: 2,694 acres (22 tracts)

1999 Buck/Doe Harvest: 1,240/1,141

1999 Archery Buck/Doe Harvest: 248/254

1999 Muzzleloader Buck/Doe Harvest: 10/90

Forested Square Miles (FSM): 214

1999 Buck Harvest/FSM: 5.8

Winter Deer Density/FSM: 26

Desired Winter Deer Density/FSM: 16

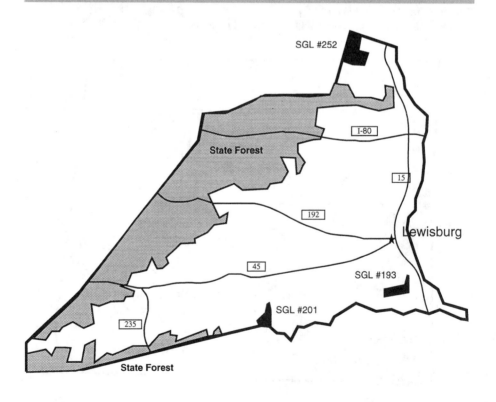

SOUTHCENTRAL REGION

"The Southcentral Region is a land of diversity. Rugged game-filled ridges rising from broad farming valleys dominate much of Southcentral Pennsylvania. The fertile land of both field and forest supports abundant big and small game populations. The great contrast of ridges on one hand and rich farming land on the other is the key to the area's game resources. All 11 counties have ample whitetail populations but Huntingdon, Bedford and Perry counties normally have the highest kill. However, the agricultural counties, particularly Adams, generally produce the heaviest whitetails."

**Wes Bower,
Pennsylvania
Game Commission**

Pennsylvania Game Commission
Southcentral Region
P.O. Box 537
Huntingdon, PA 16652
Phone: Toll free 1 (877) 877-9107; (814) 643-1831; (814) 643-1835
Adams, Bedford, Blair, Cumberland, Franklin, Fulton, Huntingdon,
Juniata, Mifflin, Perry and Snyder

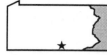

ADAMS COUNTY

Located on the southern border of Pennsylvania, Adams County covers 521 square miles with 59 percent in farmland, more than most other southwestern counties. Crops include corn, wheat and potatoes along with apples and peaches. Abundant pasture lands also rim its woodlands.

Availability of croplands provides Adams County hunters with, arguably, the heaviest whitetails in the Southcentral division.

The county holds broad highlands and ridges of primarily deciduous hardwoods. Compared to the rest of the region, however, it holds only one state gameland – SGL No. 29. It covers 1,942-acres, near Biglerville.

A focal point for many hunters during the deer seasons is Michaux State Forest near Caledonia with 21,897 acres of public hunting grounds.

Food, lodging and services, contact: Gettysburg Convention and Visitors Bureau, 35 Carlise St., Gettysburg, PA 17325. Phone: (800) 337-5015 or (717) 231-7788.

IN BRIEF:

State Gamelands: 1,942 acres

State Parks & Forests: 21,897 acres

Farm-Game Co-op: 25,178 acres (232 farms)

Forest-Game Co-op: None

Safety Zone Lands: 42,452 acres (120 tracts)

1999 Buck/Doe Harvest: 1,829/1,335

1999 Archery Buck/Doe Harvest: 352/243

1999 Muzzleloader Buck/Doe Harvest: 5/61

Forested Square Miles (FSM): 173

1999 Buck Harvest/FSM: 10.6

Winter Deer Density/FSM: 58

Desired Winter Deer Density/FSM: 24]

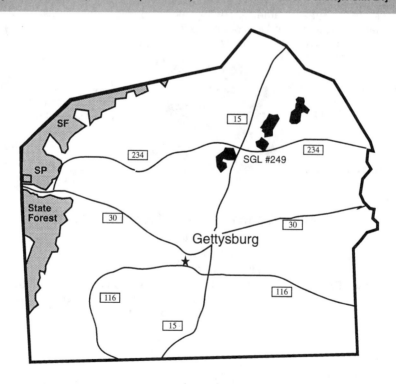

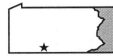

BEDFORD COUNTY

Wooded ridges and open valleys cut through Bedford in a northeast to southwest direction. Ridges covered in hardwoods and scattered groves of conifers rise 1,500 feet and more above valley floors,

Seventy-two percent of the county's 1,017 square miles is forested with elevations varying from 740 to 3,136 feet. Portions of the county are dramatically steep and rocky.

Cattle production is king in farm country with alfalfa, corn and oats on harvested lands.

Two state forest tracts, less than 3,000 acres each, and expansive Buchanan State Forest with 29,603 acres (near Chaneysville) hold numerous deer. Good whitetail hunting is also to be had on Bedford's eight gamelands varying in size from 2,626 acres to 13,878 acres. The largest is SGL No. 73 near Martinsburg. SGL No. 26 near Pavia stretches across 11,926 acres. From the Maryland border to the Pennsylvania Turnpike a hunter can roam contiguous, deer-rich forests.

Food, lodging and services, contact: Bedford County Conference and Visitors Bureau, 141 South Juliana St., Bedford, PA 15522. Phone: (800) 765-3331 or (814) 623-1771.

IN BRIEF:

State Gamelands: 62,477 acres
State Parks & Forests: 34,942 acres
Farm-Game Co-op: 42,792 acres (351 farms)
Forest-Game Co-op: 123 acres
Safety Zone Lands: 69,011 acres (394 tracts)

1999 Buck/Doe Harvest: 5,177/4,512
1999 Archery Buck/Doe Harvest: 468/512
1999 Muzzleloader Buck/Doe Harvest: 29/473
Forested Square Miles (FSM): 726
1999 Buck Harvest/FSM: 7.1
Winter Deer Density/FSM: 29
Desired Winter Deer Density/FSM: 25

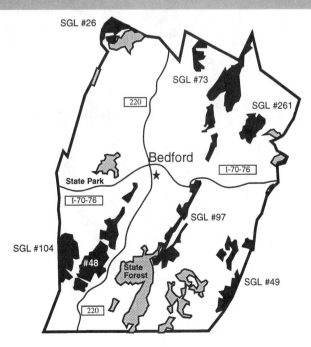

BLAIR COUNTY

Covering 527 square miles, Bedford's northwest is hilly, often mountainous. To the southwest, long valleys sweep through rugged mountain ridges. Many oak, maple and cherry ridges, rugged in many spots, have been ravaged by gypsy moths in recent years. Timber salvage operations have opened lands to sunlight and heavy undergrowth, prime for whitetails.

Some 64 percent of the county is forested with elevations ranging from 720 to 3,000 feet. Farms occupy about one-fourth of the county with over half in harvested croplands of corn, oats and alfalfa. The remainder holds cattle and poultry.

No state forest lands are available in Blair but six gamelands take up the slack, ranging in acreage from 352 to 6,421. The largest is SGL No. 166 near Canoe Creek. SGL No. 147 near Martinsburg holds 6,073 acres with 5,932 acres composing SGL No. 118 near Williamsburg.

Food, lodging and services, contact: Allegheny Mountains Convention and Visitors Bureau, Logan Valley Mall, Route 220 & Goods Lane, Altoona, PA 16602. Phone: (800) 84-ALTOONA or (814) 943-4183.

IN BRIEF:

State Gamelands: 26,439 acres
State Parks & Forests: None
Farm-Game Co-op: 53,366 acres (398 farms)
Forest-Game Co-op: 9,005 acres
Safety Zone Lands: 42,309 acres (225 tracts)

1999 Buck/Doe Harvest: 2,511/1,766
1999 Archery Buck/Doe Harvest: 368/331
1999 Muzzleloader Buck/Doe Harvest: 11/178
Forested Square Miles (FSM): 338
1999 Buck Harvest/FSM: 7.4
Winter Deer Density/FSM: 40
Desired Winter Deer Density/FSM: 22

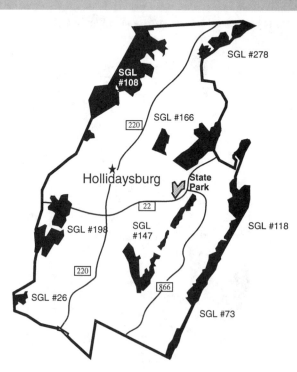

CUMBERLAND COUNTY

Located west of Harrisburg, the Appalachian Ridge cuts through Cumberland's 547 square miles. The region's rolling hills and rich, fertile, limestone valleys grow wheat, corn, barley and apples, providing desirable deer food in many areas.

Woodlands cover 35 percent of the county with farms occupying the rolling lowlands, making up 47 percent of the topography. Cumberland's 547 square miles range in elevation from 291 to 2,240 feet.

Michaux State Forest surrounding Pine Grove Furnace and Tuscarora State Forest near Doubling Gap combine for 34,665 acres of public land. Two state gamelands, one near Newville (No. 169 with 2,317 acres) and the other at Carlisle Springs (No. 230 containing 1,082 acres), offer additional hunting grounds.

Food, lodging and services, contact: PA Capital Regions Vacation Bureau, Inc., Town House Suites, Suite 1419, 14th floor, 660 Boas St., Harrisburg, PA 17120. Phone: (717) 2249-4801.

IN BRIEF:

State Gamelands: 3,399
State Parks & Forests: 34,665 acres
Farm-Game Co-op: 70,537 acres (623 farms)
Forest-Game Co-op: 698 acres
Safety Zone Program Acreage — 13,235 (78 farms)

1999 Buck/Doe Harvest: 1,732/1,441
1999 Archery Buck/Doe Harvest: 352/319
1999 Muzzleloader Buck/Doe Harvest: 11/92
Forested Square Miles (FSM): 194
1999 Buck Harvest/FSM: 8.9
Winter Deer Density/FSM: 37
Desired Winter Deer Density/FSM: 17

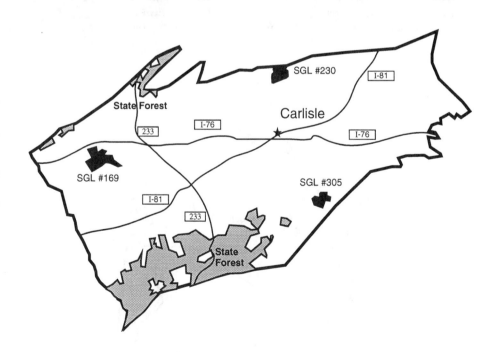

FRANKLIN COUNTY

Rimmed on its south by Maryland, Franklin's 774 square miles are made up of 44 percent woodland and 50 percent farmland. Elevations range from 400 to 2,440 feet.

The landscape in the eastern portion of the county is largely fertile, rolling lowlands. The western section, holding the Appalachian's Blue Ridge, is considerably more mountainous with long, narrow sandstone ridges and shale and limestone valleys.

Farmland areas are diverse with stands of corn and alfalfa, apples and peaches or cattle and hogs.

Coincidentally, Franklin's 1993 deer season's harvest of antlered and antlerless deer was split equally; 1,760 of each.

Michaux (at Caledonia) and Buchanan (at Upper Strasburg) state forests cover 38,258 acres of wooded public hunting grounds. SGL No. 235 at Fort Loudon stretches across 6,062 acres and SGL No. 76, near Roxbury, covers 4,323 acres.

The Letterkenny Army Depot's 8,000 acres is open for special deer hunts.

Food, lodging and services, contact: PA Capital Regions Vacation Bureau, Inc., Town House Suites, Suite 1419, 14th floor, 660 Boas St., Harrisburg, PA 17120. Phone: (717) 261-1200.

IN BRIEF:

State Gamelands: 10,385 acres

State Parks & Forests: 38,258 acres

Farm-Game Co-op: 98,278 acres (712 farms)

Forest-Game Co-op: 1,134 acres

Safety Zone Lands: 23,412 acres (92 tracts)

1999 Buck/Doe Harvest: 2,443/1,867

1999 Archery Buck/Doe Harvest: 289/316

1999 Muzzleloader Buck/Doe Harvest: 29/123

Forested Square Miles (FSM): 336

1999 Buck Harvest/FSM: 7.3

Winter Deer Density/FSM: 34

Desired Winter Deer Density/FSM: 27

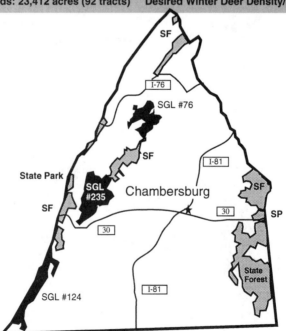

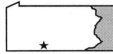

FULTON COUNTY

Bordered on the south by Maryland, Fulton's forests cover 69 percent of the 438 square mile county. Cattle and corn, alfalfa, oats and wheat dominate the numerous farmlands.

Wooded ridges and cleared, often deep, valleys, extend in a northeast to southwest direction across the county. Elevations range from 420 to 2,440 feet across the Appalachian Ridge.

Three tracts of Buchanan State Forest — at Sideling Hill, Cowans Gap and Big Cove Tannery — provide 29,187 acres of public whitetail country. Of Fulton's four gamelands, three exceed 5,900 acres. The largest is 6,835-acre SGL No. 124 near Mercersburg. SGL 53, locally called the "Meadow Grounds," is 5,927 of regrown farmland, a popular hunting tract.

Food, lodging and services, contact: Fulton County Tourist Promotion Agency, 112 North Third St., McConnellsburg, PA 17233. Phone: (717) 485-4064.

IN BRIEF:

State Gamelands: 20,530 acres
State Parks & Forests: 29,187 acres
Farm-Game Co-op: 14,693 acres (90 farms)
Forest-Game Co-op: 6,379 acres
Safety Zone Lands: 16,293 acres (73 tracts)

1999 Buck/Doe Harvest: 2,133/1,637
1999 Archery Buck/Doe Harvest: 163/202
1999 Muzzleloader Buck/Doe Harvest: 33/146
Forested Square Miles (FSM): 302
1999 Buck Harvest/FSM: 7.1
Winter Deer Density/FSM: 30
Desired Winter Deer Density/FSM: 20

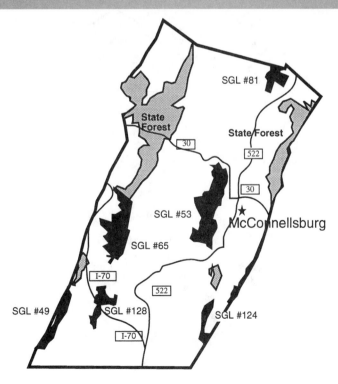

HUNTINGDON COUNTY

Best known for Raystown Lake and its surrounding, game-rich mountains, Huntingdon's 877 square miles range in elevation from 520 to 2,400 feet.

Three-fourths of the county is forested with the "lay of the land" notably a series of ridges and valleys running in a northeast-southwest direction. Corn, grain, alfalfa, oats and wheat comprise a portion of the scattered farmlands although cattle lands dominate.

There's never a problem finding accessible public hunting lands here. Within Rothrock State Forest, south of State College, 66,272 acres are available with 20,000 acres of Corps of Engineers land bordering Raystown Lake.

Eight gamelands all hold viable deer populations. The most notable include 5,724-acre SGL No. 67 around Broad Top City, 5,679-acre SGL No. 112 near Huntingdon and 4,121-acre SGL No. 71 near Mapleton Depot.

Food, lodging and services, contact: Huntingdon County Visitors Bureau, RR #1, Box 222A, Seven Points Road, Hesston, PA 16647. Phone: (888) Raystown or (814) 658-0060.

IN BRIEF:

State Gamelands: 27,354 acres
State Parks & Forests: 66,452 acres
Farm-Game Co-op: 33,552 acres (203 farms)
Forest-Game Co-op: 19,896 acres
Safety Zone Lands: 36,701 acres (158 tracts)

1999 Buck/Doe Harvest: 4,922/3,540
1999 Archery Buck/Doe Harvest: 416/448
1999 Muzzleloader Buck/Doe Harvest: 19/202
Forested Square Miles (FSM): 657
1999 Buck Harvest/FSM: 7.5
Winter Deer Density/FSM: 40
Desired Winter Deer Density/FSM: 21

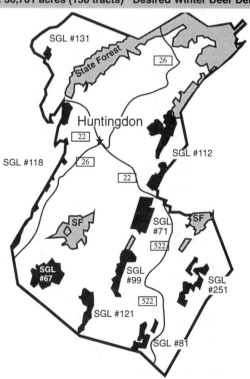

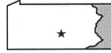

JUNIATA COUNTY

Northwest of Harrisburg, Juniata's 392 square miles are mountainous with long, narrow sandstone ridges alternating with equally long valleys. Elevations go from 383 to 2,260 feet.

Two-thirds of the county is forested with the remainder largely in cattle, fruit and field crop production. Apple and peach orchards and corn, alfalfa, oats and wheat are the main crops.

Tuscarora State Forest holds 17,337 acres north of Reeds Gap with three game-lands tracts inside county borders. The biggest is SGL No. 107 near Mifflintown with 6,560 acres. The Tuscarora Mountain region of Juniata links it with four other counties. Much of it is in public hunting lands which attract sportsmen in the bow, buck and doe seasons.

Food, lodging and services, contact: Juniata-Mifflin Counties Tourist Promotion Agency, 152 East Market St., Ste. 103, Lewistown, PA 17044. Phone: (877) 568-9739.

IN BRIEF:

State Gamelands: 8,909 acres
State Parks & Forests: 17,337 acres
Farm-Game Co-op: 13,731 acres (94 farms)
Forest-Game Co-op: 5,117 acres
Safety Zone Lands: 38,826 acres (196 tracts)

1999 Buck/Doe Harvest: 1,545/1,223
1999 Archery Buck/Doe Harvest: 206/168
1999 Muzzleloader Buck/Doe Harvest: 2/53
Forested Square Miles (FSM): 259
1999 Buck Harvest/FSM: 6.0
Winter Deer Density/FSM: 34
Desired Winter Deer Density/FSM: 18

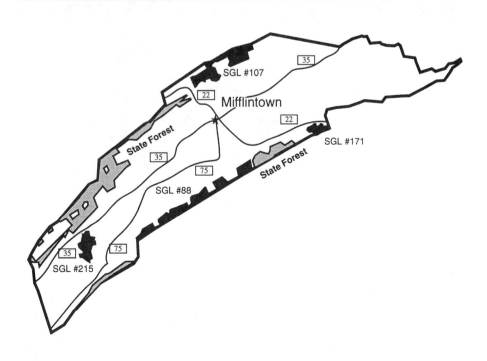

MIFFLIN COUNTY

Southeast of State College, Mifflin's 413 square miles lie in the rich Appalachian Ridge and Valley Region. The mountain-valley terrain ranges from 440 to 2,340 feet.

Long, narrow sandstone ridges and long valleys with deep soils hold rich, deciduous forest vegetation. Farms occupy about 34 percent of the land with over half in livestock and livestock products. Primary vegetables are corn and tomatoes with apples and peaches on orchard lands.

Two state forests — Bald Eagle and Tuscarora — provide more than 57,000 acres of public deer hunting grounds. Only one gameland of less than 500 acres is found near Strodes Mills.

However, Mifflin's Farm-Game and Safety Zone cooperators allow hunting on private lands, which exceed 57,000 acres. Mifflin's deer numbers in the mid-1990s were close to its goal of 22 whitetails per square forested mile.

Food, lodging and services, contact: Juniata-Mifflin Counties Tourist Promotion Agency, 152 East Market St., Ste. 103, Lewistown, PA 17044. Phone: (877) 568-9739 or (717) 248-6713.

IN BRIEF:

State Gamelands: 534 acres

State Parks & Forests: 57,361 acres

Farm-Game Co-op: 8,275 acres (54 farms)

Forest-Game Co-op: 581 acres

Safety Zone Lands: 61,971 acres (455 tracts)

1999 Buck/Doe Harvest: 1,734/1,081

1999 Archery Buck/Doe Harvest:298/247

1999 Muzzleloader Buck/Doe Harvest: 2/53

Forested Square Miles (FSM): 296

1999 Buck Harvest/FSM: 5.9

Winter Deer Density/FSM: 32

Desired Winter Deer Density/FSM: 22

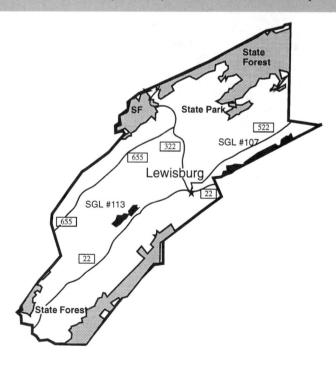

PERRY COUNTY

Elevations here range from 310 to 2,240 feet within the Appalachian Ridge and Valley Region of the state. Of Perry's 557 square miles, 64 percent is wooded. The mountain country holds long, narrow sandstone ridges penetrated by long valleys.

Farms occupy nearly one-third of the county with corn, alfalfa, oats and wheat on most harvest lands. More than 500 of these private holdings are in Game Commission co-op programs.

Tuscarora State Forest's 41,098 acres in the New Germantown area and six gamelands comprise Perry County's public hunting lands. Of the latter, SGL No. 170 near Marysville is the most expansive followed by SGL No. 88 at Ickesburg with 6,930 acres.

Food, lodging and services, contact: Gettysburg Convention and Visitors Bureau, Town House Suites, Suite 1419, 14th floor, 660 Boas St., Harrisburg, PA 17120, Phone: (717) 231-7788.

IN BRIEF:

State Gamelands: 20,461 acres
State Parks & Forests: 41,098 acres
Farm-Game Co-op: 30,204 acres (248 farms)
Forest-Game Co-op: 1,415 acres
Safety Zone Lands: 43,141 acres (285 tracts)

1999 Buck/Doe Harvest: 2,824/2,514
1999 Archery Buck/Doe Harvest: 485/367
1999 Muzzleloader Buck/Doe Harvest: 6/100
Forested Square Miles (FSM): 355
1999 Buck Harvest/FSM: 8.0
Winter Deer Density/FSM: 37
Desired Winter Deer Density/FSM: 17

SNYDER COUNTY

As is typical of the region, Snyder's mountainous landscape is sliced by long ridges and narrow valleys. Half of the county is forested with about 45 percent of the 329 square miles in farmland. Crops include tobacco and apples with hog and cattle raising on some parcels.

Elevations range from 400 to 2,165 feet.

Units at Beaver Springs and Troxelville, parts of Bald Eagle State Forest, provide 28,684 acres of deer habitat. Three gamelands combine for over 25,000 additional hunting territory; the largest SGL No. 188 near Beavertown.

Annual buck and doe harvests average about 2,000 with deer numbers above carrying capacity, according to commission biologists.

Food, lodging and services, contact: Susquehanna Valley Visitors Bureau, RR 2, 219D Hafer Rd., Lewisburg, PA 17837. Phone: (800) 525-7320 or (570) 524-7234.

IN BRIEF:

State Gamelands: 2,714 acres
State Parks & Forests: 28,684 acres
Farm-Game Co-op: 53,823 acres (460 farms)
Forest-Game Co-op: 224 acres
Safety Zone Lands: 26,706 acres (196 tracts)

1999 Buck/Doe Harvest: 1,152/908
1999 Archery Buck/Doe Harvest: 291/247
1999 Muzzleloader Buck/Doe Harvest: 7/47
Forested Square Miles (FSM): 169
1999 Buck Harvest/FSM: 6.8
Winter Deer Density/FSM: 33
Desired Winter Deer Density/FSM: 18

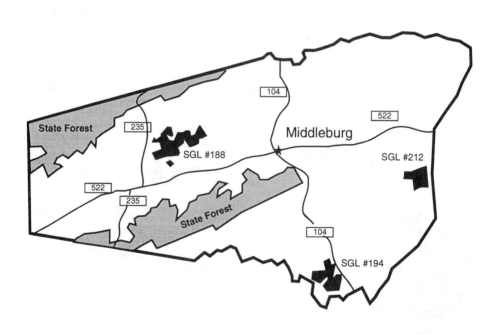

NORTHEAST REGION

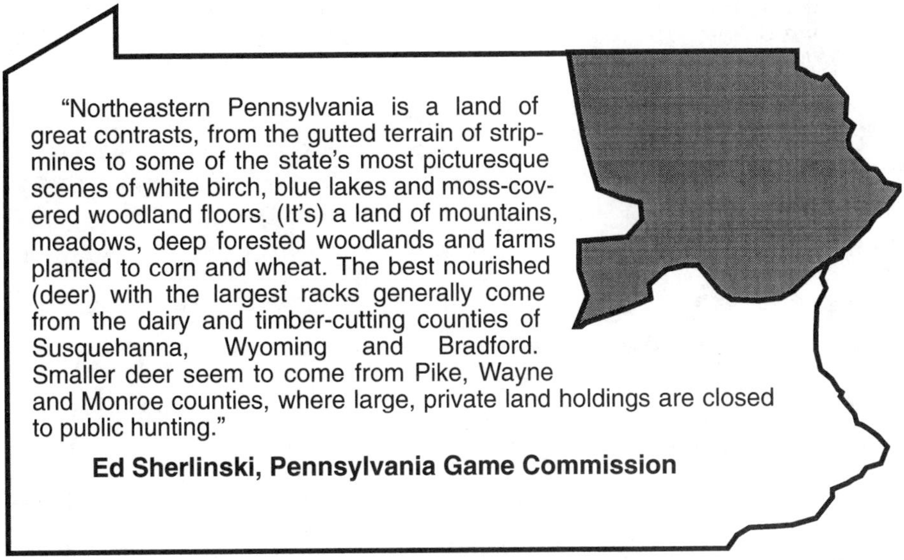

"Northeastern Pennsylvania is a land of great contrasts, from the gutted terrain of strip-mines to some of the state's most picturesque scenes of white birch, blue lakes and moss-covered woodland floors. (It's) a land of mountains, meadows, deep forested woodlands and farms planted to corn and wheat. The best nourished (deer) with the largest racks generally come from the dairy and timber-cutting counties of Susquehanna, Wyoming and Bradford. Smaller deer seem to come from Pike, Wayne and Monroe counties, where large, private land holdings are closed to public hunting."

Ed Sherlinski, Pennsylvania Game Commission

Pennsylvania Game Commission

Northeast Region
P.O. Box 220
Dallas, PA 18612
Phone: Toll free 1 (877) 877-9357; (570) 675-1143; (570) 675-1144
Bradford, Carbon, Columbia, Lackawanna, Luzerne, Monroe, Montour, Northumberland, Pike, Sullivan, Susquehanna, Wayne and Wyoming counties.

BRADFORD COUNTY

Bradford provides the best of both worlds for the deer hunter, offering farm-pasture habitats and forested mountains and valleys. The county's north, approaching the New York border, is rolling and hilly with the south largely rugged with high plateaus.

The county covers 1,152 square miles with elevations ranging from 640 to 2,420 feet.

Fifty-nine percent of Bradford is wooded with numerous beef cattle and dairy farms throughout, typically in scenic valleys rimmed by highland forests. Hay, corn, alfalfa and oats comprise the harvestable crops with pasture lands supporting a thriving dairy business.

Bradford typically makes the state's annual top 10 list in both deer harvest numbers and the amount of bucks taken per square mile of woodland.

Only 3,838 acres of Tioga State Forest, north of Canton, overlap into Bradford but the lack of public forest land is made up by 11 state gamelands. Near Tioga S.F. is SGL No. 12 with 23,289 acres. SGL No. 36 near Towanda covers 18,929 acres with 5,618-acre SGL No. 219 at Warren Center.

Food, lodging and services, contact: Endless Mountains Visitors Bureau, 712 Route 6 East, Tunkhannock, PA 18657. Phone: (800) 769-8999 or (570) 836-5431.

IN BRIEF:

State Gamelands: 55,178 acres

State Parks & Forests: 3,838 acres

Farm-Game Co-op: 14,544 acres (79 farms)

Forest-Game Co-op: None

Safety Zone Lands: 95,322 acres (538 tracts)

1999 Buck/Doe Harvest: 6,056/6,353

1999 Archery Buck/Doe Harvest: 956/873

1999 Muzzleloader Buck/Doe Harvest: 27/342

Forested Square Miles (FSM): 676

1999 Buck Harvest/FSM: 9.0

Winter Deer Density/FSM: 42

Desired Winter Deer Density/FSM: 22

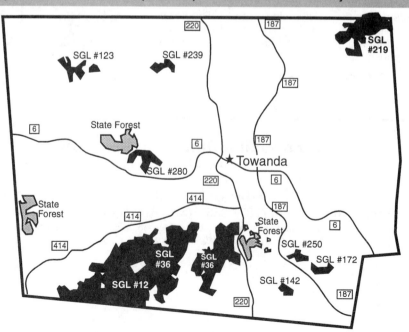

CARBON COUNTY

This Appalachian Mountain county covers only 384 square miles but it offers abundant public hunting lands. With elevations of 370 to 2,220 feet, Carbon's landscape is 75 percent wooded with only eight percent occupation by farms. Corn, oats, barley and hay are the chief crops with cattle farming a secondary business.

Bordered on the south by the Blue Mountain with heavily glaciated uplands, Carbon is both scenic and rugged. The Lehigh River cuts through the county and gamelands.

Hickory Run State Park is popular year-around with anglers, campers and sightseers and a fall and winter attraction for hunters. The park east of White Haven, totals 15,398 acres.

Five gamelands, the largest SGL No. 141 near Jim Thorpe, spans 17,047 acres. SGL No. 40 at White haven offers another 6,118 acres.

Food, lodging and services, contact: Carbon County Tourist Promotion Agency, Railroad Station, P.O. Box 90, Jim Thorpe, PA 18229. Phone: (888) 546-8467 or (570) 325-3673.

IN BRIEF:

State Gamelands: 26,337 acres
State Parks & Forests: 17,351 acres
Farm-Game Co-op: 983 acres (6 farms)
Forest-Game Co-op: 5,811 acres
Safety Zone Lands: 37,842 acres (87 tracts)

1999 Buck/Doe Harvest: 1,411/1,040
1999 Archery Buck/Doe Harvest: 239/213
1999 Muzzleloader Buck/Doe Harvest: 12/133
Forested Square Miles (FSM): 286
1999 Buck Harvest/FSM: 4.9
Winter Deer Density/FSM: 27
Desired Winter Deer Density/FSM: 23

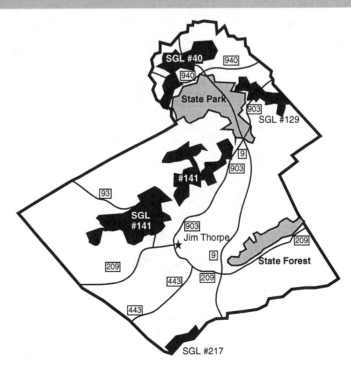

COLUMBIA COUNTY

Mountainous Columbia County holds long, narrow ridges with elevations of 460 to 2,450 feet. Spanning only 486 square miles with 53 percent of its surface forested, little Columbia produces abundant and occasional big bucks.

Farms cover about 39 percent of the terrain, mostly in croplands yielding oats, soybeans, corn and hay.

In terms of buck harvest per square mile of forest, Columbia ranks exceptionally high, particularly for a "mountain" county.

Despite being heavily forested, no state forest or park lands are present in the county. However, hunters are welcome on 12,538-acre SGL No. 58 near Catawissa, 4,335-acre SGL No. 226 near Millville and on three smaller tracts.

More than 30,000 acres of private holdings are open to hunters on safety zone and farm-game cooperatives.

Food, lodging and services, contact: Columbia-Montour Tourist Promotion Agency, Inc., 121 Paper Mill Rd., Bloomsburg, PA 17815. Phone: (800) 847-4810 or (570) 784-8279.

IN BRIEF:

State Gamelands: 20,345 acres
State Parks & Forests: None
Farm-Game Co-op: 13,892 acres (145 farms)
Forest-Game Co-op: None
Safety Zone Lands: 16,641 acres (130 tracts)

1999 Buck/Doe Harvest: 2,452/2,177
1999 Archery Buck/Doe Harvest: 487/378
1999 Muzzleloader Buck/Doe Harvest: 6/114
Forested Square Miles (FSM): 257
1999 Buck Harvest/FSM: 9.5
Winter Deer Density/FSM: 46
Desired Winter Deer Density/FSM: 19

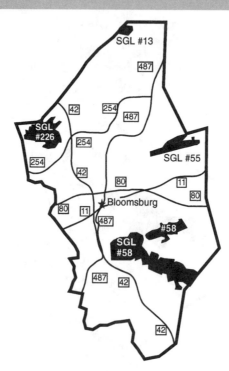

LACKAWANNA COUNTY

Encompassing Scranton, Lackawanna provides good hunting within a short drive of the city. The county's 461 square miles are 68 percent forested.

This is the heart of the anthracite region with its trademarked high, upland, dissected character. Farms cover only 16 percent of the county with both croplands and cattle operations to be found. The main crops include hay, corn, oats and wheat.

Three gamelands — the biggest 3,984-acre SGL No. 300 near Carbondale and 3,430-acre SGL No. 135 near Gouldsboro — are open to deer hunters. Lackawanna State Forest provides another 6,024 acres, west of Thornhurst.

Food, lodging and services, contact: Northeast PA Convention and Visitors Bureau, 99 Glenmaura National Blvd., Moosic, PA 18507. Phone: (888) 546-8467 or (570) 325-3673.

IN BRIEF:

State Gamelands: 8,913 acres
State Parks & Forests: 6,024 acres
Farm-Game Co-op: None
Forest-Game Co-op: None
Safety Zone Lands: 14,697 acres (100 tracts)

1999 Buck/Doe Harvest: 1,694/1,203
1999 Archery Buck/Doe Harvest: 275/185
1999 Muzzleloader Buck/Doe Harvest: 2/132
Forested Square Miles (FSM): 311
1999 Buck Harvest/FSM: 5.5
Winter Deer Density/FSM: 32
Desired Winter Deer Density/FSM: 23

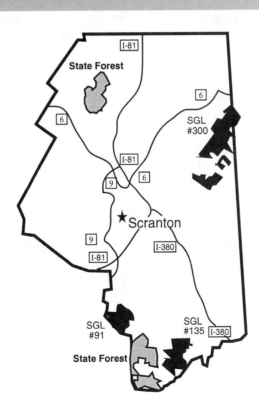

LUZERNE COUNTY

Luzerne's 891 square miles include the city of Wilkes-Barre and plentiful mountain and valley woodlands. Forests encompass two-thirds of the county throughout the rugged, dissected plateaus. Elevations range from 480 to 2,463 feet.

Farmland covers 12 percent of the county with just over half in harvested crops and the remainder in cattle production. Potatoes, alfalfa, corn and oats lead the "grocery" list.

Luzerne is rich in both state forests and gamelands. The public woodlands include 8,085 acres of Ricketts Glen State Park at Red Rock and 1,416 acres of Lackawanna State Forest west of Plymouth.

Ten gamelands are scattered about the county. The most notable is SGL No. 91 at Bear Creek with 14,390 acres followed by SGL No. 187 near White Haven (8,186 acres) and SGL No. 119 at Mountain Top (7,963 acres).

Food, lodging and services, contact: Luzerne County Tourist Promotion Agency, 56 Public Square, Wilkes Barre, PA 18701. Phone: (888) 905-2872 or (570) 819-1877.

IN BRIEF:

State Gamelands: 47,278 acres
State Parks & Forests: 9,501 acres
Farm-Game Co-op: 15,193 acres (159 farms)
Forest-Game Co-op: None
Safety Zone Lands: 20,527 acres (176 tracts)

1999 Buck/Doe Harvest: 3,909/2,844
1999 Archery Buck/Doe Harvest: 662/502
1999 Muzzleloader Buck/Doe Harvest: 22/234
Forested Square Miles (FSM): 586
1999 Buck Harvest/FSM: 6.7
Winter Deer Density/FSM: 33
Desired Winter Deer Density/FSM: 17

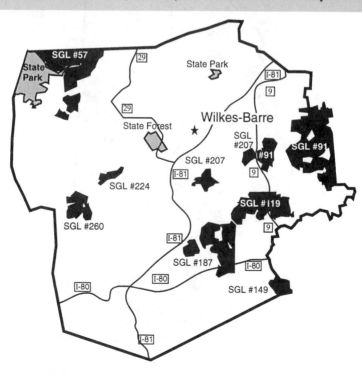

MONROE COUNTY

In the heart of the tourist-rich Poconos, Monroe borders the Delaware River and New Jersey. The land in the northern portion of the county is hilly with more mountainous features along the Blue Mountain, rimming its southern line. Elevations go from 300 to 2,220 feet.

This is not an area of rugged mountains and tall peaks. Its high, forested upland is interspersed with numerous glacial lakes. Forests cover three-fourths of Monroe County.

Only eight percent of the county is farmland, planted in hay, corn, wheat and oats or used for cattle production.

In the Canadensis-Tannersville region is the 8,637-acre tract of Delaware State Forest. State parklands at Tobyhanna and Gouldsboro offer hunters 5,485 acres with Big Pocono State park contributing another 1,017 huntable public grounds.

Six gamelands, topped by 25,527-acre SGL No. 127 near Tannersville also offer visiting hunters good whitetail habitat.

Food, lodging and services, contact: Pocono Mountains Visitors Bureau, Inc., 1004 Main St., Stroudsburg, PA 18360. Phone: (800) 762-6667 or (570) 421-5791.

IN BRIEF:

State Gamelands: 38,378 acres
State Parks & Forests: 15,139 acres
Farm-Game Co-op: 10,935 acres (108 farms)
Forest-Game Co-op: None
Safety Zone Lands: 433 acres (6 tracts)

1999 Buck/Doe Harvest: 1,908/996
1999 Archery Buck/Doe Harvest: 267/153
1999 Muzzleloader Buck/Doe Harvest: 21/130
Forested Square Miles (FSM): 461
1999 Buck Harvest/FSM: 4.1
Winter Deer Density/FSM: 22
Desired Winter Deer Density/FSM: 18

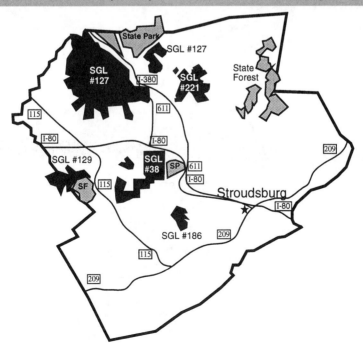

MONTOUR COUNTY

One of the state's smallest counties with only 131 square land miles, tiny Montour is a consistent buck and doe producer. It is a mountainous region with 27 percent woodland, producing a relatively high buck harvest.

Fifty-eight percent of Montour is in farmland, accounting for well-fed and numerous deer. Nearly two-thirds of the farms are in crop production (tobacco, alfalfa, corn, oats and soybeans) with the remainder hosting hogs and cattle.

Elevations here run from 440 to 1,380 feet.

As might be expected, no state forest lands penetrate the county and only one small (227-acre) gameland (SGL No. 115 near Danville) is available. Deer hunting here is best done by contacting private landowners, as those in farm co-op and safety zone programs.

Due to the abundance of farmland with adjacent woods, buck harvests are exceptionally high, in some years exceeding 13 bucks taken per square mile of woodland.

Food, lodging and services, contact: Columbia-Montour Tourist Promotion Agency, Inc., 121 Paper Mill Rd., Bloomsburg, PA 17815. Phone: (800) 847-4810 or (570) 784-8279.

IN BRIEF:

State Gamelands: 227 acres

State Parks & Forests: None

Farm-Game Co-op: 10,260 acres (67 farms)

Forest-Game Co-op: None

Safety Zone Lands: 7,253 acres (53 tracts)

1999 Buck/Doe Harvest: 474/492

1999 Archery Buck/Doe Harvest: 104/70

1999 Muzzleloader Buck/Doe Harvest: 2/34

Forested Square Miles (FSM): 36

1999 Buck Harvest/FSM: 13.1

Winter Deer Density/FSM: 72

Desired Winter Deer Density/FSM: 30

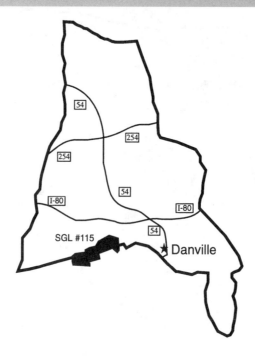

NORTHUMBERLAND COUNTY

Northumberland's 461 square miles are 50 percent forested. Elevations range from 400 to 1,760 feet across the northern Appalachian Ridge countryside.

Broad valleys broken by north-south running ridges characterize the land. Farm country composes about 42 percent of the landscape with cropland dominating. Wheat, soybeans, corn and alfalfa are the chief crops with pig farming another important business.

As with neighboring Montour, Northumberland has no state park or state forest holdings. However, four gamelands, with SGL No. 84 near Treverton the biggest at 8,154 acres, are available, all with good deer populations. Montour also has more farm-game cooperatives than any other Northeast Region county.

Food, lodging and services, contact: Susquehanna Valley Visitors Bureau, RR 2, 219D Hafer Rd., Lewisburg, PA 17837. Phone: (800) 525-7320 or (570) 524-7234.

IN BRIEF:

State Gamelands: 10,735 acres
State Parks & Forests: None
Farm-Game Co-op: 66,716 acres (741 farms)
Forest-Game Co-op: None
Safety Zone Lands: 11,019 acres (44 tracts)

1999 Buck/Doe Harvest: 1,244/1,406
1999 Archery Buck/Doe Harvest: 258/211
1999 Muzzleloader Buck/Doe Harvest: 11/62
Forested Square Miles (FSM): 228
1999 Buck Harvest/FSM: 5.5
Winter Deer Density/FSM: 26
Desired Winter Deer Density/FSM: 23

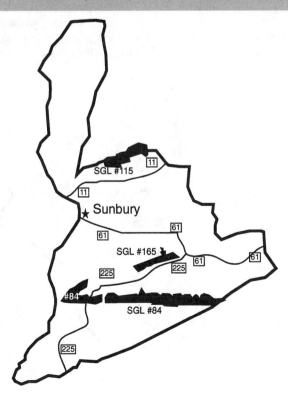

PIKE COUNTY

Another Pocono Mountain county with numerous lakes, ponds and public hunting lands, Pike borders portions of New Jersey and New York to the east. It spans 550 square miles. Numerous wetlands penetrate the 82 percent of the countryside with forests, serving as home for plentiful black bears as well as whitetails.

Many private hunting clubs and woodland vacation and resident developments cover the county, accounting for an under-harvest of deer and animals smaller in size than many other counties. This is one of few counties in the state which, in the mid-1990s, held deer numbers below carrying capacity.

Only two percent of the county is in farms, mainly holding livestock. Crops include hay, corn and oats.

Many deer hunters head to the county's scattered tracts, totaling 62,983-acres, of Delaware State Forest lands for buck season. Also popular is the 1,450-acre bear and deer-rich Promised Land State Park, north of Canadensis.

Five state gamelands offer another 21,000-plus acres with SGL No. 180 near Greely the most expansive.

Food, lodging and services, contact: Pocono Mountains Visitors Bureau, Inc., 1004 Main St., Stroudsburg, PA 18360. Phone: (800) 762-6667 or (570) 421-5791.

IN BRIEF:

State Gamelands: 21,564 acres

State Parks & Forests: 64,433 acres

Farm-Game Co-op: None

Forest-Game Co-op: None

Safety Zone Lands: 85 acres (1 tract)

1999 Buck/Doe Harvest: 2,122/1,390

1999 Archery Buck/Doe Harvest: 234/205

1999 Muzzleloader Buck/Doe Harvest: 2/117

Forested Square Miles (FSM): 451

1999 Buck Harvest/FSM: 4.7

Winter Deer Density/FSM: 22

Desired Winter Deer Density/FSM: 19

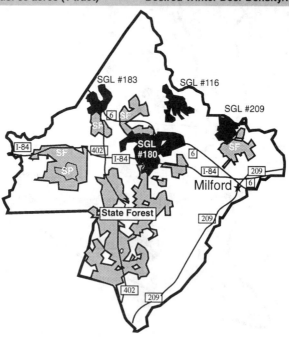

SULLIVAN COUNTY

This is the second least populous county in the state, made up of 86 percent forest land. Covering 451 square miles, elevations run from 779 to 2,593 square feet.

Deep gorges and varying valleys cover Sullivan although much of its forests are elevated, accounting for geologists' descriptions as a "high relief" area.

Farms occupy about 12 percent of the land, most holding livestock. Crops include hay, corn and oats.

Sullivan's deer numbers far outnumber its human residents although populations swell in the hunting seasons as visitors escape to their backwoods cabins and lodges.

Wyoming State Forest's 39,013 acres, in the Forksville and Hillsgrove areas, entice many visiting sportsmen with a few preferring the 920-acres of scenic World's End State Park next to Forksville.

State gamelands number four with extensive (45,529 acres) SGL No. 13 near Sonestown the largest. SGL No. 66 near Lopez is another popular deer hunting site.

Food, lodging and services, contact: Endless Mountains Visitors Bureau, 712 Route 6 East, Tunkhannock, PA 18657. Phone: (800) 769-8999 or (570) 836-5431.

IN BRIEF:

State Gamelands: 57,182 acres

State Parks & Forests: 39,933 acres

Farm-Game Co-op: None

Forest-Game Co-op: None

Safety Zone Lands: 12,648 acres (47 tracts)

1999 Buck/Doe Harvest: 1,635/1,232

1999 Archery Buck/Doe Harvest: 209/202

1999 Muzzleloader Buck/Doe Harvest: 2/118

Forested Square Miles (FSM): 387

1999 Buck Harvest/FSM: 4.2

Winter Deer Density/FSM: 27

Desired Winter Deer Density/FSM: 16

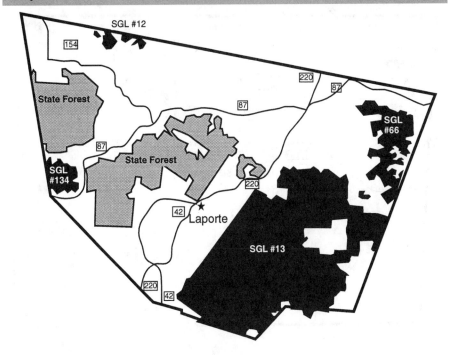

SUSQUEHANNA COUNTY

Bordering New York on the north, Susquehanna County's 826 square miles are 65 percent forested. Mountain elevations span 760 to 2,693 feet.

Another completely rural county, cattle and dairy products are the focus on most of the 34 percent of landscape in farmland. Hay, corn and oats are the main crops.

Rolling and hilly, Susquehanna, like neighboring Bradford, has larger deer than most northern tier counties because of crop and pasture lands and numerous timber-cuts. The latter yield the sapling and second growth habitat which is more conducive to good deer country than mature forests.

No state forests or parks are found here but there's plenty of hunting grounds — more than 60,000 acres — on safety zone and co-op farms. Add to that five gamelands open to public hunting. SGL No. 35 near Hallstead with 7,739 acres is the biggest although two others exceed 2,000 acres.

Food, lodging and services, contact: Endless Mountains Visitors Bureau, 712 Route 6 East, Tunkhannock, PA 18657. Phone: (800) 769-8999 or (570) 836-5431.

IN BRIEF:

State Gamelands: 14,324 acres

State Parks & Forests: None

Farm-Game Co-op: 41,277 acres (256 farms)

Forest-Game Co-op: None

Safety Zone Lands: 20,450 acres (89 tracts)

1999 Buck/Doe Harvest: 3,743/3,482

1999 Archery Buck/Doe Harvest: 463/365

1999 Muzzleloader Buck/Doe Harvest: 4/213

Forested Square Miles (FSM): 531

1999 Buck Harvest/FSM: 7.1

Winter Deer Density/FSM: 37

Desired Winter Deer Density/FSM: 25

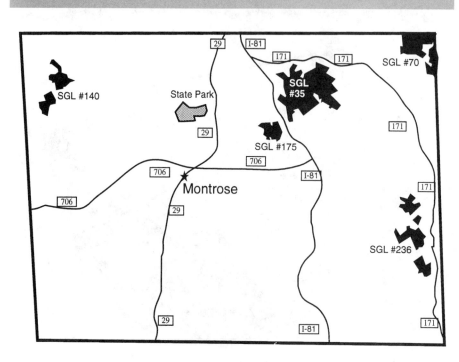

WAYNE COUNTY

Bordering New York on its east, Wayne covers 731 square miles with elevations from 680 to 2,654 feet. Two-thirds of the county is wooded.

Farms occupy much of the remainder of the county with livestock and livestock products dominating. Hay, oats and corn are the main crops.

Wayne's topography, typical of the Poconos, consists of high wooded hills with hundreds of small, forest-encircled glacial lakes.

Prompton State Park, east of Honesdale, is the county's only state-owned park-land with 850 acres. The biggest public tract (9,367 acres) is SGL No. 159 at Lookout. SGL No. 70 near Susquehanna contributes another 3,766 acres. Two other smaller gamelands are located at Starlight and Archbald. More than 14,000 acres of private farms are also available to sportsmen.

Food, lodging and services, contact: Pocono Mountains Visitors Bureau, Inc., 1004 Main St., Stroudsburg, PA 18360. Phone: (800) 762-6667 or (570) 421-5791.

IN BRIEF:

State Gamelands: 14,167 acres
State Parks & Forests: 850 acres
Farm-Game Co-op: 734 acres (8 farms)
Forest-Game Co-op: None
Safety Zone Lands: 13,314 acres (90 tracts)

1999 Buck/Doe Harvest: 3,589/2,367
1999 Archery Buck/Doe Harvest: 274/311
1999 Muzzleloader Buck/Doe Harvest: 5/109
Forested Square Miles (FSM): 480
1999 Buck Harvest/FSM: 7.5
Winter Deer Density/FSM: 38
Desired Winter Deer Density/FSM: 20

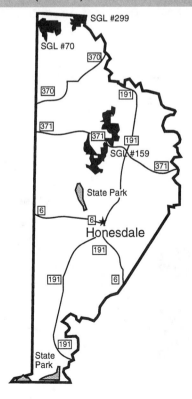

WYOMING COUNTY

Another totally rural county, Wyoming covers 399 square miles with 62 percent in forest. Elevations range from 560 to 2,380 feet.

About 30 percent of the county is in farmland, primarily used for livestock. Hay, corn and oats are grown on tilled lands.

Northeast of the Susquehanna River, this county duplicates the ecological and geographic features of neighboring Bradford and Susquehanna counties. Southwest of the river, topography rises rapidly to 2,000 feet, forming a rugged, forested plateau interrupted by stream-bottom gorges.

A unit of Lackawanna State Forest with 1,273 acres overlaps into Wyoming with SGL No. 57, near Noxen, offering 28,242 acres. More than 20,000 acres of co-op lands can also be found.

Food, lodging and services, contact: Endless Mountains Visitors Bureau, 712 Route 6 East, Tunkhannock, PA 18657. Phone: (800) 769-8999 or (570) 836-5431.

IN BRIEF:

State Gamelands: 28,272 acres
State Parks & Forests: 1,273 acres
Farm-Game Co-op: 9,258 acres (46 farms)
Forest-Game Co-op: 1,350 acres
Safety Zone Lands: 10,942 acres (56 tracts)

1999 Buck/Doe Harvest: 1,663/1,617
1999 Archery Buck/Doe Harvest: 239/202
1999 Muzzleloader Buck/Doe Harvest: 15/88
Forested Square Miles (FSM): 247
1999 Buck Harvest/FSM: 6.7
Winter Deer Density/FSM: 30
Desired Winter Deer Density/FSM: 23

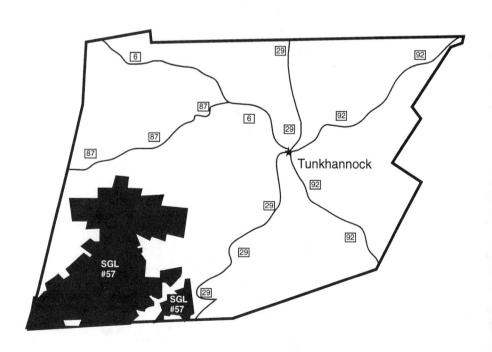

SOUTHEAST REGION

"Nearly a third of the hunting licenses sold in the common-wealth are purchased in this region, which isn't too surprising as it contains nearly half of the state's population. The Southeast's deer population is excellent. Many areas are suffering from an overabundance of whitetails. Countless resident hunters annually travel to the more popular deer hunting territory of the northern tier counties when deer season opens. More often than not, they leave behind farm-fed whitetails which weigh more and have larger antlers that those found farther north. Farmers here often complain about excessive crop damage and posting is often the cause. If hunters don't have access, they can't harvest deer causing the damage."

Mike Schmit,
Pennsylvania Game Commission

Pennsylvania Game Commission
Southeast Region
RD 2, Box 2584
Reading, PA 19605
Phone: Toll free 1 (877) 877-9470; (610) 926-3136; (610) 926-3137
Berks, Bucks, Chester, Dauphin, Delaware, Lancaster, Lebanon, Lehigh, Montgomery, Northampton, Philadelphia, Schuylkill and York

BERKS COUNTY

In terms of bucks taken by hunters per square mile of woodland, Berks leads the list just about every year. Abundant and fertile farmland plays no small part in the county's deer populations and sizes. Add to that (unusual in the Southeast) abundant public hunting grounds totaling nearly 27,000 acres and another 70,000 in landowner-game commission co-ops.

Covering 861 square miles with 134 to 1,680-foot elevations, the county is 35 percent forested. The rolling, hilly lowlands of southern Berks contrast sharply with the Blue Mountain on its northern edge.

Farms occupy about 47 percent of the county, nearly three-quarters in cropland and the remainder cattle holdings. Alfalfa, hay, wheat, corn and barley are the chief crops.

French Creek State Park near Birdsboro and a small tract of Weiser State Forest are the sole Dept. of Environmental Resources holdings here. State gamelands on the Blue Mountain at Shartlesville (SGL No. 110 with 10,093 acres) and Eckville (SGL No. 106 holding 9,197 acres) and three others are popular deer hunting grounds.

Food, lodging and services, contact: Reading and Berks County Visitors Bureau, 352 Penn St., Reading, PA 19602. Phone: (800) 443-6610 or (610) 375-4085.

IN BRIEF:

State Gamelands: 21,130 acres
State Parks & Forests: 5,790 acres
Farm-Game Co-op: 64,164 acres (576 farms)
Forest-Game Co-op: 4,300 acres
Safety Zone Lands: 5,773 acres (49 tracts)

1999 Buck/Doe Harvest: 4,046/4,089
1999 Archery Buck/Doe Harvest: 1,423/964
1999 Muzzleloader Buck/Doe Harvest: 25/245
Forested Square Miles (FSM): 300
1999 Buck Harvest/FSM: 13.5
Winter Deer Density/FSM: 60
Desired Winter Deer Density/FSM: 21

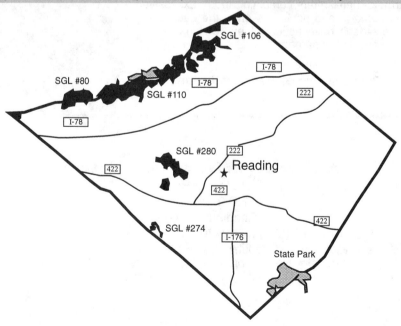

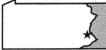

BUCKS COUNTY

Bucks, the fifth most populous county in the state, holds a surprisingly large number of whitetails. Those avoiding vehicles may grow to 3-4 years of age and more, making the county a haven for some monster bucks within its 610 square miles. The biggest human population is in the southern townships.

Set north of Philadelphia and bordering the Delaware River, Bucks county's gently rolling hills, with elevations running from sea level to 980 feet, is 26 percent forested. Farmland composes 29 percent and the remainder is covered with towns, cities and sprawling suburbia. Crops include soybeans, wheat and corn.

A part of the Special Regulations Area, season lengths here are liberal as is the issuance of antlerless deer tags to hunters with access to overpopulated habitats. Rifles are not permitted here for whitetails.

As might be expected, public hunting lands are minimal. Nockamixon State Park, west of Quakertown, covers 3,000 acres. Four gamelands (two under 310 acres each) are within county borders. SGL No. 56 at Upper Black Eddy covers 1,740 acres with SGL No. 157 near Harrow offering 2,010 acres.

Food, lodging and services, contact: Bucks County Conference and Visitors Bureau, 152 Swamp Road, Doylestown, PA 18901. Phone: (800) 836-2825 or (215) 345-4552.

IN BRIEF:

State Gamelands: 4,320 acres

State Parks & Forests: 3,000 acres

Farm-Game Co-op: 9,125 acres (119 farms)

Forest-Game Co-op: None

Safety Zone Lands: 2,064 acres (25 tracts)

1999 Buck/Doe Harvest: 1,688/3,425

1999 Archery Buck/Doe Harvest: 773/969

1999 Muzzleloader Buck/Doe Harvest: 18/152

Forested Square Miles (FSM): 160

1999 Buck Harvest/FSM: 10.6

Winter Deer Density/FSM: N/A

Desired Winter Deer Density/FSM: 5

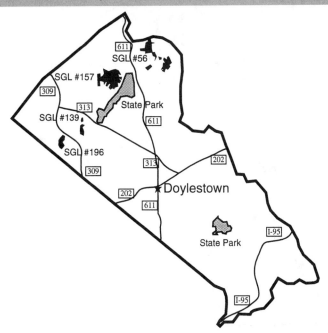

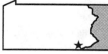

CHESTER COUNTY

A personal note here: Given one county on which to have hunting access in buck season, I'll choose Chester. Not a big woods county (28 percent is forested), the many "gentlemen's farms" — some sizable — provide haven for big-racked bucks and fat does with ready access to crops and the protection of posted refuges. Finding land on which to hunt here is difficult. Seasons and doe tags are liberal, as part of the Special Regulations Area.

Chester's elevations range from 66 to 1,020 feet across its vast 758 square miles. The north is largely composed of broad highlands and ridges with gently rolling lowlands to the south. Farms occupy 45 percent of the county with tobacco, soybeans, corn, alfalfa and barley the prime money-crops.

Marsh Creek State Park's 1,000 acres near Eagle is the only Dept. of Environmental Resources holding in the county. The sole gameland is SGL No. 43 at Elverson, totaling 1,819 acres.

Food, lodging and services, contact: Chester County Conference and Visitors Bureau, 601 Westtown Rd., West Chester, PA 19382. Phone: (800) 228-9933 or (610) 344-6365.

IN BRIEF:

State Gamelands: 1,819 acres
State Parks & Forests: 1,000 acres
Farm-Game Co-op: 18,685 acres (187 farms)
Forest-Game Co-op: None
Safety Zone Lands: 307 acres (3 tracts)

1999 Buck/Doe Harvest: 2,069/4,283
1999 Archery Buck/Doe Harvest: 906/1,375
1999 Muzzleloader Buck/Doe Harvest: 9/170
Forested Square Miles (FSM): 208
1999 Buck Harvest/FSM: 10.0
Winter Deer Density/FSM:
Desired Winter Deer Density/FSM:

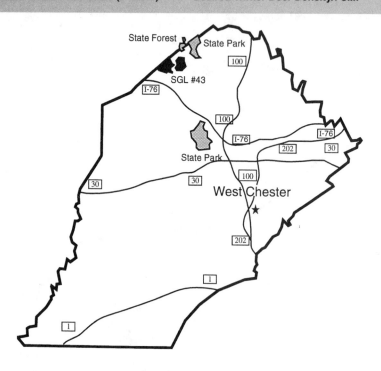

DAUPHIN COUNTY

Encompassing the state capital, Dauphin's 528 square miles vary from mountains in its central and north to rolling lowlands in its south.

Elevations range from 280 to 1,760 feet with fully half of the county in forest. Ridge country typifies northern Dauphin with rich farmlands and rolling hills southward. Livestock and crops are grown on the 33 percent of the county in farmland. Tobacco, barley, corn and hay grow on nearly two-thirds of the harvest soils.

The biggest of three public deer hunting tracts in the county is 41,392-acre SGL 211 near Dauphin. SGL No. 210 at Lykens provides another 11,061 acres. Two tracts of Weiser State Forest are within Dauphin's borders, both adjoined by SGL 210.

Food, lodging and services, contact: PA Capital Regions Vacations Bureau, Inc.,Town House Suites, Suite 1419, 14th floor, 660 Boas St., Harrisburg, PA 17120. Phone: (717) 231-7788.

IN BRIEF:

State Gamelands: 54,273 acres
State Parks & Forests: 8,357 acres
Farm-Game Co-op: 39,624 acres (402 farms)
Forest-Game Co-op: None
Safety Zone Lands: 10,040 acres (62 tracts)

1999 Buck/Doe Harvest: 1,620/1,501
1999 Archery Buck/Doe Harvest: 526/411
1999 Muzzleloader Buck/Doe Harvest: 10/122
Forested Square Miles (FSM): 265
1999 Buck Harvest/FSM: 6.1
Winter Deer Density/FSM: 27
Desired Winter Deer Density/FSM: 23

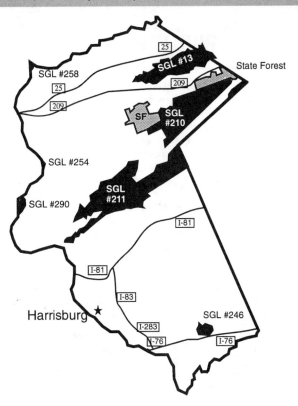

DELAWARE COUNTY

With more than 3,000 residents per square mile, Delaware County's minimal (11 percent) amount of woodland and six percent of farmland offers little space for free-roaming deer. Nevertheless, the county, like most of the lower Southeast, has an overabundance of the adaptable animals and few open lands on which to hunt them.

Sportsmen with permission of private landowners and farmers take only about 500-600 deer annually. Many are bucks, accounting for a variable "per forested square mile" harvest which in recent years has ranged from 5.9 to a phenomenal 13.1.

Elevations rise from the flat lowlands at sea level with rolling lowlands rising to 500 feet. Crops produced here include alfalfa, hay, corn and soybeans.

The relatively small, densely populated suburban county offers no farm-game or safety zone programs. It's within the Southeast's Special Regulations Area.

Food, lodging and services, contact: Brandywine Conference and Visitors Bureau, 200 East State St., Suite 100, Media, PA 19063. Phone (800) 343-3983 or (610) 565-3679.

IN BRIEF:

State Gamelands: None

State Parks & Forests: None

Farm-Game Co-op: None

Forest-Game Co-op: None

Safety Zone Lands: None

1999 Buck/Doe Harvest: 333/983

1999 Archery Buck/Doe Harvest: 180/387

1999 Muzzleloader Buck/Doe Harvest: 2/7

Forested Square Miles (FSM): 20

1999 Buck Harvest/FSM: 16.7

Winter Deer Density/FSM: N/A

Desired Winter Deer Density/FSM: 5

PHILADELPHIA COUNTY

To many people's surprise, deer hunting (bowhunting only) is permitted within the city's borders. Covering 136 square miles, the county (city) ranges in elevation from sea level to 440 feet.

As the ninth most populated city in the nation it seems incongruous that whitetails would be present, but they cause severe damage to vegetation in some places and present hazards when crossing thoroughfares. A few farms within city limits produce corn, a special attractant to whitetails. It's also forested, at places.

In 1999, bowhunters tagged 144 deer within city limits. Many more were killed by vehicles.

No public lands are available for hunting nor does the game commission attempt to manage whitetails in Philadelphia. Most bowhunting is done on private estates.

Food, lodging and services, contact: Philadelphia Convention and Visitors Bureau, 1515 Market St., Suite 2020, Philadelphia, PA 19102. Phone: (800) 537-7676 or (215) 636-3300.

IN BRIEF:

State Gamelands: None

State Parks & Forests: None

Farm-Game Co-op: None

Forest-Game Co-op: None

Safety Zone Lands: None

1999 Buck/Doe Harvest: 34/110

1999 Archery Buck/Doe Harvest: 34/110

1999 Muzzleloader Buck/Doe Harvest: 0/0

Forested Square Miles (FSM): N/A

1999 Buck Harvest/FSM: N/A

Winter Deer Density/FSM: N/A

Desired Winter Deer Density/FSM: N/A

LANCASTER COUNTY

This is farm-country pure and simple with many handsome Amish farms dotting the county. A full 69 percent of the land is in farms, accounting for vast acreage in corn, tobacco, alfalfa, wheat, barley and corn plus pastures and orchards. Numerous deer tap the bounty.

Lancaster's 952 square miles are characterized by broad highlands and ridges in the north and rolling lowlands to the south. Its bordered by the Susquehanna River to the west.

Woodland covers only 13 percent of the county which ranges in elevation from 109 to 1,200 feet. Its deer density per forested square mile is among the highest in the state.

Six gamelands tracts are scattered across this Pennsylvania Dutch landscape. The biggest is SGL No. 46 (5,027 acres) near Hopeland with another 4,537-acres inside the borders of SGL No. 156 at Elstonville.

More than 100,000 acres are available through co-op and safety zone projects.

Food, lodging and services, contact: Pennsylvania Dutch Convention and Visitors Bureau, 501 Greenfield Rd., Lancaster, PA 17601. Phone: (800) 723-8824 or (717) 299-8901.

IN BRIEF:

State Gamelands: 11,287 acres
State Parks & Forests: None
Farm-Game Co-op: 82,320 acres (987 farms)
Forest-Game Co-op: 3,500 acres
Safety Zone Lands: 19,848 acres (181 tracts)

1999 Buck/Doe Harvest: 1,611/1,638
1999 Archery Buck/Doe Harvest: 726/544
1999 Muzzleloader Buck/Doe Harvest: 18/157
Forested Square Miles (FSM): 125
1999 Buck Harvest/FSM: 12.9
Winter Deer Density/FSM: 57
Desired Winter Deer Density/FSM: 19

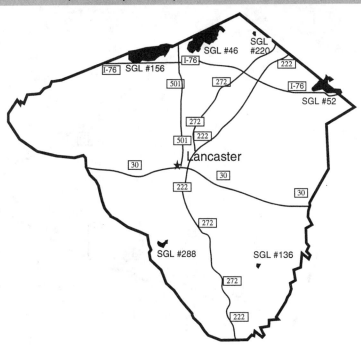

LEBANON COUNTY

Half of Lebanon's 363 square miles is devoted to farming with another 34 percent in woodlands. Its southern three-quarters consists of rolling lowlands dotted with farms. The northern part of the county is more mountainous with elevations spanning 340 to 1,660 feet.

Farms make up half of the fertile, limestone land, mainly in harvestable crops including tobacco, corn, barley and soybeans with plentiful cattle lands, as well.

A portion of Swatara State Park's 3,600 acres is shared with Schuylkill County. SGL No. 145 at Mt. Gretna with its 2,792 acres is the bigger of two gamelands in the county.

Food, lodging and services, contact: PA Capital Regions Vacation Bureau, Town House Suites, Suite 1419, 14th floor, 660 Boas St., Harrisburg, PA 17120. Phone: (717) 272-8555.

IN BRIEF:

State Gamelands: 3,539 acres
State Parks & Forests: 3,000 acres
Farm-Game Co-op: 24,678 acres (242 farms)
Forest-Game Co-op: 600 acres
Safety Zone Lands: 8,882 acres (68 tracts)

1999 Buck/Doe Harvest: 1,021/945
1999 Archery Buck/Doe Harvest: 393/544
1999 Muzzleloader Buck/Doe Harvest: 0/90
Forested Square Miles (FSM): 122
1999 Buck Harvest/FSM: 8.4
Winter Deer Density/FSM: 38
Desired Winter Deer Density/FSM: 23

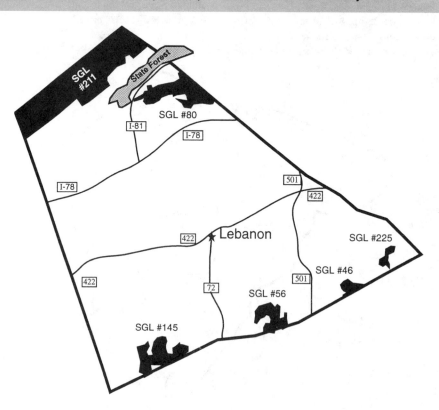

LEHIGH COUNTY

Lehigh's 348 square miles include 43 percent farmland and 29 percent woods, ranging in elevations from 220 to 1,640 feet. Gently rolling hills and farmlands are rimmed in the north by the Blue Mountain. The south is also hilly with abundant farms and country homesites.

Harvested cropland yields wheat, potatoes, barley and corn with numerous peach and apple orchards scattered across the county.

There aren't any state parks or forests here and only two gamelands — SGL No. 217 near Slatedale (4,070 acres) and SGL 205 near Schnecksville (1,303 acres).

Lehigh annually yields some large corn-fed whitetails including trophy quality bucks, among them the state record non-typical bow-buck. It regularly ranks in the top 10 counties for bucks taken per square mile of woodland.

Food, lodging and services, contact: Lehigh Valley Convention and Visitors Bureau, Inc., 2200 Avenue A, Bethlehem, PA 18017. Phone (800) 747-0561 or (610) 882-9200.

IN BRIEF:

State Gamelands: 5,373 acres

State Parks & Forests: None

Farm-Game Co-op: 15,369 acres (184 farms)

Forest-Game Co-op: None

Safety Zone Lands: 3,126 acres (23 tracts)

1999 Buck/Doe Harvest: 1,291/1,165

1999 Archery Buck/Doe Harvest: 484/320

1999 Muzzleloader Buck/Doe Harvest: 7/75

Forested Square Miles (FSM): 100

1999 Buck Harvest/FSM: 12.9

Winter Deer Density/FSM: 66

Desired Winter Deer Density/FSM: 22

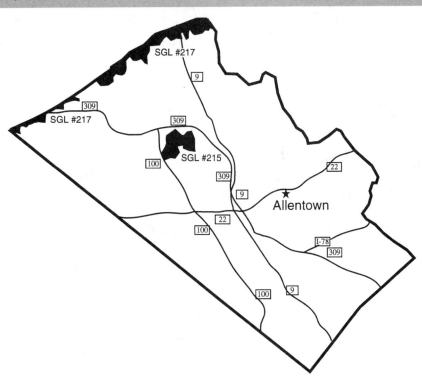

MONTGOMERY COUNTY

Characterized by a belt of ridges and broad highlands, Montgomery is 18 percent forested with another 24 percent in farms. As the third most populous county in the state (more than 1,300 people per square mile), little public hunting land is available even though whitetails live throughout the region.

Elevations within the 486 square mile county run from 20 to 700 feet. Soybeans, corn, hay and wheat cover much of the farm region.

Evansburg State Park's 1,000 acres near Collegeville is the only Dept. of Environmental Resources land in Montgomery and only one small gameland is to be found. The county is part of the Special Regulations Area.

Food, lodging and services, contact: Valley Forge Convention and Visitors Bureau, 600 West Germantown Pike, Ste. 130, Plymouth Meeting, PA 19462. Phone (888) 847-4883 or (610) 834-1550.

IN BRIEF:

State Gamelands: 158 acres

State Parks & Forests: 1,000 acres

Farm-Game Co-op: 10,992 acres (128 farms)

Forest-Game Co-op: None

Safety Zone Lands: 4,459 acres (31 tracts)

1999 Buck/Doe Harvest: 893/1,887

1999 Archery Buck/Doe Harvest: 556/801

1999 Muzzleloader Buck/Doe Harvest: 13/32

Forested Square Miles (FSM): 89

1999 Buck Harvest/FSM: 10.0

Winter Deer Density/FSM: N/A

Desired Winter Deer Density/FSM: 5

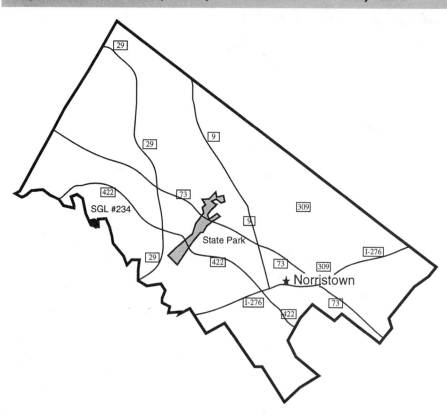

NORTHAMPTON COUNTY

Bordering the Delaware River and New Jersey to the east, Northampton County's 376 square miles are covered 34 percent in forest and 42 percent in farms. Elevations range from 140 to 1,660 feet from its rolling, farm-country lowlands north to the rim of the Appalachian Mountains.

Farms support beef and dairy cattle, primarily, with croplands growing wheat, corn, alfalfa, oats and soybeans. Numerous peach, apple and pear orchards can also be found.

With neighboring Lehigh, Northampton County annually ranks in the top 10 counties for bucks harvested per square wooded mile.

Jacobsburg State Park near Belfast is the sole Dept. of Environmental Resources land in the county, offering hunters 1,000 acres. SGL No. 168 near Wind Gap stretches along the Blue Mountain across 5,173 acres.

Food, lodging and services, contact: Lehigh Valley Convention and Visitors Bureau, Inc., 2200 Avenue A, Bethlehem, PA 18017. Phone (800) 747-0561 or (610) 882-9200.

IN BRIEF:

State Gamelands: 5,173 acres
State Parks & Forests: 1,000 acres
Farm-Game Co-op: 40,297 acres (435 farms)
Forest-Game Co-op: None
Safety Zone Lands: 3,924 acres (17 tracts)

1999 Buck/Doe Harvest: 1,471/1,158
1999 Archery Buck/Doe Harvest: 453/234
1999 Muzzleloader Buck/Doe Harvest: 10/68
Forested Square Miles (FSM): 127
1999 Buck Harvest/FSM: 11.6
Winter Deer Density/FSM: 51
Desired Winter Deer Density/FSM: 27

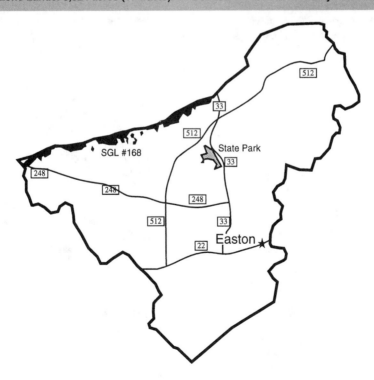

SCHUYLKILL COUNTY

More like the northeastern counties in some of its natural and topographic features, 71 percent of Schuylkill's 782 square miles hold forests. The land is mountainous, yielding in many places to gently rolling farmlands. Elevations span 380 to 2,094 feet.

Agricultural interests occupy 20 percent of the land with nearly two-thirds in crops including potatoes, corn, hay, oats and wheat along with peach and apple orchards.

In a recent year more than three dozen Schuylkill farms registered as "deer damage farms," permitting January hunting for antlerless deer while attesting to the their raids on crops.

Locust Lake State Park near Mahanoy City (1,045 acres), Tuscarora State Park near Barnesville (1,100 acres) and more than 9,000 acres in scattered tracts of Weiser State Forest, all offer good whitetail numbers.

Ten gamelands are scattered across Schuylkill. The largest include: SGL No. 110 near Auburn with 10,093 acres; SGL No. 106 at Drehersville, 9,197 acres; and SGL No. 80 near Rock with 8,236 acres.

Food, lodging and services, contact: Schuylkill County Visitors Bureau, 91 South Progress Road, Pottsville, PA 17901. Phone: (800) 765-7282 or (570) 622-7700.

IN BRIEF:

State Gamelands: 38,099 acres
State Parks & Forests: 11,878 acres
Farm-Game Coop: 68,880 acres (669 farms)
Forest-Game Co-op: 20,236 acres
Safety Zone Lands: 10,317 acres (76 tracts)

1999 Buck/Doe Harvest: 3,871/3,863
1999 Archery Buck/Doe Harvest: 946/789
1999 Muzzleloader Buck/Doe Harvest: 36/227
Forested Square Miles (FSM): 551
1999 Buck Harvest/FSM: 7.0
Winter Deer Density/FSM: 37
Desired Winter Deer Density/FSM: 20

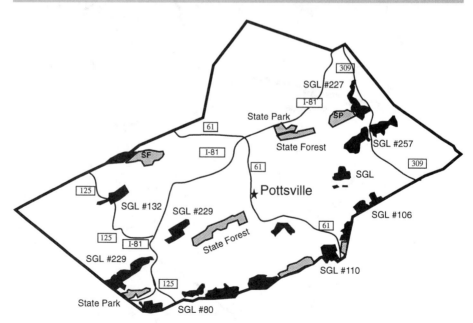

YORK COUNTY

York's hilly and mountainous north yields to rolling lowlands in its south. It's bordered by the Susquehanna River on its east. Elevations run from 109 to 1,440 feet.

Woodland covers 27 percent of the county which is largely farm country. Cattle and croplands compose 52 percent of its 906 square miles. York's rich fields produce barley, soybeans, corn, potatoes, and tobacco.

Four gamelands, including 1,517-acre SGL No. 242 at Rossville and 1,166-acre SGL No. 243 at Franklintown, hold deer. York also holds Cordurus and Pinchot state parks but has no state forest lands.

In terms of buck kills per square wooded mile, York annually ranks among the top counties. The county's woods and farms support an overpopulation of whitetails according to Game Commission biologists, to the dismay of most farmers.

Food, lodging and services, contact: York County Convention and Visitors Bureau, 1 Market Way East, York, PA 17401. Phone: (800) 673-2429 or (717) 848-4000.

IN BRIEF:

State Gamelands: 4,014 acres
State Parks & Forests: 5,662 acres
Farm-Game Co-op: 74,232 acres (667 farms)
Forest-Game Co-op: None
Safety Zone Lands: 25,808 acres (194 tracts)

1999 Buck/Doe Harvest: 3,421/3,033
1999 Archery Buck/Doe Harvest: 1,241/908
1999 Muzzleloader Buck/Doe Harvest: 16/219
Forested Square Miles (FSM): 244
1999 Buck Harvest/FSM:14.0
Winter Deer Density/FSM: 69
Desired Winter Deer Density/FSM: 18

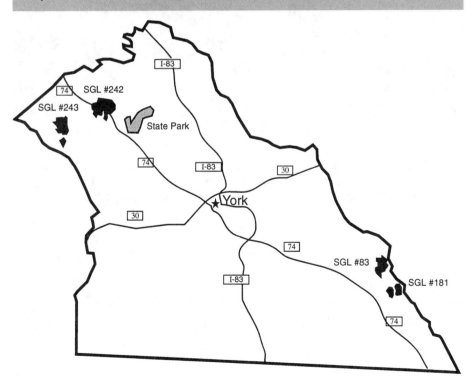

SECTION V
BONUSES OF THE HUNT

The eastern coyote has been documented in every Pennsylvania county.

CHAPTER 26

THE WILDLIFE EXPERIENCE

Coyotes, Bears, Bobcats and Birds

Wildlife education for many people comes from sitting on a couch and watching nature shows on television. Others feed birds in the backyard or drive through parks where they see elk, deer, waterfowl and other game and non-game species.

But it's those of us who get into the woods, waters and fields on regular occasion and become a part of nature, whose observations are most intense and meaningful.

Hunters are privileged to cross paths with more than just whitetails during the hunting seasons. Often it's the interactions with anything from foxes to snowshoe hares that make our days — and fill our memories.

I vividly recall a frigid morning in 1974, while buck hunting in Carbon County, when a beautiful charcoal-and-black coyote wandered from a cluster of pines, sniffed the snow beneath an oak tree, then pranced over the rise and out of sight.

It was my first sighting of a Pennsylvania coyote and one I'll never forget. Ditto for the bobcat which slipped by on a snowy December afternoon near Roulette in Potter County or the great-blue heron I flushed from a pile of cuttings on a flintlock hunt in Berks County. The fact that the long-necked waterbird was in a woodland during a snowstorm in the middle of winter remains a mystery.

Of course, there have been other encounters of note, from a tiny screech owl sharing my treestand to fat black bears waddling by below. Add to that chickadees that perched on my gun barrel and nuthatches and creepers passing inches away from my face while traveling their tree-trunk turnpikes.

It's these wildlife encounters which, in time, become as memorable and joyous as the hunt itself.

You never know what you'll meet in the woods and fields during any of the hunting seasons but an encounter with any of these wild animals will surely leave an impression — and a memory.

Eastern coyote

Few animals are as intriguing to the sportsman and naturalist as the coyote. Once considered only a resident of the American West, it's now a solid citizen of the entire East, including every county in Pennsylvania.

Coyotes are at the core of one of the more laughable rumors promulgated by hunters over the years. That is, Colorado coyotes were "secretly" stocked by the Game Commission for many years to control burgeoning deer herds.

"We deal with those rumors all the time," said Bruce Whitman of the commission's information and education staff. "I always ask why coyotes are present in all other states (surrounding Pennsylvania) if we had to stock them here."

More accurately, the wild canines are believed to have moved into the state after extending their ranges north of the Great Lakes, then entering New York, New England and eventually Pennsylvania via Ontario and Quebec. Coyotes are known to have bred in the states Northwest in the late 1960s with stories of "brush wolves" stretching back to the pre-World War II years.

Pennsylvania specimens, which have been recorded in every county, are more wolf-like than their western counterparts, weighing 30-60 pounds. Their colors are varied, ranging from cream to blonde-red and splotched gray to pure black. Most are gray-black mixes, similar to the colors of a German shepherd.

At this point in their recent Pennsylvania history coyotes have not had much of an effect on deer populations, although they are known to take fawns and will, as in Maine, kill yarded deer in winter.

Retired Game Commission biologist Arnie Hayden said evidence of deer show up in about 55 percent of coyote scat. However, he's quick to note that much of it comes from carrion, deer killed and not retrieved by hunters, gut piles and whitetails injured in vehicle collisions which wander off and die.

PGC biologist Tom Hardisky, now in charge of coyote research and management, said coyote numbers were estimated at about 10,000 to 15,000 in the early 90s but there's strong evidence their populations may have doubled since.

Coyotes are legal game throughout the year, except Sundays, with exception. Coyotes may be taken during the buck and doe and spring gobbler seasons only by those hunters still holding valid deer tags or unfilled spring turkey tags.

An ongoing Game Commission study is focusing on coyote food habits and the effect of disease on the packs. Hayden said about 40 percent of the coyotes taken by trappers and hunters show signs of mange.

"We still have plenty to learn" said the Wellsboro biologist. "It's been here (in Pennsylvania) since the 1950's at least but we really don't know a whole lot about it."

Rocky Mountain elk

If you hunt in hunt Elk, Cameron, Clinton, Clearfield, Potter or Tioga counties, you may cross paths with the whitetails' larger cousin, the Rocky Mountain elk.

These aren't the same elk which roamed Pennsylvania into the mid-1800s, although they were probably genetically similar. The native eastern elk were slowly extirpated via non-regulated hunting and habitat loss and showed serious declines in populations by the 1750s. By 1800, the elk was gone from southeastern Pennsylvania and they were eliminated from the Poconos by 1845. It's believed that a full-blooded Indian by the name of Jim Jacobs killed the last Pennsylvania elk east of St. Marys (where today's herd lives) in November, 1867.

Between 1913 and 1926, some 177 Rocky Mountain elk were brought from Yellowstone National Park and bought from private propagators, then released in various parts of the state. Only the Cameron-Elk counties releases took a long-term hold. Over the years their numbers grew steadily, but minimally.

In January, 1994 the Pennsylvania elk population totaled 224, the highest of anytime in the century up to that point. The January 2000 survey revealed 566 elk composed of 99 branch-antlered bulls, 52 spikes, 288 cows and 120 calves. Thick cover prevented the sex determination of seven elk.

Each year elk are lost due to winter mortality, accidents, brainworm and vehicle collisions or poached and/or shot for crop damage. Nevertheless, their numbers jumped by a phenomenal 15 percent between the winters of 1999 and 2000.

The elk herd in northcentral Pennsylvania exceeded 550 individuals in January 2000.

The Game Commission is currently involved in a management plan to reduce conflicts in agricultural areas and create more enticing habitat on state forests and gamelands in the vast Northcentral Region where the animals roam. The elk range expanded over the past couple years with the trap-and-transfer of bulls, cows and calves into new areas.

Each fall the Elk-Cameron region draws tourists by the thousands, all hoping for a glimpse of the majestic animals or the opportunity to hear the spine-tingling bugles that again echo throughout the mountains.

As this is being written, plans are being made to conduct the first limited elk hunt in Pennsylvania since 1931, possibly to take place in 2001 or 2002.

"Based on recent trends, we believe the elk herd will reach 735 by the fall of 2001," said Rawley Cogan, the Game Commission's elk biologist, "and it could be nearly 1,300 by 2005."

"Increased use of deterrent fencing in farming areas and aggressive habitat improvement programs (with financial aid from the Rocky Mountain Elk Foundation) on public lands have caused population gains by reducing elk conflicts," Cogan said.

"If we do not prepare for an elk hunt, we should expect to face more conflicts with landowners, more vehicle collisions and potential habitat destruction and competition between elk and other wildlife," Cogan cautions.

Following releases in other counties, the elk range now encompasses some 835 square miles.

Bobcats

Yet another animal of intrigue and occasional but rare sighting is Felis rufus, the bobcat. I've been blessed to have seen five Pennsylvania wildcats in my lifetime, four of them while deer hunting in Potter, Sullivan, Pike and Clinton counties. Yet another Pike County cat was caught in my headlights as it streaked across the road late on an October night.

The "bob" gets its name by virtue of its relatively short tail, which is typically 4-6 inches but may grow to 7-1/2 inches. The tail holds three or four brownish-black bars, the last of which is broadest and darkest.

It's estimated that Pennsylvania's breeding population of bobcats numbers about 3,500 statewide.

The bobcat has historically been absent from the Southeast and the western fifth of the state (although a few have been reported there in recent years) with greatest numbers in the remote northcentral mountains. They're known to occasionally wander into areas where they haven't been seen for hundreds of years. Largely nocturnal, it's sometimes seen during daylight hours.

Often mistakenly referred to as "lynx," the Pennsylvania bobcat's ear tufts are considerably shorter than those of its larger Canadian cousin's. Also, the bobcat's foot pads lack fur.

On rare occasion bobcats will breed with house cats. In documented cases it has been the male "wildcat" which has bred with the female domestic cat. The progeny can include both bob-tail kittens and siblings with long tails.

Forest clearcuts, which provide rabbits, mice, woodchucks and birds — such as turkey and grouse — are of as much benefit to bobcats as to deer.

For the first time since 1970, the Game Commission approved a limited — if not controversial — bobcat hunting and trapping season beginning in the fall and winter of 2000. It is estimated that the adult breeding bobcat population may consist of as many as 3,500 cats statewide. Population growth has been 4 to 6 percent annually with 60 to 100 killed on Keystone roadways every year.

Black bears

Well over four dozen of the state's 67 counties have yielded bears since 1949. Bear sightings are often made during the bow, buck and doe seasons but it's during the three-day Thanksgiving week hunt that they become elusive, often heading to the safety of cover, especially swamps, and staying there.

"I've been bear hunting 23 years and I've never seen one while I was after them," said a white-whiskered Carbon County hunter on the opening day of buck season a few years back. " This morning I saw four of them."

The estimated Pennsylvania bear population at the recent turn of the century was estimated at 10,000. Their numbers are kept in check by the 1,400 to 2,600 or

Many black bears are denned by the beginning of buck season.

so taken during each November's 3-day season. The record was set in 1998 when hunters tagged 2,598 bruins.

Bear numbers are highest in the northcentral and northeastern counties. Successful breeding in both areas has accounted for a growing range as bears are today moving back into places they haven't been seen for 50 years and more.

Indeed, it's the availability of food and the catholic tastes of bruins that have adapted to them well to life in a state with a population exceeding 12 million people.

Dr. Gary Alt lists blueberries, blackberries, raspberries, wild cherries, acorns and beechnuts as the main wild fare but some "domestic" menu items are also considered important.

"Feeding bears is a sport for many people, especially in the Poconos," said Dr. Alt of the northeast's vacationland bruins. "Man and bears live here in higher densities than anywhere in the world."

It's a common sight in the Poconos and in the Northcentral sector of the state to see mounds of shelled corn, donuts and pastries, stale bread and suet behind a cabin or home. Bears tap the supplies regularly, providing viewing pleasure for the observers and fat and protein for the visiting bruins. The practice is discouraged by Game Commission officials because bears soon become accustomed to humans, making them dangerous to be around.

Add to that regular raids on cornfields, particularly in August when the kernels are sweet, along with apples and other foods which also appeal to Pennsylvania whitetails. Even garbage cans and dumps add considerably to their caloric intake in certain locales.

Bears have also developed a taste for birdseed, usually knocking down and/or ruining bird feeders in the process.

"A lot of people think that bears come out of the dens in the spring of the year very skinny and gain weight the whole year but that's not true," according to Dr. Alt.

Bears will continue to lose weight after denning, considering spring's meager offerings. But some will gain more than 200 pounds in 90 days as summer's smorgasbord is set. Studies show larger bears will consume over 20,000 calories a day when food is in abundance, such as blueberries.

"We know we have the fastest-growing bears in all of North America," explains Dr. Alt. "In most of the country cubs will weigh between 30 to 50 pounds but ours average about twice that. We've had some cubs weigh over 150 pounds in the fall and look almost identical to their mother."

Of course, not all bears are behemoths. Many 75-200 pounders are harvested each season as are a good number in the 200-350 pound range and some exceeding 500 pounds. Females, of course, are always considerably smaller than their mates.

Like deer, Pennsylvania bears are highly adaptable. Studies show that during meager food years females may den as early as October to cut their energy expenditure — also making them unavailable during the hunting season.

"The decision to hibernate is determined by energetics," Dr. Alt explains. "If a bear must expend more fat than it can store by feeding it will stay in its den and hibernate."

Typically, cubs stay with their mothers for 18 months, breeding every two years. Male yearlings often set out on long-distance excursions, showing up in towns and cities far from their birthplaces. Eventually they wander back home or set up housekeeping in more suitable habitat but not before frightening some suburbanites and backyard poodles out of their wits.

Bear hunting in Pennsylvania nowhere near approaches the popularity of whitetail hunting as less than 10-12 percent of the million licensed hunters buy the $10 bear permits. Nor do most hunters employ laborious techniques or preparations, other than casual scouting, for the abbreviated season.

The biggest bear of 1998 was a 730-pounder shot in Lackawanna County. The heaviest bear known to have been shot in Pennsylvania was an 826-pounder taken in Carbon County in 1994. The Boone & Crockett record book is filled with Pennsylvania bears, which qualify by skull measurements.

Birds of the deer woods

While the sighting of a downy woodpecker or a tufted titmouse doesn't stir the adrenaline as does an elk, coyote or bear, the deer woods surely wouldn't be the same without the presence of birdlife.

Go ahead and curse the blue jays for giving away your position, but praise them for returning a favor when a heard of deer is coming your way.

From turkeys and grouse to pileated woodpeckers and barred owls — even the occasional chickadee alighting on your gun barrel — deer woods birds add yet another dimension to spending the day on a treestand. Dozens of times a day I'll raise my binocular to check out what's scouring an oak or flying above my head, when I probably should be focusing my attention on finding deer parts among the grasses and trees.

While you may not want to carry it afield at hunting time, on scouting trips I always keep a copy of Roger Tory Peterson's *A Field Guide to the Birds (East of the Rockies)* or the Golden Field Guide's *Birds of North America* in my daypack.

Every deer camp needs a bird book. Having one available provides the observant hunter a quick reference for identification of these constant companions of the deer woods.

Black, gray and red squirrels, gray and red foxes, minks and weasels, otters and hares, red-tailed and Coopers hawks, great-horned and screech owls, pileated and red-headed woodpeckers and dozens of other species all contribute to making the hours spent in treestands, or hunched against mountaintop oaks, much more pleasurable.

The pileated woodpecker is a welcome sighting in the deer woods.

Gamelands Grilled Chops

CHAPTER 27

DOUBLE YOUR PLEASURE
Favorite Venison Recipes

By Betty Lou Fegely

Thousands of Pennsylvania families rely on a deer or two in the freezer each year. This low-cholesterol meat is healthy and nutritious, no matter how it's prepared.

In our home, venison shows up in everything from hamburgers and spaghetti sauces to grilled steaks and chops, chip steak sandwiches, ring bologna and gourmet meals when "company comes."

Our kids grew up with venison and now are serving it on their own tables.

Of course, this entire book could be filled with venison recipes and many books contain just that. To whet your tastebuds a bit, try one or all eight of these delights from the Fegely dinner table.

BASIC VENISON MEATBALLS

2 eggs
1/2 cup milk
2 lbs. ground venison
1 cup chopped onions
1/4 cup dry bread crumbs

1 tsp. salt
1/4 tsp. McCormick's pepper
1 tsp. Worcestershire sauce

Heat oven to 400 F. In large bowl combine eggs and milk; blend well. Stir in remaining ingredients; mix well. Shape into balls 1 to 1 1/2 inches in diameter. Place in an ungreased 15x10x1-inch pan and bake at 400 F. for 15-20 minutes or until lightly browned and thoroughly cooked. Can be frozen and used later in various recipes. Great for parties and appetizers.

VENISON MEATBALL STROGANOFF

1 tb. oil
2 cups frozen snow peas
1/3 cup red bell pepper strips
1/3 cup chopped onion
1 garlic clove, minced

1 (10 oz) can condensed cream of chicken soup
1/4 cup water
1 tb. Worcestershire sauce
18-20 venison meatballs
1 cup dairy sour cream

Serve over hot cooked noodles

Heat oil in large skillet over medium heat. Add peas, bell pepper, onion and garlic; cook and stir until onion is tender. Stir in soup, water, Worcestershire sauce and meatballs; bring to a boil. Reduce heat to low; cover and simmer 15 minutes or until the meatballs are thoroughly heated and peas are tender, stirring and turning meatballs occasionally.

Stir in sour cream; heat over low heat until warm, stirring occasionally. To serve, spoon stroganoff mixture over noodles. 4-6 servings.

Kids love it, too.

GAMELANDS GRILLED CHOPS

6-8 venison chops or tenderloins
1 bottle (12 oz.) Lawry's Teriyaki with Pineapple Juice Marinade
Lawry's Garlic Powder

Cut venison into 1-1/2-inch thick slices. In a resealable plastic bag, combine chops and marinade. Close bag and refrigerate at least 3 hours (or up to three days). Spray grill with cooking spray. Preheat grill and then cook 5 to 7 minutes on each side. Baste with leftover marinade and sprinkle with garlic powder while cooking, turning once. Do not overcook. Serve with baked potato and fresh tossed salad. Feeds 4-6.

VENISON SHISHKABOB

Marinade	*1 tsp. basil*
1 cup salad oil	*parsley*
1 clove garlic, smashed	*salt and pepper*
3/4 cup white wine	*1 lb. boneless venison steak, cut in 2*
1 tsp. oregano	*inch cubes*

Mix all seven ingredients and place in zip-lock type bag with venison cubes. Marinade at least three hours in refrigerator. In a hurry? Use one of Lawry's bottled marinades: Seasoned, Mesquite or Teriyaki.

10 cubes sweet onions	*10 cherry tomatoes*
10 cubes green pepper	*10 mushroom caps*

Alternate cubes of venison, onion, green pepper, mushroom caps and cherry tomatoes on skewers. Brush lightly with marinade. Grill, turning once, for 3-5 min. on each side. Serves four. Serve with grilled potatoes, carrots and salad. Great for company.

CAROL'S VENISON FINGERS

Marinade	*1 lb. venison steaks*
1/2 cup olive oil	*1 cup unseasoned cracker-meal or*
1/4 cup red wine vinegar	*seasoned Italian bread crumbs*
1 tsp. dried oregano	*1/4 cup olive oil*
1 tsp. dried basil	*4 tb. margarine-butter will burn too*
1 clove garlic, crushed	*easily*

Combine oil, vinegar, garlic, and seasoning for marinade. Cut steak into finger-sized strips. Place single layer in a glass dish or in a sealable bag and cover with marinade. Marinate in refrigerator overnight or a few days. Remove the meat and dredge in cracker-meal. Pat the meal firmly into meat on all sides. Bring olive oil and margarine to 325 degrees (medium heat) in an electric frying pan. Saute the strips until golden. Drain on paper towels. Serve hot as an appetizer or in larger pieces for entree. Serves 4 as an entree. 6-8 as appetizer.

Unique and delicious.

POCONO PARTY STEAK

4-6 venison steaks

2 cups prepared bread stuffing

12 oz. Mozzarella cheese, sliced

btl. Lawry's Red Wine Marinade

1 cup spaghetti sauce

1/3 cup grated Parmesan cheese

Add marinade to steaks in zip-bag and refrigerate. Remove steaks and saute in medium-hot pan in a little olive oil. Remove browned steaks to a deep baking dish. Place a 1/4 cup of stuffing on each steak and flatten with a fork. Cover with a spoon of spaghetti sauce, top with a slice of mozzarella and sprinkle with Parmesan cheese. Cover loosely with foil. Bake at 300 F for one hour. Great with rice, a favorite vegetable and warm bread. Serves 4-6.

SPORTSMAN'S STROGANOFF

1 tb. oil

2 cups frozen snow peas

1/3 cup red bell pepper strips

1/3 cup chopped onion

1 garlic clove, minced

1 (10-1/2-oz.) can condensed cream of chicken soup

1/4 cup water

1 tb. Worcestershire sauce

1 cup dairy sour cream

20 Italian Venison Meatballs

Heat oil in large skillet at medium heat. Add peas, bell pepper, onion and garlic. Cook and stir until onion is tender. Stir in soup, water, Worcestershire sauce and meatballs. Bring to a boil. Reduce heat to low. Cover and simmer 15 minutes or until meatballs are heated through and peas are tender. Stir occasionally to turn meatballs. Add sour cream over low heat until warm. Ladle stroganoff over cooked noodles. Serve with cornbread. Feeds 4-6.

BRADFORD COUNTY VENISON CASSEROLE

8 oz. pkg, medium noodles

1-1/2 lb. ground or cubed venison

8 oz. cream cheese

1/2 cup sour cream

1/3 cup green pepper, chopped

1 tb. butter

2 (8 oz.) cans tomato sauce

1 cup cottage cheese

1/2 cup chopped onion

2 tb. melted butter

Cook noodles according to package directions. Brown venison in butter. Add tomato sauce. Combine cottage cheese and sour cream with the softened cream cheese. Add onions and green pepper. Butter a large casserole and spread half the noodles on the bottom. Cover with cheese mixture. Put the remaining noodles on top and pour melted butter over noodles. Top with the tomato-venison mixture. Place casserole in pre-heated 350 F. oven for about 20 minutes or until heated through. Serves 4-5.

DEER CAMP POT ROAST

2-3 lb. venison roast

2 tb. oil

2 tb. margarine

salt and pepper

1 large onion

1 tb. garlic powder

1 can beer

2 pkgs. onion gravy mix

1 tb. brown sugar

1 cup water

1 tb. Worcestershire sauce

Melt oil and margarine in pan. Roast until brown on all sides. Place roast in crock pot and add remaining ingredients. Slow-cook at low to medium setting for 6-12 hours. Prepare before bedtime, cook all night and it will be ready for lunch. Add carrots, peas, potatoes and celery for a tender, tasty, hardy stew.

Reading the annual edition of the camp logbook is a highlight in many deer camps.

CHAPTER 28

THE CAMP LOG BOOK
A History of the Hunts

Many of the hunting camps in which I've had the pleasure of being a guest across Penn's Woods had some sort of a written record of the previous years' hunts. Most consisted of old rosters, faded snapshots, some shirt-tail stubs trimmed from plaids worn when the big one was missed, an anecdote or two scribbled in a ruled notebook and other memorabilia.

On occasion, I also saw camp logs that were more fittingly "history books" — detailed, illustrated accounts of happenings at deer camps past. They were the sometimes-detailed happenings of times spent in of the "palaces in the popple" as the late outdoor writer John Madson called deer camps.

Up until 1990, I was a member of Green Tree Lodge in Carbon County, a loosely-organized bunch of hunters who took pride in their serious approach to the sport and who lived for buck season. In the late 60s someone began taking notes and snapping photos of the happenings at our deer camp, then turned it into a "typed up" story with pictures and anecdotes.

That began a series of annual additions to the Green Tree Logbook, a work that was to become cherished over the years. Each season a different camp member was appointed "outdoor writer."

That began a challenge of "can you top this" entries. Over some 30 years the annual accounts filled three volumes, which (thanks to the evolution of copy machines) we eventually "published" so that each camp member could have his own ready reference.

The book was a highlight of each year's camp. Old-timers chuckled as their memory banks were tickled. Kids in camp for the first time delighted at the antics and tales highlighted in each season's story and looked forward to making their debuts in its pages.

It soon turned into a piece of history. Sad is the camp without such a cherished treasure.

You need not be a skilled writer or top-notch photographer to record the hunt in a professional manner. But there are a few considerations that must be made to produce a log book camp members won't be able to put down until they've read it start to finish.

Creating the Camp Log
Here are some tips for starting your own camp log — a history book that becomes more and more valuable as the seasons slip by.

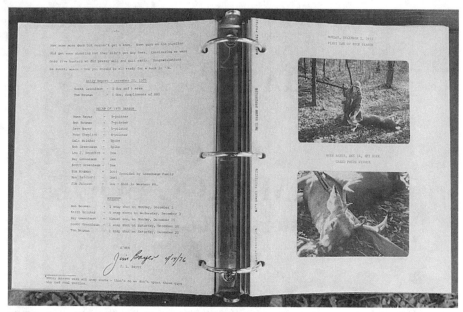

Neatly typed text, accurate accounts of what happened the year before and plenty of photos eventually make the logbook into an invaluable history book.

- While at camp, take 10 or 15 minutes at day's end to jot down the day's happenings. Don't rely on your memory. It may be clearly inscribed in your mind at the time, but two months later most of the details will have become blurred.
- Collect copies of the camp roster, the daily menu, and any other incidentals that should be included in the book.
- Be sure at least one camp member takes photos of each day's harvests and all the happenings (especially humorous situations) in camp. It pays to have a couple photographers for a variety of shots (and as insurance should the other guy's camera be out of order.) A month or so after the season, contact the photographers and have each contribute duplicates or 3x5 and 5x7 prints. Remember that photos are the highlight of a camp log.
- Set aside a night or two to concentrate on creating your written masterpiece. Don't rush things. If you don't own a computer or typewriter, find someone who does.
- If someone in camp is good at artwork, have him or her draw up a few cartoons based on happenings at camp (like Ol' Fred running barefoot to the outhouse or Ben starting his socks on fire while drying them too close to the woodstove.)
- You may want to "lift" cartoons from outdoor magazines and add your own captions. You can also adapt layout ideas from such magazines as "Pennsylvania Game News" and write the logbook as if it were a special edition of the magazine, as I did on my appointed year as editor of the "Greentree Lodge Game News."
- Make neatness your byword. Your work will be read time and again throughout the years by the parade of hunters that pass through the camp doors. Slip each page into a transparent, plastic protective sheet for longevity.
- Because the members of our camp took pride in their work, each year's "editor" used one page to express personal thoughts on deer camp and the fellows who meet each year to enjoy the Pennsylvania ritual. Most were presented as

"editorials." Reading them often revealed a side of the author you may not have known before. This is the "signature" you put on your efforts.

- One more suggestion: Don't forget anyone. Even though everyone enjoys reading about friends and relatives, you can bet your best scope that each camp member will also be looking for the part about himself. Forgetting to include a reference to someone in camp is a cardinal sin — no matter if he or she is honored for getting the top buck or teased for falling out of the top bunk.

The Photo Finish

Along with the colorful descriptions of events that transpire in camp, some colorful photography is also a necessity. The "colorful" part comes from each photographer's eye for the unusual and a flair for pushing the shutter at just the right time — or simply having a camera in hand when things happen.

Whether the final results are from a Polaroid or a top-of-the-line 35mm camera, use these few tips for photographing your hunting friends and telling the photo-story.

- The prime rule for getting more interesting shots than the deer-hanging-on-the-meat-pole or back-of-the-pickup-truck variety is to carry your camera afield and snap photos "on the scene." There's always an extra corner in your hunting coat or daypack to carry one of the new 35mm compacts. The "on location" shots will beat the ones you pose on the front porch when someone downs a nice 10-pointer.

Creativity in tastefully photographing the camp's kills add professionalism and zest to the annual entries.

A good flash is necessary for photographing the hunters who return to camp after dark, such as Glenn Lindaman of Whitehall with his Pocono Mountain 8-pointer.

- Get candid shots of your hunting buddies. Shoot their portraits when they're off guard. There's time for this when the next drive is being organized, when you meet at the creek for lunch, or when you come upon a friend posted in his tree stand or hunkered down under his favorite pine tree.
- Photographs of dead game, especially deer, require special attention to avoid the "blood 'n guts" pic showing a spread body cavity and the tongue drooping from a deer's mouth. If you're on the scene prior to the time the deer is field dressed, that's when your "hero" shots should be snapped. If the animal's body is bloody in a particular spot, pose the hunter and his kill so that part isn't visible or clean the area with leaves or tissue. Take a few minutes to tuck in the tongue and position the animal so unattractive aspects are de-emphasized.
- Get in tight with the camera, filling the frame with hunter and antlers. The biggest mistake amateur photographers make is using only a small portion of the frame. Close-up shots are best.
- Be creative. One of my personal favorite photos is of a friend who downed a nice 8-pointer. I posed him, dressed in blaze orange garb and gun in hand, far behind his trophy, then framed him in the deer's antlers (see page 287). A wide-angle lens works best for such compositions by providing a broad depth of focus.
- Study the image in your viewfinder. A twig growing out of your buddy's ear may evoke a laugh later on but it's not one he or she will be proud to own. Watch all aspects of the background and try to avoid anything unnatural. If shots are posed back at camp, drag the deer to a spot where a patch of rhododendron or an open field comprises the backdrop. Too often gremlins such as garbage

cans, automobiles, outhouses and other objects taint an otherwise good photograph. Forget about posing the kill in the back of the pick-up or hanging by the neck on the meat pole.

- Make certain there's a functional flash on the camera. Often the crew gets back to camp after dark, particularly if a deer had to be dragged from deep in the woods. Rather than wait until morning for photos (when rigor mortis has set in or the deer is frozen hard as a rock), it's best to pose the pictures right then. Of course, shots inside the cabin also may need a flash but it may be possible to get by in natural light with some of the new 400-1000 speed print film. Fill-flash, which is an option on many of the modern snap-and-shoot cameras, will erase heavily-shadowed areas in the photo, such as the shaded eyes under hat brims, even in bright sunlight.
- You'll also want to have the camp photographer up front at shirt-tail clipping time when the "honor" is bestowed on the hunters who had their chances — but missed.

Deer camp is a fun time. A bonus of the actual hunt is the fellowship and friendship in spending a few days away from the daily grind. A top-quality logbook — a history book, really — will make it possible for every man, woman and child in camp to relive those pleasant memories with the arrival of each new season.

Keep in the back of your mind the possibility that sometime — 30, 40 and maybe even 50 or more years down the line — someone will pick up the dusty logbook and enjoy a taste of what deer camp was like "back then."

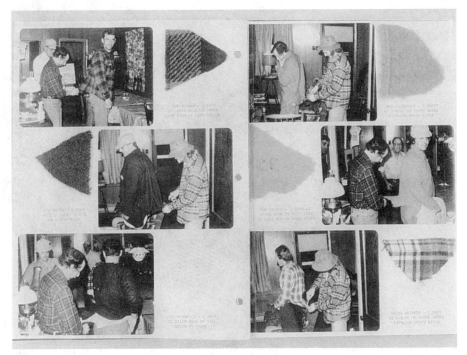

The camp ritual – snipping shirttails of those whose shots were errant – is duly recorded in this logbook, along with snipped tails and accompanying photos of the "shirt surgery."

Deer camp then...

...and now

Chapter 29

DEER CAMP REVISITED
Palaces In The Popple

Pennsylvania deer camps, like the hunters who inhabit them, come in a variety of sizes, shapes, smells, sounds and personalities. But they share one characteristic: They're palaces to hunters who annually migrate to them for buck hunts.

No matter if the "camp" is carpeted, water flows at the twist of a handle and the bathroom is walled with tile or the structure is subject to northwinds that sneak through holes in the siding, water's carted from a nearby spring and the nearest "relief room" is a tumbledown outhouse 25 cold and snowy paces from the cabin door, or it's simply a tent set on the edge of the deer woods, countless sportsmen know them as the places where memories are born.

Today, unlike the past, many deer camps also have ladies in residence. Once totally a male bastion, an increasing number of girls and women are now sharing in the joys of deer camp.

Here in Pennsylvania, deer camp is solid tradition. While referred to as "camps," few can hold up to the turn-of-the-century whitetail encampments when canvas tents or log shacks, open fires and oak meat poles were standard items. Creature comforts, such as beds with mattresses and spigots with water, were luxuries.

I'm not old enough to have experienced deer camps of the 1920s and earlier. Few of us are. But I vividly recall the more modern versions of the buckskin camps where blaze orange would have been scorned, duck coats or Woolrich suits being the standard dress for the hunt.

Today, I'm pleased to report, the camp in which several friends and I spend the opening days of the annual hunt is considerably more comfortable.

But I'm privileged to have experienced a sampling of the rough `n tough deer camp of the past when several friends and I set up shop in tents for a buck season hunt.

Like heirlooms handed down generation to generation, kids exposed to deer camps seldom throw away the memories, themselves adopting their own friends and camps as they grow older.

Most hunters gain entry to a camp courtesy of a father, uncle or some special person who thought enough of them to share the experience and the mystique — passing on the tradition.

I can still remember my first night at Dad's deer camp, the same in which my late grandfather was a member. I was 18 and a freshman at Lock Haven State College (now University) in Clinton County. Dad hosted me for the opening day of buck season at Tall Maples Hunting Lodge in Sullivan County, about a 90-minute drive east of school. I even managed a second day of hunting by getting lost along the Loyal-sock on the opener, wandering around in the dark for over four hours, and finally being found too late to go back to school that night.

As I vividly recall, the camp was alive with action, from long-johned members making hasty runs to the two-holer, to cigar-munching poker players surrounding the long wooden dining table. Another contingent sitting in the small living room, near the woodstove, told tales which grew taller by the year. Bucks got bigger and wiser and hunters grew hardier and smarter as the night wore on.

Hands caringly stroked the stocks of guns new and old as they were polished and oiled. The old standards, largely .32 Winchester Specials or some other type of "brush guns," many without the high-power scopes that today top deer rifles, lined a stand-up rack along the far wall like soldiers at attention, awaiting their call.

On the eve of the opener talk was always of past hunts and happenings that took place in camp before and after the actual hunting expeditions. Jokes and pranks flowed as easily as the Seagrams and Ballantine stocked in the camp refrigerator.

With it all there was a certain anxiety; an experience one seeks to savor and not let go until the early hours of morning when the subconscious finally relinquishes dreams of big-racked bucks and sleep comes reluctantly. Most often it's an abrupt nap with the dreamer jarred to consciousness by the clanging of a broad-faced alarm clock.

The smells of bacon and fresh-brewed coffee drifted up the spiraling stairs, expediting the task of dressing on a morning where a peek through the window revealed a new-fallen blanket of tracking snow.

As I write this it's that time of year again. Tonight the fires will burn bright, curling woodsmoke into the crisp night throughout the northwoods. Tomorrow, before first light, the bobbing beams of flashlights will pilot orange-coated hunters to their favored stands in the woods and field edges. By dusk, camp poles will hang heavy with deer. If not, talk of the day's misses and the ritual of snipping shirt-tails will fill the hours and thereafter sleep will come more gently.

I'd like to have been part of a 1900 deer camp, mainly to verify my belief that little has changed among avid deer hunters and the spirit of deer camp over the near century. Certainly, accommodations are more comfortable now and camps are easier to access. Four-wheel-drive trucks and Jeeps now fill the front yards of the mountain camps. No longer need anyone curse getting stuck in the snow and mud with the Old Model T, or hiking and mule-tripping into the hinterlands as our forefathers did.

Hunters dress differently, too, and deer are more abundant than when our great-grandfathers took to the forests. Variable scopes enhance shiny guns, some with plastic stocks of which my grandfather would surely make comment. The arsenal is stacked on the camp rack and the line-up of Cordura and Goretex boots in front of the door underscores a modern time.

But I'll bet anticipation's the same as it was in those wind-blown tents of a century past. And the smells are similar, too. Whether the alluring odor of Hoppes No. 9 or the addictive scent of frying bacon and black coffee wafting through the camp kitchen, an escape to deer camp satisfies and stimulates all of the senses.

I like it that way. It takes me back to the time of the lumberjacks, miners and hard-working townsfolk who labored hard above ground and under to feed their families. But once each year they'd band together to play hard in the backwoods deer camps, bringing home venison as a bonus.

This is the season that urges me to draw the late John Madson's *The White-Tailed Deer* (Winchester, 1961) from my bookshelf and once again read his poem, "Palace In The Popple," shared here with John's personal blessing.

"Palace In The Popple"

It's a smoky, raunchy boars' nest
With an unswept, drafty floor
And pillowticking curtains
And knife scars on the door.
The smell of a pine-knot fire
From a stovepipe that's come loose
Mingles sweetly with the bootgrease
And the Copenhagen snoose.
There are work-worn 30-30s
With battered, steel-shod stocks,
And drying lines of longjohns
And of steaming, pungent socks.
There's a table for the Bloody Four
And their game of two-card draw,
And there's deep and dreamless sleeping
On bunk ticks stuffed with straw.
Jerry and Jake stand by the stove,
Their gun talk loud and hot.
Bogie has drawn a pair of kings
And is raking in the pot.
Frank's been drafted again as cook
And is peeling some spuds for stew
While Bruce wanders by in baggy drawers
Reciting "Dan McGrew."
No where on earth is fire so warm
Nor coffee so infernal
Nor whiskers so stiff, jokes so rich
Nor hope blooming so eternal.
A man can live for a solid week
In his old underbritches
And walk like a man and spit when he wants
And scratch himself where he itches.
I tell you, boys, there's no place else
Where I'd rather be, come fall,
Where I eat like a bear and sing like a wolf
And feel like I'm bull-pine tall.
In that raunchy cabin out in the bush
In the land of the raven and loon,
With a tracking snow lying new to the ground
At the end of the Rutting Moon.

Deer camp!
May woodsmoke forever curl from its chimney.

CHAPTER 30

LAST WORD
The Immortal Buck

January 30, 2000
It's the time of the year I like to kick back, sit in front of a blazing fire with a few friends as snowflakes drift by the window and tell deer hunting stories.
One tale that I've shared only a handful of times but have thought about on hundreds of occasions occurred in the fall of 1963 in southern New York, not far from the Pennsylvania border.
This is the way I remember it.

The buck still walks through my dreams now and again.

I'm no longer certain after 35 years that my return to that overcast November day continues to accurately reflect what really happened.

Or if it happened at all, I've come to admit.

It remains surreal, as if I'd been a spectator, not a participant.

The place was a farm in southern New York, not far from the Pennsylvania border, which I saw for the first time that steel-gray morning as the sky reluctantly yielded to a hazy dawn. My host had placed me on the edge of an old apple orchard with a harvested cornfield off to my left and a sapling-choked woodlot to my immediate right.

It seemed an ideal place to spend opening morning, here in the tight cover and only a few steps from prime deer food. Indeed, this could be the day I'd break the spell of too many buck-less seasons.

My 12-gauge, Ithaca double-barrel shotgun, loaded with a pair of "punkin balls," would need to suffice. My meager school teacher's pay didn't allow for a deer gun — new or used — in my budget back then, although each time I wandered downtown I'd pause at the window of the Goodyear store and eye up the shiny, new Ithaca Deerslayer so enticingly displayed in the window.

Instead, I had to make do with the shotgun Uncle Russell gave to me upon my graduation from high school.

Before leaving me alone in the darkness, my host, Dan, advised: "Hang in there even if you don't see anything." From being there past opening days, he knew hunters on the adjacent farm would start driving the far woods about 10 a.m.

By 9, I'd watched three does trace the edge of the woods and was briefly entertained by a lone 'possum, probably heading home after a night of feasting on fallen persimmons and fresh roadkills.

A half-hour later my churning stomach reminded me that I had sandwiches — three as a matter of fact — stuffed into my game pouch. Drawing one — bologna and American cheese, as I recall — from the wrapper, I took a bite, then casually glanced back to the place I'd seen the does an hour earlier.

That moment remains deeply etched in my mind. No other aging memory is as vivid. The scene is always the same, as if I'm witness to a drama, looking on from somewhere else in the abandoned orchard.

I see me, sandwich in hand and dressed in a dark-red Woolrich coat and hat, and the buck, a fat-necked 10-pointer with eyes of coal, little more than 15 yards away. Neither of us is moving. We lock eyes for a half-minute, perhaps longer.

In time the buck turns. Seemingly unconcerned, he casts a glance into the orchard, takes a half-dozen slow steps, then leaps over the barbed wire fence separating the cornfield from the apple orchard.

With a final twitch of his white tail, he disappears ... and I am again alone.

Why I made no attempt to lift the old shotgun, which lay across my lap, or otherwise react to the buck's presence, I shall never know.

The events of that long-ago morning are as puzzling now as they were then.

Had I dozed off for a moment and only dreamed that the magnificent buck — 10 points with bronzed beams arching well beyond each ear and a notably rust-colored forehead — was real?

Or was it a classic case of buck fever, so intense that I became paralyzed at the appearance of the handsome stag. Under different circumstances, it might have been my first-ever buck.

The bologna sandwich, perhaps, adds a necessary touch of comic relief. Minutes after the giant buck disappeared and with my thoughts in disarray, I lifted my clenched hand to nibble at my sandwich. It wasn't until then that I realized I'd squeezed it to the size of a walnut.

It took a bit of time, but reality and rational thought began their slow returns. I spent the next 30 minutes searching for his tracks. But all I found was a cedar tree rubbed raw, accounting, perhaps, for the buck's russet forehead.

The drivers began shouting precisely at 10, pushing several does across the cornfield, as Dan promised. He showed up a while later.

"See anything?" Dan asked.

I paused, searching for a way to explain what had occurred, but could only mutter "Yeah, a few does but that was it."

Why I couldn't bring myself to tell Dan or anyone else what happened remains a source of inner searching to this day.

Since then, the Red Gods have been kind. My wanderings in the deer woods near and far have brought trophies and more than my fair share of memories.

But none remain as ingrained or intense or as puzzling as the silent, immortal ghost that continues to walk in my dreams.

BIBLIOGRAPHY

Bell, Bob, Betsy Maugans, Bob Mitchell, *Pennsylvania Big Game Records (1965-1986)*. Harrisburg: Pennsylvania Game Commission, 1988.

Doutt, J., C. Heppenstall, J. Guilday. *Mammals of Pennsylvania*. Harrisburg: Pennsylvania Game Commission, 1977.

Flying The Colors: Pennsylvania Facts. Dallas, TX: Clements Research, Inc., 1987.

Kosack, Joe. *The Pennsylvania Game Commission*: 100 Years of Wildlife Conservation. Harrisburg: Pennsylvania Game Commission: 1995.

Lewis, Don. *The Shooter's Corner*. Harrisburg: The Pennsylvania Game Commission, 1989.

Liscinsky, S., C. Cushwa, M. Puglisi and M. Ondik. *What Do Deer Eat?* Reprinted from Pennsylvania Game News. Harrisburg: Pennsylvania Game Commission.

Merritt, Joseph F. *Guide to the Mammals of Pennsylvania*. Pittsburgh: University of Pittsburgh Press, 1987.

Powell, D. and T. Considine. *An Analysis of Pennsylvania's Forest Resources*. United States Department of Agriculture: Resource Bulletin NE-69, 1982.

Rue, Leonard Lee, III. *The Deer of North America*. Danbury: Grolier Book Clubs, Inc., 1989.

Shissler, Bryon. *White-tailed Deer Biology and Management In Pennsylvania*. Conestoga: Wildlife Managers, 1985.

Weiss, John. *The Advanced Deer Hunter's Bible*. New York: Doubleday, 1993.

PHOTO CREDITS

All photos by the author unless otherwise credited.

Betty Lou Fegely: 20, 26, 34, 62, 63, 83, 90 (left), 100, 129, 144, 146, 149, 180, 290 (bottom), 298.

Pennsylvania Game Commission: 2, 9, 11, 29, 182 (bottom), 275.

Pennsylvania Historic & Museum Comm.: 6. Dr. Gary Alt: 21, 22. Horton Manufacturing Co.: 56, 57. Olin-Winchester: 72. Knight Rifles: 73. Realtree 78 (Left). Mossy Oak: 78 (right). Georgia Boot: 79. Fieldline: 80. Imperial Schrade: 81 (top). Karl Power: 99. Penn's Woods Products: 120, 124. Dick Laros: 121. Primos Game Calls: 122. John Phillips: 128 (left). Bob & Linda Steiner: 132 (center), 145, 157. Jim Fitser: 165. U.S. Fish & Wildlife Service: 176. Mike Haviland: 297.

TOM FEGELY BIO

Tom Fegely has been making his full-time living as an outdoor writer, photographer and broadcaster since 1976 when he accepted a position as outdoors editor of The Morning Call in Allentown, Pennsylvania.

Prior to that he taught environmental education and ecology in the public schools for 14 years. He holds a Bachelor of Science degree from Lock Haven University and received a Master's degree in education and the biological sciences from Kutztown University.

He has written eight books, five of them for children.

Tom has received more than 85 awards for his work, including the Associated Press Enterprise Award three times. Each week his newspaper features and columns are carried on the wire services and appear in many state and national papers.

He hosted "Call Of The Outdoors" on NBC-affiliate WGAL-TV in Lancaster from 1980 to 1987 and "Escape To The Outdoors," a syndicated daily radio show which aired on 375 stations in the eastern U.S. He has also hosted and/or scripted and narrated seven deer, turkey and African hunting videos for King Video Adventures.

Currently, Tom is on the masthead of, Buckmasters, Keystone Outdoors, Whitetail Hunting Strategies, North American Hunter and Whitetail News. He is past president of the Pennsylvania Outdoor Writers Association and has been a member of the Outdoor Writers Association of America (OWAA) since 1969.

His wife, Betty Lou, is also an outdoor writer/photograph with whom he shares his travels, which have included whitetail and/or turkey hunts in 32 states and four provinces.

They make their home in southeastern Pennsylvania with their chocolate Lab, Max. Four of their five children are avid hunters.

The author and his grandson Mason Kostick take time to talk things over on a walk in the deer woods